Chinese Language in Law

Chinese Language in Law

Code Red

法言法语

Deborah Cao

LEXINGTON BOOKS
Lanham • Boulder • New York • London

Published by Lexington Books
An imprint of The Rowman & Littlefield Publishing Group, Inc.
4501 Forbes Boulevard, Suite 200, Lanham, Maryland 20706
www.rowman.com

Unit A, Whitacre Mews, 26-34 Stannary Street, London SE11 4AB

British Library Cataloguing in Publication Information Available

Library of Congress Cataloging-in-Publication Data

Names: Cao, Deborah, author.
Title: Chinese language in law : code red / Deborah Cao.
Description: Lanham : Lexington Books, [2017] | Includes bibliographical references and index.
Identifiers: LCCN 2017038111 (print) | LCCN 2017037444 (ebook) | ISBN 9781498503969 (Electronic) | ISBN 9781498503952 (cloth : alk. paper)
Subjects: LCSH: Law—China—Language. | Chinese language—Semantics. | Semantics (Law)
Classification: LCC KNQ92 (print) | LCC KNQ92 .C359 2017 (ebook) | DDC 340/.14—dc23
LC record available at https://lccn.loc.gov/2017038111

∞™ The paper used in this publication meets the minimum requirements of American National Standard for Information Sciences—Permanence of Paper for Printed Library Materials, ANSI/NISO Z39.48-1992.

Printed in the United States of America

To Larry Tedesco who has helped to open my eyes to the world beyond China and to the world of other beings.

Contents

Preface and Acknowledgments

It is commonly acknowledged that China is not a country of the rule of law, but China says it is, now describing itself as *fazhi Zhongguo* (rule of law China). China also says that it has a political system based on "people's democracy," but common sense tells us that China is not a democratic country in the sense that the word "democracy" is normally understood. In Chinese, *zhengfa* (politics and law) is a phrase found in the names of many Chinese universities specializing in law and the name of a government branch of judicial institutions including the judicial, prosecutorial, and law enforcement departments, and it is no coincidence that *zheng* (politics) always precedes law. In recent years, the Confucius Institute has been promoted by the Chinese government around the world especially in Western countries as a spearhead to showcase and expand China's soft power. Despite the fact that China blocks and censors the *New York Times*, the Chinese government frequently quotes the *New York Times* for allegedly saying that "Confucius Institute is the best Chinese export yet." However, extensive searches of the *New York Times* failed to find any such praises in English or Chinese. Is this a fake translation and do people know that it is a fake?

Humans are creative "signifying animals." Through deliberate choice of words and use or abuse of language, linguistic manipulation as illustrated in the above examples reveals as much as it conceals. As we are reminded, "If something cannot be used to tell a lie, conversely it cannot be used to tell the truth: it cannot in fact be used 'to tell' at all" (Eco, 1976, p.7). Language is one such thing, especially when two languages are involved.

This book explores some of the intricacies, dilemmas, and idiosyncrasies of the Chinese language used in the legal context, analyzing linguistic matters in both monolingual Chinese context and cross-linguistically when Chinese and English are compared. It investigates the linguistic and cultural landscape through an examination of a number of keywords and linguistic usages associated with Chinese law. The chapters in the book are independent, but they are all connected with and contribute to the overall theme of the book, that is, language matters. To understand Chinese society and law, we need to learn about the rich and idiosyncratic Chinese language and cultural traditions and the legal and political context and subtext, and also to be cognizant of the tension and interaction between legal norms and cultural and linguistic values. The book is a collection of my thinking about the Chinese legal language, as an interpreter and a user of this ancient and changing language. In short, the book considers the interaction and intersection between language and law in Chinese culture and society and highlights the significance and signification of the language in the talking, writing, and doing of law.

As for the arrangement of the book, chapter 1 outlines the general theme and background for the book. It problematizes the main issues and outlines some of the challenges and areas that have been obscured in the study of Chinese law.

Chapter 2 examines the key Chinese characters or words associated with law: *fa* (law), *xing* (punishment, criminal law) and *lü* (statutes). *Fa, xing* and *lü* were first used over two thousand years ago when the Chinese conception of law and its dominant philosophical thoughts took shape. These Chinese characters are still used today and their core meanings remain despite the enormous and profound changes that took place in modern and contemporary Chinese society. Examining the origins of the key Chinese legal concepts and tracing their evolutionary core meanings can assist in our understanding of the developing conception and functioning of law in contemporary Chinese society.

Chapter 3 focuses on the translation between English and Chinese of legal words or words used in legal contexts, and the manipulation of language in translation between English and Chinese. It first discusses the translation of Chinese institutional terms from imperial China into English, followed by a comparison of *yi* and "justice" and a presentation of the meanings of *yi*. Lastly, it considers some of the implications in cross-cultural legal communication.

Chapter 4 examines *yuan*, a word with a long history in Chinese culture that can give us a glimpse of some of the largely hidden aspects of the criminal justice system in China. The linguistic meanings of *yuan* and its classical and modern usage and associated words are first discussed, followed by outlining the possible reasons why *yuan* should be considered a keyword in Chinese law against the backdrop of the imperial Chinese criminal system and its modern counterpart. It is proposed that *yuan* has both ordinary and legal usages with different meanings and functions, and importantly, *yuan* is a keyword in Chinese law, used as speech acts with illocutionary forces in the Chinese legal process.

Chapter 5 proposes that classical Chinese language did not have an equivalent word to the English word "rights" and classical Chinese culture did not have an equivalent concept of "rights." The word for "rights" was introduced into Chinese from the West in the second half of the nineteenth century with a new word *quanli*. The meaning of *quanli* is not identical to "rights," and is still evolving, reflecting the culture, society, and thinking of the indigenous Chinese.

Chapter 6 discusses legal speech acts and examines statutory laws of China and Taiwan to document and compare the similarities and differences of this pragmatic feature of Chinese legal language. After elaborating on legal speech acts and illocutionary forces in legislative texts and corresponding linguistic forms in legal English, the main part of the chapter describes illocutionary forces in legislative texts in Chinese in China and Taiwan and the legal performative modal verbs in the legislation of China and Taiwan.

Chapter 7 addresses the question of linguistic uncertainty of Chinese legislative language. It first identifies certain inherent linguistic features of Chinese that tend to render the Chinese language prone to uncertainty. It then discusses drafting issues in Chinese law that may have contributed to ambiguity and vagueness. Lastly, it considers the pragmatic legal implications of the contention that the Chinese legal language is more ambiguous and vague than English.

I acknowledge the following publishers for their permission to use parts of my articles previously published by them:

Legal Speech Acts as Intersubjective Communicative Action, in A. Wagner, W. Werner and D. Cao (eds.), *Interpretation, Law and the Construction of Meaning*, Springer, 2007: 65–82. Copyright © 2007, Springer. Reprinted with permission of Springer;

Is the Chinese Legal Language More Ambiguous and Vaguer? in A. Wagner and S. Cacciaguidi-Fahy (eds.), *Obscurity and Clarity in the Law,* Ashgate, 2008:109–125. Copyright © 2008, A. Wagner and S. Cacciaguidi-Fahy. Reprinted with permission of Ashgate/Routledge;

Illocutionary acts of Chinese legislative language, *Journal of Pragmatics*, 2009, 41:1329–1340. Reprinted with permission of Elsevier;

On the Universality of "Rights": Absence and Presence of "Rights" in the Chinese Language, *Intercultural Pragmatics*, 2017, 14(2). Reprinted with permission of De Gruyter Mouton.

For a section quoted in chapter 2 from *Luxuriant Gems of Spring and Autumn* translated by Queen and Major. Copyright © 2015, Columbia University Press. Reprinted with permission of the Columbia University Press.

NOTE

1. For the words of praise supposedly said by the *New York Times* as used by the Chinese: http://culture.people.com.cn/GB/22226/69556/177071/10582919.html. Similarly, the Chinese government official body that runs Confucius Institute also cites Western media praising the Confucius Institute but no such praises in English can be found in those Western media outlets: http://www.hanban.edu.cn/article/2015-12/22/content_627909.htm, and http://english.hanban.org/article/2015-12/30/content_628684.htm.

Chapter 1

Linguistic Dimensions in Chinese Law

Problems and Perspectives

On March 1, 2014, a small group of knife-wielding attackers launched a frantic and violent assault on ordinary travelers at the train station of Kunming, the capital of Yunnan Province in southwest China, killing 29 people and wounding over 140 more. Immediately after the attack, China and Chinese people were voicing condemnation and anger, and foreign governments were also expressing solidarity with the Chinese people and condemning the violence. Of these, the embassy of the United States in China posted a translated message in Chinese without the original English on its official Weibo account, the Chinese Twitter-like popular social media:

> 美国谴责这一可怕且毫无意义的在昆明的暴力行为。我们向死难者的家人表示哀悼，并向所有被这场悲剧殃及的人们致以慰问。
>
> The U.S. condemns this horrific and senseless violence in Kunming. We extend our condolences to the families of those killed and sympathies to all those who have been affected by this tragedy.

Astonishingly, and contrary to expectations, this message fueled the outrage of Chinese bloggers. Most of the more than 50,000 comments left on the embassy Weibo post accused the United States of a double standard, with many angry Chinese verbally abusing and condemning the country for its message. Some Chinese bloggers agitated by the Chinese government and media write frequent abusive comments on American and other Western government Weibo accounts but, apart from the usual nationalist sentiments, one apparent irritation to many Chinese bloggers in this case stemmed from the phrase *haowu yiyi* in the Chinese message—a literal translation of the word "senseless" used in the embassy's English statement.[1] *Haowu yiyi* means "not meaningful," "no meaning at all," or "totally meaningless," rather than conveying the original sense of the English "senseless" in the statement.

"Senseless violence" has been a common English phrase in political discourse in recent times. For instance, it was used by the Obama administration to describe the 2012 attack on the U.S. Consulate in Benghazi, the shooting incident at a Sikh temple in Wisconsin and the terrorist attack in the Woolwich district of London. President Obama's statement to commemorate International Holocaust Remembrance Day in 2013 also used the phrase "senseless violence." Much earlier, in 1983, President Reagan used "senselessly" in a statement remembering Holocaust survivors. But in 2014, tens of thousands of ordinary Chinese bloggers interpreted the Chinese translated phrase "senseless violence" in the Chinese way, taking it to mean that the U.S. embassy was not only disrespectful but also somehow sympathetic to the assailants of a terrorist attack in China and was trivializing a horrific tragedy. Many Chinese bloggers fumed that if the Kunming attack was said to be "meaningless" (as the literal rendering of the word "senseless"), then the 9/11 terrorist attack on the United States could be described as a "meaningless traffic accident." Many Chinese also asked what, then, would constitute "meaningful" violence if the Kunming attack had been considered "meaningless." It is apparent that ordinary Chinese bloggers would not have known the common English term "senseless violence" and the meaning of "senseless" in such a context. In Chinese, violence or tragedy is never described or modified by words such as senseless or meaningless. The translator must not have thought of the nuances of the Chinese word, leading to the subsequent torrent of verbal abuse. It was a case of unintended and serious cross-cultural misunderstanding.

This situation can be described by a popular Chinese idiom, *huo cong kou chu*—meaning "troubles or calamities come through the mouth," that is, through the words that one uses. Language can indeed stir up troubles as well as help to solve them. In 2001, during the United States-China spy plane diplomatic standoff, the Chinese government adamantly demanded an apology from the U.S. government, while the American government was equally adamant that it would not apologize. In the end, when the U.S. government presented a letter to China, the letter read in part that both President Bush and the U.S. Secretary of State expressed their "sincere regret" over the missing Chinese pilot and aircraft, they were "very sorry for their loss," and they were also "very sorry" that the entry into China's airspace and the landing in China did not have the verbal clearance of the Chinese authorities. This was widely reported in the Chinese media. The letter was consistently referred to as *daoqian xin* (letter of apology) by both the Chinese government and the Chinese media. As we know, the English word "sorry" is ambiguous, and it can mean both regret and apology. The American "sorry" letter intended the meaning of "regret," but the Chinese chose to understand it to mean "apology."

I cite these examples to illustrate the fact that language matters and words have consequences. Many of us know this simple fact intuitively, but some may not have realized its wider ramifications. This realization has long existed in Chinese culture; indeed, it can be traced back to Confucius (551–479 BCE), who famously said:

> If names be not correct, language is not in accordance with the truth of things. If language be not in accordance with the truth of things, affairs cannot be carried on to success. (Legge, 1970, pp. 263–264)

This Confucian teaching has long been internalized by the Chinese people and become part of the Chinese language and way of thinking. The Chinese people know that language—or what one says and writes—is vitally important, and that one therefore must speak properly and appropriately. The Chinese people have further learned that if one does not speak properly, one's words may indeed bring calamities—as the idiom says, sometimes bringing about one's loss of freedom or life physically and figuratively ending one's career, and social and other relationships. Words can become hard evidence for alleged or real serious acts of crime throughout Chinese history, including contemporary times.[2]

For our purpose, language—careful use of language and choice of words—is considered to be particularly important to law.[3] Law is expressed in language and performs its functions through language: "Law would not exist without language" (Danet, 1980, p. 448). Similarly, it is said that, "Language plays a central role in the operation of law that is different from, even if not necessarily greater than, the role it plays in facilitating many other forms of human interaction" (Schauer, 1993, p. xii). Interestingly and relevantly, such acknowledgment, commonly pronounced in relation to law and Western legal studies in Western cultures, is not part of the Chinese legal culture or tradition. To the Chinese, as stated above, language is always important; however, the language used in law is not distinguished or singled out for any special attention. It is all regarded as part of the official language from authorities. Analyzing the language used in law is a very recent academic interest in China that has emerged only in the last decade or so. Perhaps this is because law never enjoyed a high status in the evolution of Chinese society and culture, and never attracted extensive reflection, scrutiny, and probing by philosophers in Chinese history—unlike the situation in Western civilization. This is also what originally motivated me to pursue research in the language of law in China and to write this book. I wanted to tag and track words associated with Chinese law, in order to consider the interactions and intersections between language and law in Chinese culture, and to highlight the significance and signification of the language in the talking, writing, and doing of law. In this book, the phrase "Chinese legal language" refers to the language of the law and legal process of China and associated words and usages.

This book therefore is an extension of my interest and research in language used in law, a sequel to my earlier work, *Chinese Law: A Language Perspective* (2004). While the previous book is more broadly anchored, touching on the various aspects of the communicative acts involving law, this book is more specific and narrower in focus. It examines a number of keywords and linguistic usages associated with Chinese law, and explores some of the dilemmas and idiosyncrasies of the Chinese language in the legal context, analyzing the linguistic issues in both a monolingual Chinese context and cross-linguistically when Chinese is compared with English. The chapters in the book are independent, but there are a number of broad themes running throughout the book that connect them.

First, this work begins with the basic assumption that language matters; further, linguistic signs as representations of the world and connections to the world are not neutral, but rather culture specific and distinct. Such language, learned and nurtured together with our language socialization, forms an important—if not the most important—part of our cultural resources; it also renders each culture distinct (Cao, 2004). Language is a semiotic system, and law is also a system of signs. Even seemingly simple everyday words are understood differently with diverse connotations for users from different languages and cultures. Take the word "red," used in the title of the book. In modern English, the word "red" and the color red are often used to signify communism—red communism, red scare, reds under the beds, and Red China. However, for the Chinese, the color red has had a much longer history associated with the Chinese culture than the latecomer communism.[4] Many people in the West may not know that red is a Chinese color first, and communist red falls a distant second. Red has always been a traditional Chinese color symbolizing good fortune; it is a festive, auspicious, and joyful color. On the Chinese stock exchange, the color for rising stocks is red, while green is for falling stock prices, the opposite to stock market indicative colors in Western countries. It is rather odd when Western market commentators announce on a particularly day that the Chinese market is dominated by red, describing a falling Chinese stock market, while the accompanying vision on television of the Chinese stock exchange display screen showing a sea of green.[5] Literally, when a Westerner sees red, a Chinese would see green.[6] This is the case despite the fact that in contemporary China, the stock market was only established in the late 1980s and was a Western capitalist import.

Similar examples of cultural differences involving words and language abound in our daily life:

> As individuals, we often see things differently because we are different persons, with different interests, preoccupations, and assumptions. As speakers of different languages we see them differently because every language equips its speakers with a particular set of cognitive tools for seeing and interpreting the world. This applies both to the literally visible world of colors and light, and the "invisible" world of emotions, relationships, social structures and mental life. (Wierzbicka, 2014b, p. 3)

I would add legal life to that list. There are many instances of meaning differences found in the language used in law when we consider legal language cross-culturally. Additionally, how words are used in relation to law and the legal process is also indicative of the different legal cultures and traditions. For example, at the most basic level, linguistically we have a legal word and concept of "law" in English, while we have three Chinese counterparts for it: *fa*, *xing*, and *lü*. Conceptually and pragmatically, they embody, signify, and convey different meanings to the users of their respective language (see chapter 2). In other instances, ordinary words used in the legal process may also represent different meanings in life and culture in subtle ways. I remember watching on CNN a live broadcast of a manhunt for two fugitives in 2015. A New York government official said in a media briefing something to the effect that, "Mr. Matt and Mr. Sweat . . . were convicted killers and have been on the run for three weeks," and that it was necessary to "bring these gentlemen into custody." These English words were nothing extraordinary. However, if we think about these words cross-culturally, and translate them into Chinese, the comment would read and sound extraordinary to Chinese eyes and ears. To begin with, a Chinese—either a Chinese individual or a Chinese official representing the state would never call convicted criminals and dangerous escapees "gentlemen" and would never address them as "Mr." Suppose we translate the media briefing of the U.S. law enforcement officers into Chinese. Including the words "gentlemen" and "Mr.," the translated Chinese version would be jarring, and would read unnaturally and awkwardly. It would sound strange to most Chinese and many may feel uncomfortable or offended by the words in such a context. For a comparable Chinese situation, in the media briefing or press releases about manhunts or indictments and prosecutions of criminals or corrupt Chinese officials, the Chinese would never use the words "gentlemen" or "Mr." For crimes related to corrupt officials, whether or not the word "Comrade" is used depends on the seriousness of the case. Sometimes people can literally tell how serious the charges are based on whether or not the word "Comrade" is in the government statements detailing the alleged crimes and misdemeanors of disgraced officials. Related to this is the fact that suspects in criminal proceedings were referred to and described as *fan* (offenders, criminals) in imperial and modern China until very recently. It is only over the last ten years or so that a new neutral word, *xianyiren*, has been coined to refer to "suspects." Previously, *xianyifan* (suspect offenders or criminals), or simply *fanzui fenzi* (criminals), would have been used. In Chinese indictments, court documents, and judgments, the words "Mr." and "Comrade" are not used. Only people's names (sometimes just surnames) and other personal details are given. This is not limited to mainland China, but also applies to Taiwanese court judgments. We should not over-interpret this as an indication of a just or unjust legal system of one place or the other, or see it as a sign of China's lack of the principle of presumption of innocence in its criminal justice system.[7] Nevertheless, we do not need to be critical discourse analysis gurus to realize that such language use conveys more than just the literal words. It imparts and communicates much about the cultures with meaningful pragmatic connotations, even though such meanings are not always shouting in bold type and often people are oblivious to them:

> 'Language [is] a symbolic guide to culture,' Sapir (1949, p.162) famously said, and perhaps a little less famously, 'vocabulary is a very sensitive index of the culture of a people' (1949, p. 27). Words shared by people speaking a given language are both reflections of, and guides to, these people's shared ways of thinking. That is, of course, not words as such, but the meanings of words. (Wierzbicka, 2014b, p. 40)[8]

For this reason, I believe that legal words or keywords are particularly worthy of our attention. Keywords, as Raymond Williams (1976) describes them, are significant, binding words in certain activities and in their interpretation; they are significant, indicative words in certain forms of thoughts. As Williams further points out, many issues cannot be understood simply by the analysis of words, and most of the social and intellectual issues persist within and beyond the linguistic analysis, yet at the same time, some issues cannot really be thought through unless we are conscious of the words as elements of the problems. For this purpose, four chapters in the book focus on the meanings of keywords associated with Chinese law: *fa/xing/lü* in chapter 2, *yi* and its comparison with the English word "justice" in chapter 3, *yuan* (injustice) in its common usage and in the legal context in chapter 4, and *quanli* (rights) and its linguistic and cultural meanings in chapter 5.

In this connection, I believe that something seldom commented upon in the English literature about law and Chinese law is the hazards of English as a default language. In the linguistic study of English, Anna Wierzbicka has documented and argued over the years that while English is a language of global significance, it is not a neutral instrument; she warns that English could become a conceptual prison, and one could become a prisoner of one's own language (Wierzbicka, 2014b, p. 4). In linguistics, and humanities and social sciences in general—and, I would add, law—commentators writing in English tend to treat English as a standard in relation to which all other languages and cultures can be analyzed and interpreted, and to assume that what is true in English tend to be generalized as universal across most or all languages and cultures (Wierzbicka, 2014b). This leads to various forms of Anglocentrism in English-based human sciences, not only in description, but also in theory formation (Wierzbicka, 2014b, p. 4). Wierzbicka asks whether the dominant conceptual framework of the humanities and social sciences is not "trapped" in the language of the "Default Country" (England) and the "Default Culture" (Anglo culture) (Wierzbicka, 2014b, p. 10). Of course, as she points out:

> If a language other than English were to be treated as the default language of the humanities and the standard for interpreting other languages and cultures, this would also lead to conceptual distortions. But the fact is that in this day and age it is English, rather than any other language, that is being treated as such a standard. (Wierzbicka, 2014b, p. 10)

In the analysis of and commentary on law in general and Chinese law in particular, I suggest that there is also such a tendency when the writings are produced not only in English but also in Chinese. English and Anglo-American law and legal concepts are regarded as the standard and the yardstick to be applied everywhere. Notwithstanding the fact that Western law and legal order constitute the most coherent legal system that human societies have produced so far, using Euro-American law as the standard sometimes may blind us to things in other legal cultures that are not found, or that are not prominent, in this standard and in this language, that is, English; conversely, sometimes English legal words and concepts are taken as universal, while it is not always necessarily the case. As rightly pointed out, the path of the Chinese legality from antiquity to modernity cannot be understood unless one is willing to venture beyond a Eurocentric conceptualization of law, the rule of law, and the legal system (N. He, 2014, p. 10). For my second point, an example is the concept of rights that originated in Western civilization and law. "Rights" are not universally conceived, developed, or constructed as some Western commentators suggest (see chapter 5). For my first point, an example is that, in the vast number of works written about Chinese law, a unique and important Chinese word, *yuan* (generally translated as "injustice") has largely escaped the attention of scholars in both Chinese and English; I propose that *yuan* is a keyword in Chinese law and legal culture (see chapter 4). One possible reason could be that most scholars commenting on Chinese law are not linguistics specialists, and Chinese linguists writing about language matters are not particularly familiar with law. In all likelihood, though, in the academic discussions of Chinese law in both China and outside, there is a tendency to discuss Chinese law with reference to Western legal concepts and English terminology. English does not have a word similar to *yuan*, and this may have contributed to the lack of attention given to the Chinese word. So, in this sense, my chapter on *yuan* is original and also preliminary.

Another issue relating to the dominance of English and English legal language is that in translating and commenting on Chinese law—especially imperial Chinese law—there is a tendency of domestication or acculturation—that is, making words conform to the culture of the language being translated into, and in our case, making Chinese law—particularly imperial Chinese law and traditional Chinese legal culture—sound like Western law in familiar English. An early case is Staunton's 1810 translation of the Great Qing Code, where the translator bends over backward to make the translation of the imperial Chinese law comprehensible to his English readers (André, 2004). He omits, adds, and changes negative Chinese words into affirmative English legal terms, and makes imperial Chinese law sound more logically organized, well reasoned, universal in scope, and non-contradictory; he also introduces a distinction between civil and criminal law that does not exist in the Chinese code, and even writes extremely long sentences in his translation to reproduce the legal style of nineteenth-century England, transforming the Chinese text into a form in English that would be familiar, intelligible, and acceptable to English readers (André, 2004; see chapter 3). Even for other English conventional and moderate writings and translations of imperial Chinese law, such a tendency to domesticate exists, for instance translating local officials *xianling* (and its variations) as "magistrate" and *Xing bu* as "Ministry of Justice" instead of the original meaning of "Board of Punishments" (see chapter 3). This may not only involve the loss of authenticity from the original Chinese; it can sometimes also be misleading. We know that imperial China and its criminal law and legal process in the eighth or the eighteenth century were nothing like the modern-day English courts with lawyers, judges, and courts playing a role in the administration of justice. Of course, a translation needs to take the readability of the English reader as paramount importance, but I regard this tendency to homogenize and Anglicize as a hazard of the default English language and English law.

Language is the universal medium in which understanding is realized, and it is at the core of understanding. Problems with interlingual and intercultural understanding and misunderstanding are common when words in Chinese and English are used seemingly interchangeably, including keywords in areas such as law, philosophy, and international relations. This is related to the presumption of equivalence. As pointed out a long time ago:

> A moderate skill in different languages will easily satisfy one of the truth of this, it being so obvious to observe great store of words in one language which have not any that answer them in another.[. . .]Nay, if we look a little more nearly into this matter, and exactly compare different languages, we shall find that, though they have words which in translations and dictionaries are supposed to answer one another, yet there is scare one of ten amongst the names of complex ideas[. . .]that stands for the same precise idea which the word does that in dictionaries it is rendered by. . . . These are too sensible proofs to be doubted. (Locke, 1959 [1690] cited in Wierzbicka, 2014b, p. 31)

As we have seen in the case of a literal translation of "senseless" and words such as "red" alluded to earlier, those simple words are not so simple, and they cannot be assumed to be identical and understood in the same way in English and Chinese. For our purpose, legal concepts such as law, justice, and rights present more challenges and often cause confusion in translation. This fact can never be emphasized enough when we read writings about China and Chinese law in English. In a way, just as Wierzbicka (2010b) tries to make the familiar English words look foreign in the sense of "othering" or "denaturalizing" English, explicating and revealing the cultural contents, assumptions, and values embedded in English, this book is attempting to do the same in a different and roundabout way: to explicate and interpret the meanings of familiar legal words in Chinese and such words translated into familiar English, illustrating in the process that those Chinese words in English are nevertheless very Chinese.

We must pause here and note that this may be dismissed as a form of Chinese exceptionalism. Linguistically, the Chinese language is unique and exceptional in terms of its linguistic property, its cultural status, and its history. By the same token, all languages are unique and exceptional in their own ways. Nevertheless, we are all humans, and human societies have more in common with each other than what divides us. Thus the study of Chinese language and law can illuminate and offer insight not only for the study of subject-matter specific to China but also for the study of language, law, and human society in general (Cao, 2004). Additionally, the long history of Chinese culture and civilization is also unique and exceptional, but the present and the future must not be seen as being determined by the past. Although I suggest that the influence and effects of the past are with us and are likely to remain with us, and that language plays a major role in sustaining such effects, because language is the medium in which the past and the present are fused, and language—particularly the Chinese language—bears the stamp of the past, I do not see the past or tradition as immutable in determining human destiny, and I do not argue or imply that Chinese culture, society, and language are incapable of change and innovation (Cao, 2004). One example of such a linguistic change is the word *quanli* (rights) (see chapter 5).

Whether or not one admits it, or whether or not one is aware, language entails power. Words can be powerful—or as the saying goes, words are mightier than the sword. These days, the young Chinese "little pink army," as the youth are called, is not taking to the street as the Red Guards did. Instead, its members are armed with social media and iPhones, literally waging relentless wars of words on people who they believe offend China and the Chinese sensibility because of what they say about China or the Chinese. They populate Chinese social media, and now also cross over the "Great Fire Wall" onto Facebook and Twitter. When in English cyberspace, many of them resort to Google Translate, literally translating their insults, and as a result puzzling and causing headaches as well as laughs to English speakers who are the targets of their online denunciations in garbled English in verbal onslaught in their tens of thousands. A genre of online Chinglish is emerging, mainly used for insulting people in tortured English. On another level, language can also exert power in subtle and imperceptible ways, *qian yi mo hua*, influencing people without them realizing it—a form of indoctrination. Language has the power to reveal as well as conceal; it has the power to inform and enlighten as well as to misinform and mislead. In this regard it is noted that one linguistic feature of the Chinese legal language is vagueness and ambiguity, as manifested in Chinese law and legal discourse. Explicit and implicit manipulation of language utilizes the ambiguous properties of the Chinese language and the linguistic habits of the language users, and it can be indicative of the state of the rule of law or the lack thereof. A prime example is the currently ubiquitous *xun xin zi shi* (picking quarrels and provoking fights) provision in the criminal law for the elastic and ever-expanding list of crimes under this category (see chapter 7). It may be an exaggeration to say that to understand the language of Chinese law requires a well-developed sense of guessing (Karlgren, 1949, cited in Finkelstein, 1970, p. 189), but I believe that the Chinese legal language is more vague and ambiguous than its English counterpart, made so by both the inherently linguistic nature of Chinese and the manipulative use of the language. This is idiosyncratic of the Chinese legal language.

Much of this book delves into China's past and traditional Chinese legal culture. So why write about old Chinese words? I believe that an understanding of China's legal tradition and culture—especially its language—can teach us much about China today and that not enough attention has been paid to the language associated with law. In this regard, Chinese political leaders have always had a habit of quoting and recycling old verses, sayings, and phraseology. For instance, in the late 1800s and early 1900s, political reformers such as Kang Youwei and Sun Yat-Sen advocated the idea of *datong* (one harmonious world), and the idea originated from Confucius. In the more recent past, the Chinese leadership has promoted the ideas of *tian ren he yi*

(Heaven or nature and humans as one) and the goal of achieving *xiaokang* (moderately well-off) for the Chinese people by the year 2020. Both phrases derive from ancient Chinese philosophical thoughts. In the past few years, the Chinese government started to promote the "correct notion of *yi li*" in China's foreign policy as an initiative and new policy direction for the current Chinese president, Xi Jinping,[9] and the *yi* and *li* (righteousness vs personal interest) dichotomy originated from the pre-imperial philosophical debates in early China (see chapter 3). Furthermore, the Chinese also have a long-standing tradition of using history to comment on contemporary events, *yi gu feng jin* (using the past to satirize the present).[10] This was often used by the literati and intellectuals in the past, and this tradition lives on today among ordinary Chinese in their everyday commentary in cyberspace about current Chinese politics and the government—sometimes in jest, and importantly to avoid censorship and political harassment. On the popular Weibo, every day bloggers talk about *tianchao* (celestial empire), *shengzhi* (royal decree), *shengshang* (emperor), and *taijian* (eunuch)—all referring to today's China. Old habits die hard and old Chinese words never die. Most Chinese words used today have a rich past, including those related to law.

Finally, I wish to quote something I wrote earlier:

> In Chinese culture, the language is the carrier of knowledge and meanings, and has provided a mental bond as well as a stage, a backdrop, and resources and means for communicating and continuing with its cultural tradition. Conversely, the Chinese language is also the product of forces of cultural unification and centralization, a set of cultural practices. Moreover, it is a system of communication that allows for intersubjective representations of the Chinese social order and helps people to use such representations for constitutive social acts. Equally importantly, we recognize that culture is coherent and consistent, not random bits and pieces diffused across the landscape. Culture forms consistent wholes and its composite elements fit in leading to an organically patterned worldview (Block, 2000). This by no means excludes contradictory or conflicting variants of views. Law is part of the larger coherent culture as a system of signs, not just a set of norms and rules. For our purpose, Chinese legal culture is part of an integrated whole, "a system of symbols, language, and diffusely shared attitudes that produced a common set of legal assumptions and beliefs" (Macauley, 1998, p. 14). Thus, cultural contextualization of Chinese law is both necessary and crucial. (Cao, 2004, p. 4, with modification)

I believe that to understand Chinese society and law, we need to understand the rich and idiosyncratic Chinese language and cultural traditions, and the political context and subtext, and to be cognizant of the tension and interaction between legal norms and cultural and linguistic values in their legal realization in the changing Chinese society. This is the case for both Chinese native and nonnative language users interested in Chinese law.

NOTES

1. Pinyin Romanization of the Chinese language and simplified Chinese characters are used throughout the book unless otherwise indicated or quoting others. The Chinese language consists of characters, not words. Despite the difference, for convenience, "word" is used in this book to describe Chinese characters.

2. Starting from October 1, 2016, Chinese authorities investigating criminal cases have the right to request information posted on social media, including WeChat and Weibo, and to use such data as evidence in court according to the new rules issued by the Supreme People's Court, the Supreme People's Procuratorate and the Ministry of Public Security—Rules on Collection, Request, Review and Assessment of Electronic Data in Criminal Cases: http://www.spp.gov.cn/zdgz/201609/t20160921_167425.shtml. See also http://www.bloomberg.com/news/articles/2016-09-22/tencent-s-wechat-social-media-posts-count-as-criminal-evidence.

3. In a recent court case, *O'Connor v. Oakhurst Dairy*, No. 16-1901 (1st Cir. 2017), the U.S. Court of Appeals for the First Circuit made a ruling involving the ambiguous use or lack of comma, which could cost a dairy company an estimated US$10 million: see https://www.nytimes.com/2017/03/16/us/oxford-comma-lawsuit.html?emc=eta1.

4. There are several words for the color red in Chinese, and commonly used ones are *hong* and *chi*. *Hong* is more commonly used than *chi*. *Hong* is always used with positive meaning, while *chi* is often used in a negative and derogatory sense. For instance, the Kuomintang used to call the Chinese communists *chifei* (red bandit), and the Chinese word for "deficits" is *chizi*, literally "red word."

5. See, for instance, http://www.bbc.com/news/business-33464903.

6. See an interesting discussion of the pronunciation of word "red" in different languages at:https://www.scientificamerican.com/article/r-is-for-red-common-words-share-similar-sounds-in-many-languages/?WT.mc_id=send-to-friend&WTmc_id=send-to-friend.

7. Some argue that Chinese criminal law now has the principle of presumption of innocence after the Criminal Procedure Law (1996) was amended in 2012, while others suggest that the amendment does not recognize the notion of presumption of innocence; for the latter, see Lewis (2012).

8. As an example of vocabulary as an index of Chinese culture and people, see Yu Hua's (2011) *China in Ten Words*. For detailed analysis of modern Chinese political or official language, see Link (2013). For discussion of the evolution of modern Chinese, see Moser (2016).

9. http://cn.chinadaily.com.cn/2016xivisiteeu/2016-06/19/content_25762023.htm.

10. Variations of the phrase include *yi gu fei ji*, using the past to attack the present, and *yi gu shi jin*, using the past to interpret the present.

Chapter 2

Keywords of Law

Yan Fu (1854–1921), one of the most influential Chinese modern thinkers and a leading translator, warned his readers in his Chinese translation of Montesquieu's *De l'esprit des lois*, published in 1913, about the difference between the Chinese *fa* (law) and Western "law":

> In the Chinese language, objects exist or do not exist, and this is called *li* [order in nature, things as they are, or the law of nature]. The prohibitions and decrees that a country has are called *fa* [human-made laws]. However, Western people call both of these "law." Westerners accordingly see order in nature and human-made laws as if they were the same. But, by definition, human affairs are not a matter of natural order in terms of existence or non-existence, so the use of the word "law" for what is permitted and what is prohibited as a matter of law of nature is a case in which several ideas are conveyed by one word. The Chinese language has the most instances in which several ideas are expressed by one word, but in this particular case the Chinese language has an advantage over Western languages. The word "law" in Western languages has four different interpretations in Chinese as in *li* [order], *li* [rites, rules of propriety], *fa* [human-made laws] and *zhi* [control]. Scholars should take careful note (Yan, 1981 [1913]).[1]

Yan Fu was not the only person who saw the linguistic difficulty and complications inherent in translating legal terminology between English and Chinese. For more than the past century, both translators and legal scholars have been pondering the question of whether *fa* is indeed the equivalent of "law." Furthermore, Chinese is certainly not the only language that presents a dilemma and challenge in translation. Examples of similar difficulties abound in the translation of basic legal concepts between most languages. For instance, one may ask whether the English "Rule of Law," the French *État de droit*, and the German *Rechtsstaat* are equivalent. Or can the English "law" reflect the German words *Gesetz* (concrete-specific law) and *Recht* (general-abstract law)? Is the French *droit* conceptually the same as "law"?

This chapter examines the Chinese characters or words associated with law: *fa* (law), *xing* (punishments, criminal law), and *lü* (statutes). *Fa, xing*, and *lü* were first used over two thousand years ago when the Chinese conception of law and its dominant philosophical thoughts took shape. These Chinese characters are still used today, and their core meanings remain despite the enormous and profound changes that have taken place in modern and contemporary China. These culturally distinctive keywords are carriers and symbols of Chinese beliefs, and also represent powerful forces that create realities in modern Chinese society. The Chinese words are indexical, referential, and evolutionary. Examining the origins of the key Chinese legal concepts and tracing their evolutionary core meanings can assist in our understanding of the developing conception and functioning of law in contemporary Chinese society. The layers of meanings of such concepts can also reveal the knowledge as well as the image of law that they represent to the Chinese language user in the distant past and today.

CLASSICAL CHINESE FOR LAW: *XING, FA, LÜ*

First, we take a look at the three key Chinese characters associated with law: *fa* (法law), *xing* (刑punishments, criminal law), and *lü* (律statutes), and outline the meanings regarding law that were formed in early Chinese history. Such reflection may help us to see how much or how little the notion of law has changed in Chinese culture and society.

Fa (law, laws), *xing* (punishments, criminal law), and *lü* (statutes, codes) are closely related. In fact, they meant more or less the same as some of the classical works testify regarding their meanings. A classical early work, *Er ya*, says: 刑, 法也 (*Xing* is *fa*); 律, 法也 (*Lü* is *fa*). The authoritative classical Chinese dictionary, *Shuo wen jie zi* (*The Origin of Chinese Characters*),[2] tells us: 法, 刑也 (*Fa* is *xing*). The Tang Code, the first major and most important imperial code in China, declares: 法, 亦律也 (*Fa* is also *lü*). In other words, the classics inform us that *xing* is *fa*, *fa* is *xing*, and *fa* is *lü*, all refer to the same object of what may be termed generally "law" or "laws." To illustrate this further, the Tang Code summarizes the earliest Chinese law and legal development in a more detailed and direct way:

> Formerly the three kings were the first to use corporal punishments, it being difficult to continue having criminals merely wear reddish-brown clothing. With the increasing distance in time from the customs of the sovereigns, simplicity

> became scattered and sincerity was left behind. Instead there came to be cutting of flesh and breaking of bones as punishments of criminals. The *Great Commentary on the Book of History* states: "The Hsia Dynasty had 3,000 punishments." The *Rites of Chou* states: "The minister of punishments had charge of the five punishments which covered 2,500 crimes." King Mu [1001–947 B.C.] of the Chou Dynasty measured the age and accordingly instituted laws. The five punishments covered 3,000 crimes.
>
> As the Chou Dynasty declined, the punishments became heavier. The Warring States [403–22 B.C.] had differing systems of laws. Marquis Wen of Wei [424–387 B.C.] studied under Li K'uei, who brought together the writings on punishments of the various states and wrote the *Canon of Laws* in six chapters. The first deal with laws on robbery, the second with laws on violence, the third with laws on imprisonment, the fourth with laws on arrest, the fifth with miscellaneous laws and the sixth with general laws. Shang Yang transmitted and expounded the *Canon of Law*, changing laws to statutes. (Johnson, 1979, p. 52, footnotes omitted)[3]

Although the three characters of *xing*, *fa,* and *lü* are used somewhat differently in modern Chinese—as often used in *falü* (law) and *xingfa* (criminal law)—nevertheless, the basic meanings of these characters have been retained. *Fa* still means "law" or "laws," and *xing* still means "criminal punishment," "criminal law," "torture," and "corporal punishment." As we know, these characters and their meanings have ancient origins, which is discussed next.

Xing 刑

Xing is believed to have been used in classical Chinese before the appearance of *fa* and *lü*. The character *xing* originated from early military practice: *xing shi yu bing* (*xing* started with the military, for punishing soldiers). Traces of corporal punishment have been found in archaeological finds of the early Chinese human remains. Corporal punishment of soldiers in ancient China included decapitation, nose cutting, leg cutting, and castration. This was before any written law was enacted. According to the authoritative classical Chinese dictionary, *Shuo wen jie zi*, *xing jing ye*—literally, "*xing* refers to the neck"—that is, to decapitate. Thus *xing* was generally used to refer to "corporal punishment" or "punishment." This meaning can also be explained in the way the character was and is written. The modern form of the character comprises the ideograph for "knife" (on the right) and balanced scale pans (on the left). The "knife" radical symbolizes "cutting" or "using a knife." In legal texts dating as far back as the Qin Dynasty (221–206 BCE), the character *xing* was used to refer to criminal penalties (see Hulsewé, 1955).

An explanation is that the modern character *xing* is a variant of its original, archaic form, which included *jing*, a radical meaning "well" in the sense of shaft in the ground for water. The character for "well" symbolizes nine plots of land farmed by eight families in ancient China. The ninth plot was farmed jointly to the benefit of the state. It was on this ninth plot that public functions—for example, executions—were held. Combined with the knife, this denotes punishment carried out by the state—usually decapitation. Thus *xing* was used to refer to criminal or lawful punishment. *Xing* later evolved to be a general term for laws that related to criminal punishment. Once written law came into existence, the meaning of *xing* was extended to include not only punishment but also any state prohibitions, the violation of which would result in punishment. In this usage, *xing* may be understood in the sense of penal law (Bodde and Morris, 1973, p. 11. See also Z. Liang, 1989, 2004; MacCormack, 1990). In short, in imperial China, criminal punishment and interrogative torture used in the legal process were referred to as *xing*, a blanket term that comprised all forms of legally sanctioned physical violence (Park, 2008, p. 37).

Another explanation for *xing*, meaning "criminal law," is offered in terms of its pronunciation. According to Schwartz, the character is often used in ancient texts interchangeably with its homonym *xing* (form), suggesting that the two characters are somehow closely associated in origin, so perhaps the punishments were thought of as means of re-forming people, and penal law as a kind of mold forcibly imposed from above to correct aberrant behavior (Schwartz, 1985, p. 322). In this sense, *xing* had the meaning of bodily remolding and reforming of the criminals, and for the Legalists, the meanings of *xing* as punishment and as shape or shaping are de facto interchangeable (Mühlhahn, 2009, p. 16).

One example of the use of *xing* is found in *The Analects of Confucius* (c. 551–479 BCE);[4] this is *qi zhi yi xing*, uniformity sought to be given them by punishments (Legge, 1970, pp. 263–264; see also Chang, 2016). An example of the use of *xing* in classical Chinese is *Xing bu* (literally, Board of Punishments—see chapter 3), referring to the department in charge of legal matters in imperial China. Another example is *wu xing* (five punishments) in traditional Chinese criminal law. The contents of *wu xing* varied in pre-imperial and imperial China. Originally it referred to the punishment of death, leg cutting, nose cutting, castration, and facial tattoo. From the Tang Dynasty to the Qing Dynasty, the five punishments stipulated in Article One of the imperial codes were the punishments of beating with light or heavy bamboo, penal servitude, exile, and death.

In modern Chinese usage, the first and most common meaning of *xing* is criminal or criminal matters. For instance, *xing fa* means criminal law. The current Criminal Law of China is named *Xing fa*. This meaning and usage is now dominant in the use of *xing*, but *xing* has also retained the earlier meaning of corporal punishment and torture. For instance, *yong xing* or *shang xing* means "to use corporal punishment" or "to use torture." Other examples of *xing* in the criminal law-related meanings include *xingshi* (criminal matter), *xingshifan* (criminals), *xingshi susong* (criminal prosecution), *xingshi zeren* (criminal responsibility), *xingchang* (execution ground), *xingfa* (penalty for criminal offence), *xingjing* (police dealing with criminal matters), *xingqi* (term of imprisonment), and *xingxun* (interrogation by torture). It is noted that *xing* has lost its traditional usage as a generic term for law in modern Chinese, which is now *fa*, which is discussed next.

Fa 法

Fa (law, the law or laws) is the most important character in Chinese legal terminology. The original meaning of *fa* is a model, pattern, or standard, or to model as a verb. A well-known use of *fa* in this sense is found in the Daoist (Taoist) classic, *Dao de jing* (*Tao Te Ching*):

> Man models [*fa*] himself on earth,
> Earth on heaven,
> Heaven on the way,
> And the way on which is naturally so. (Lau, 1963, p.82)[5]

This meaning and usage of *fa* are still current in modern Chinese. So it is said that *fa* is a model, standard, method, or procedure imposed by superior authority to which the people must conform and that they must follow (Bodde and Morris, 1973, p. 11). Guan Zi (725–645 BCE) writes that law is measurement, carpenter's ink and line, carpenter's square, utensil used for measurement [pecks and bushels], volume measure and gauge (Rickett, 1998).

The exact time when *fa* was first used is not known. In classical Chinese, according to *Shuo wen jie zi, fa* had an ancient writing form, 灋. The character consists of a "water" radical on the left, and this gives the word the meaning of "being leveled or even as the surface of water." On the bottom right of the word is the symbol *qu* (to go), which is said to symbolize that, if someone is not upright, then the person should be made to go—that is, to be removed. The ancient character *fa* also contains the symbol *zhi* on the top right. According to legend, *zhi* or *xiezhi* was a one-horned mythical beast, believed to be able to cure crooked things, giving rise to the meaning of making something or someone "straight." According to Bodde and Morris (1973), this idea of a wild animal being a referee was reflected in the costume later worn by magistrates in China. From the Han Dynasty (206 BCE–220 CE) to the end of the imperial dynasty in the early twentieth century, Chinese legal officials wore the crests of *xiezhi* on their robes and hats, a practice that signified the function of expelling the crafty and the obsequious (Bodde and Morris, 1973; see also Z. Liang, 1989). Today, *xiezi* can be seen among the carved small creatures on the eaves of the roof in *Taihe dian* in the Forbidden City in Beijing.

The modern character *fa* is a simplified version of its ancient form, in which the symbol for *zhi* has been deleted on the top right, but it is unclear exactly when this simplified character was first used. Some Chinese scholars rely on *Shuo wen jie zi*'s explanation to argue that, etymologically, the Chinese character *fa* contains the meanings of both fairness and justice, resembling the ancient meaning of law in other languages. However, Liang Zhiping argues that this theory is wrong. Citing the works of another scholar, Cai Shusheng, Liang maintains that the meaning of "being leveled as even as water" in *Shuo wen jie zi* was added by others in later generations, and that it is unreliable. Cai argues that the meaning of water is not symbolic but rather purely functional. It refers to placing a criminal on the water to drift away with the current—what is now known as banishment (Z. Liang, 1989). In ancient China, this was a very harsh punishment, so one aspect of *fa* means to prohibit and another means to command, based on the pronunciation of the ancient character (Z. Liang, 1989). Liang also points out that the word for the abstract sense of law in some Western languages, such as *il diritto* in Italian, *le droit* in French, *recht* in German, and *Jus* in Latin, contains the meaning of rights, uprightness, and justice. This is in contrast to the Chinese word *fa*, wherein such meaning is not present (Z. Liang, 1989).

For examples of the actual use and explanation of *fa* in ancient China, Han Fei, a well-known Legalist during the Warring States period, writes:[6]

> Though a skilled carpenter is capable of judging a straight line with his eye alone, he will always take his measurements with a rule; though a man of superior wisdom is capable of handling affairs by native wit alone, he will always look to the laws [*fa*] of the former kings for guidance. Stretch the plumb line, and crooked wood can be planed straight; apply the level, and bumps and hollows can be shaved away; balance the scales, and heavy and light can be adjusted; get out the measuring jars, and discrepancies of quantity can be corrected. In the same way one should use laws [*fa*] to govern the state [*yi fa zhi guo*] disposing of all matters on their basis alone. (Watson, 2003, p. 28)

In short, *fa* is a significant word in Chinese—more now than it ever was in history. In contemporary China, it is used as a lexical equivalent to the English word "law," incorporating the meanings of the modern concept of law. Nevertheless, the ancient meanings stay with the word.

Lü 律

The third most important character related to law is *lü*. In classical Chinese, the character *lü*, according to *Shuo wen jie zi*, means *junbu*, a tool for adjusting musical instruments. *Lü* carries the meaning of rhythm, standards, or rules, some common pattern for people to follow or behavior to be regulated. The original music-related meaning of *lü* is still used today in modern Chinese—for example, *xuanlü* (melody). *Lü* is a technical designation for the individual pitch-pipes, twelve in number and of graduated lengths, which were the basis for the Chinese twelve-tone scale.

The character *lü* appears rarely in a legal sense in the earliest Chinese texts. It was believed that it was in the Warring States period (475–221 BCE), particularly during Shang Yang's (390–338 BCE) law reforms that *lü* started to be used frequently, when Shang Yang changed *fa* to *lü* in both linguistic usage and actual law.[7] Since then, and throughout imperial Chinese history, *lü* was the technical designation for the major articles into which the imperial code was divided. As such, *lü* may be translated into "statute." It also refers to the entire body of such statutes as a collective entity, in which case it may be rendered as "code."

As Shang Yang reformed the legal and governmental system during the Qin State, the character *lü* became important in the law codes of imperial times (221 BCE onwards to 1911). All the legal codes in the subsequent dynasties except Xing Tong (Song Code) and Dian Zhang (Yuan Code) were named *lü*—for example, Qin Lü (Qin Code), Tang Lü (Tang Code), and Da Qing Lü (The Great Qing Code). The most important dynastic code was the Tang Code.[8] It was first enacted in 653 CE and achieved its final form in 737 CE. It was the oldest surviving Chinese code, believed to be based largely on the now-lost Sui Code of 581–583 CE. All the successive imperial codes were modeled after the Tang Code.

Due to the prominence of *lü* as the fundamental components of imperial Chinese law, in the study and interpretation of law there was a branch called *lüxue* (study of statutes or legal codes). It essentially involved annotating and interpreting the imperial codes, usually carried out by classical scholars who wrote explanations of the meanings of the statutory texts, and the annotations together with the texts and amended texts became law in later codes. This has led to the claim that there was no theoretical or systematic study of law or jurisprudence in imperial China, but only a study of codes. In modern China, *lüxue* as a component of law or legal studies no longer exists, and the word is no longer used in modern Chinese.

TRADITIONAL CHINESE CONCEPTION OF LAW

A great deal has been written in both Chinese and English about traditional Chinese law.[9] Here a few aspects regarding the meaning and conception of law in traditional China are briefly highlighted.

Fa *Equals* Xing *As Written In* Lü

Various studies show that the basic meaning of law in early China was established during the period from the Shang (1766–1122 BCE) to the Han Dynasty, in particular the Spring and Autumn and Warring States periods (770–221 BCE). It was during this period that dominant Chinese thought, and also dominant Chinese legal thought, took shape. During this creative period as described by Schwartz (1985), law and systems of punishment were established and developed together with a centralized bureaucratic system of administration, with the rulers and officials of the Qin and Han Dynasties laying the foundation of the imperial law and the penal system, forming the basic framework of law and the most of the important legal institutions (Liu, 1998, p. 2). It was also during this period that the earliest political and legal theories of traditional China emerged, the earliest written codes were promulgated, and some of the most important characteristics of traditional Chinese law formed (Liu, 1998, p. 2).

As the description of these major key characters shows, the basic notion of law in early China was that *xing* meant punishments and law as *xing* essentially entailed a system of punishment. Earlier, we saw the description of the linguistic signs of *fa*, *xing*, and *lü* highlighting such basic meanings. Now, if we look at the referential meaning of the notion of law in ancient China in terms of legal rules and legal institutions, such meaning is well sourced. Such a proposition is confirmed by the actual legal rules and laws of early China, as in the instance of the earliest codified law in *Canon of Laws* (*Fajing*) and the first imperial code of law, the Tang Code and the succeeding codes throughout Chinese history. As it has been described:[10]

> The most famous written code of the Warring States period was Li Gui's Canon of Laws. Lord Shang adopted the Canon of Laws to assist in governing the state of Qin. Canon of Laws is penal law. There were a great deal of *lü* and *ling* (ordinances) regulating the economic activities of the state. But there is little similarity between these laws and economic or civil laws because all regulations concerning prohibitions and command as used punishment to ensure their implementation. These regulations are a manifestation of the development of the concept of *xing* since the time of the Three Dynasties and they are also a reflection of the people's understanding of the concept of *fa*. The Tang Code contained twelve chapters on such varied topics as Administrative Regulations, Family and Marriage, Stables and Treasuries, and most if not all the clauses contain provisions of punishment. Civil relationships like those of relatives, marriage, inheritance, property rights, and creditor rights have all been incorporated into the system of punishments. The concept of *xing* was development to the point of excess. This phenomenon was not limited to the Tang code but was a general distinguishing feature of the ancient law right up to the Qing statutes. (Z. Liang, 1989, pp. 86–87)

As pointed out, in early China law was never perceived as a means of preserving rights, freedom, and justice (Z. Liang, 1989, p. 89).[11] Law was punishment, and it was also one of the methods of governing that could be used and constituted at will by the ruler (Z. Liang, 1989, p. 89). Given such an instrumental approach, law was a personified tool of governing, dependent on and confined by its function and of limited use (Z. Liang, 1989, p. 89). According to Liang, this model of governing can be expressed by the formula man–law–man: the king issues orders; the orders are carried out by the high and petty officials on the common people as the objects of the law's application—that is, rewards and punishment (Z. Liang, 1989, p. 89).[12] Similarly, as MacCormack (1990, p. 48) notes, traditional Chinese penal law is essentially a set of rules emanating from the emperor, which imposes punishments on officials or ordinary people who behave, or fail to behave, in certain ways; these rules are not concerned with the establishment of the rights of the individual or with the protection of individual freedom. This does not mean that civil matters and civil relations were not dealt with, however: *li* instead of *fa*—or, more precisely, *liyi* (礼义ritualized morality)—provided a body of rules regulating civil conduct. *Li* emphasized morality as the foundation of society and imposed civil obligations among the people according to their social status (see Jiang, 2015).

Hence the basic conceptualization and the basic framework of law in traditional China as it evolved from early China may be summarized as: *Fa* (law) refers to *xing* (punishments) as set out in the ritualized moral standards or norms embodied in the imperial *lü* (statutes).

The meaning of law as a system of punishment seems to be the dominant meaning and function of law in traditional China. This interpretation does not contradict the suggestion that *fa* also embodies the meaning of model and standards. Nor does this contradict the argument that traditional Chinese law contained civil law and civil elements.[13] As pointed out, civil activities in imperial China were regulated mostly by the customs or proprieties of appropriate social behaviors that reflected the moral and social values in traditional China represented by *li* (Jiang, 2015, p. 385). *Fa* embodies a range of meanings: laws backed by coercion as well as to laws linked with moral standards; to positive laws issued by the state and to the more specific rules for special skills, such as military strategy (Turner, 1992, p.13). Nevertheless, the dominant meaning of *fa* as it was understood and practiced in early and imperial China was that of coercion and punishment.[14] Violation of or deviation from the prescribed moral standards would be met with punishment according to the rules in the imperial codes.

CONFUCIANISM IN SUBSTANCE AND LEGALISM IN FORM

Further on the conceptual meanings of *fa*, the basic understanding and notion of law as a system of punishment and as a means of government were not only accepted by the Confucianists, Legalists, and other major schools of thought in early China, but were part of the dominant thinking of early Chinese philosophers and statesmen alike. As already noted, "the concept of using punishment as the foundation of law and the legal thinking reflected in the principle of ceasing what is prohibited and carrying out what is ordered had deep historical and cultural roots predating the [L]egalists" (Z. Liang, 1989, p. 81). The notion of punishment had dominated the Chinese conception of law since at least the epoch of the early Zhou, around 1,000 BCE (MacCormack, 1996, p. 28; see also Li Guilian, 1999).

The early Confucianists and Legalists differed fundamentally in their opinions about the importance of law in governance, and the ways in which it was used to achieve its designed purposes. Perhaps partly because of this, there was an absence of sophisticated discussion or basic questioning regarding the nature of law in classical Chinese writings. As Liu (1998, p. 326) points out, the Confucianists hardly put forward any positive theory concerning the origin, function, and framework of law. The Legalists, in contrast, wrote a great deal about law, but mostly on the use of law as an instrument and punishment for deterrence.[15] This can be seen from the writings from the early Confucianists and Legalists.[16] In other words, it seems that, because of the similar understanding of *fa*/law as a system of punishment, we find the biggest disagreement between the early Confucianists and Legalists not in the nature of law but rather in seeing law's role and the extent of the use of law in governing society and guiding people's behavior.

In terms of law and Confucianism, Confucius has this to say in *The Analects* regarding law and punishment:[17]

> The Master said, "If the people be led by laws,[18] and uniformity sought to be given them by punishments [*xing*], they will try to avoid the punishment, but have no sense of shame." "If they be led by virtue [*de*], and uniformity sought to be given them by the rules of propriety [*li*], they will have the sense of shame, and moreover will become good." (Legge, 1970, p. 146)[19]
>
> When proprieties [*li*] and music do not flourish, punishments will not be properly awarded. When punishments are not properly awarded, the people do not know how to move hand or foot. (Legge, 1970, p. 264)

In contrast, the Legalists focused on and emphasized *fa* as the chief means of governance. They believed that tough measures and effective deterrence in the form of law were essential for controlling the population effectively and also for political control (Bodde and Morris, 1973, p. 18, 50). Put simply, the Legalists advocated the idea that, for a state to succeed in maintaining good order and to become powerful, a vigorous and impartial application of penal rules was necessary (MacCormack, 1985, p. 334)—that is, the use of *fa*, or strict law and severe punishment.

A major point of contention between the early Confucianists and Legalists can be found in their views on *li* and *fa* and on the differentiation and use in governance.[20] *Li* and *fa* represent a conceptual dichotomy in traditional China (Lee and Lai, 1978, p. 1308). The Confucian School depended on *li* to maintain the social order by moral education, while the Legalist School invoked law for the same end, and employed punishment as the enforcing agent (Ch'ü, 1965, p. 267). Thus the views of the two major schools were in conflict: between ruling by moral influence and ruling by punishment. The solution to the conflict was *de zhu xing fu* (morality primary and punishment secondary). When Confucianism gained the upper hand during the Han Dynasty, it was thought possible to implement moral norms by sanctions, thus *li* could be enforced by moral influence and legal means (Ch'ü, 1965, p. 268).[21] This led to the eventual incorporation of the essentials of Confucianist *li* into legal codes, with Confucian conceptions dominating ancient Chinese law (Ch'ü, 1965, pp. 277–278). This resulted in the gradual process of Confucianization of law, the most significant development in the legal system of China prior to the twentieth-century modernization of Chinese law (Ch'ü, 1965, p. 280). In Confucian China, *li*, or social proprieties, was implemented according to a person's status; law functioned as a regulatory tool applicable mostly to "barbarian" people, and physical punishments became available only when *li* was broken and conscience failed (Jiang, 2015, p. 387)—that is, law as punishment was not needed if everyone in society was educated properly (Ch'ü, 1965, pp. 249–250; see also Jiang, 2015, p. 387). *Li* is also said to have developed into customary laws. Since the Han Dynasty, the spirit embodied by *li* had been the value orientation of *fa*, and the traditional *fa* was formed in some way by *li* and *fa* (Zeng and Ma, 2006, p. 42). As a result, "*li* not only gave rise to ancient Chinese law, but most importantly, embodied its spirit and value and was the habitat of its soul" (Zeng and Ma, 2006, p. 48). Apart from regulating conduct outside the jurisdiction of law, *li* also supplied the rigidity of written law with flexibilities and exceptions; *li* was regarded as a source of authority in the court of law, and as pointed out, starting from the Han Dynasty, when there was no applicable law in the statutes, the Confucian classics were cited as authority in determining guilt and punishments in imperial China (Jiang, 2015, p. 388; Zeng, 2005, p. 117).[22]

In this regard, we may say that traditional Chinese law contained significant Confucian teachings on morality, which has been described as the Confucianization of law, but the influence of the Legalists was significant and long lasting (Liu, 1998, MacCormack, 1990). One example of the influence of the Legalists in Chinese law is that, "Throughout the imperial period the emperor was accepted as the sole source of law," and "law was an expression of the emperor's will, although not all expressions of the imperial will constitute law" (MacCormack, 1990, p. 48). This practice of the emperor "as supreme ruler, promulgated various legal rules" owed its origins to the Legalists (Liu, 1998, p. 325). As MacCormack states, despite the fact that Confucianism was established as the official doctrine of the state in the Han Dynasty, "certain of the tenets of [L]egalism continued to exercise a subterranean influence—not acknowledged as such—and were in effect adopted by Confucian officials" (MacCormack, 1990, p. 37). A significant example of the process of absorption can be seen in the writings of one of the greatest Confucian thinkers, Xun Zi (c. 313–238 BCE), who accepted law as a necessary part of government (MacCormack, 1990, p. 37).[23] Yet Xun Zi differed from the Legalists in refusing to treat moral example as irrelevant to government; for him, the best solution was to combine the two techniques—moral example and law—advocating a doctrine that seems to have combined Legalist and Confucian elements (MacCormack, 1990, p. 37), achieving an "amalgam" of the two schools (MacCormack, 1996, p. 53). It is believed that Xun Zi's "thinking about law and punishment represents what was portrayed as the ideal system of government virtually throughout the whole of Chinese royal and imperial history," advocating the imposition of severe punishments for severe offences, but also the infusion of benevolence and compassion into law (MacCormack, 1990, p. 38).[24]

To sum up, in early China, *fa* by itself was deemed insufficient and inferior as a social institution, given its principal meaning as punishment. If *fa* is *yin*, the female and negative, *li* is *yang*, the positive, dominant male. *Fa* is subordinate to *li*. If *li* was not invented, something else would have been created in its place, to counteract and subdue *fa*. This is the case at least partly due to the understanding of what law was and what it was used for in the overall scheme of governing society and regulating and guiding human behavior in the eyes of the leading classical Chinese thinkers and statesmen in early Chinese civilization. History tells us that "traditional social order in China has been maintained through a set of pluralistic norms [that] include *dao* (the Way), *de* (moral precepts), *li* (rites), *fa* (law) and *xisu* (custom), and the classic Confucian view places these norms in a preferred hierarchy, with *dao* at the top, *fa* at the very bottom, and the other norms in between" (N. He, 2014, p. 10). The Confucians did not necessarily hold the concept and letter of law in contempt, but accepted that the failure of all the higher norms in preventing crime and unethical behavior would lead to the unfortunate use of law as a last resort (N. He, 2014, p. 11). As a result, in the content of the law, the penal codes give effect to the Confucian system of values, and in the form of the law, we find evidence of the Legalist influence (MacCormack, 1990, p. 38). Indeed, it is said that the Confucian spirit and Legalist system constituted the primary content of traditional Chinese law—or, more precisely after the mid-Han Dynasty, *fa* was the body and *li* was the soul (Zeng and Ma, 2006, p. 49,

51). We can summarize the traditional Chinese law in the following way, as stated by an ancient Chinese historian:

> The sages, being enlightened and wise by nature, inevitably penetrated the mind of Heaven and Earth. They shaped the rules of proper behavior (*li*), created teachings, established laws (*fa*), and instituted punishments [*xing*], always acting in accordance with the feelings of the people and patterning and modeling themselves on Heaven and Earth. (Bodde and Morris, 1973, p. 15, quoting Pan Ku, Han Shu, *History of the Han Dynasty*)

This brings us to another distinctive feature of traditional Chinese law, law and nature, and the origin of law: *dao fa ziran*.

Dao fa ziran

Dao fa ziran 道法自然 can mean "*Dao* models itself on nature" as used in the Daoist classic cited earlier, but it can also be read as "*Dao*, law and nature," although the latter reading is not the commonly used orthodox reading. For either interpretation, *dao* 道 or the Way and *ziran* 自然, or natural order, are of fundamental importance to law in all persuasions of classical Chinese philosophy. It is suggested here that the *li* and *fa* dichotomy, as described earlier, may be underpinned by the notions of *dao* and *ziran*, which constitutes an overarching, underlying, and prevailing earlier philosophical thought on the cosmic order in ancient China, predating both Confucianism and Legalism. The pairing of *li* and *fa* as institutions governing human behavior and society may be related to the fact that the early Chinese conception of law and governance was influenced by the Chinese conception of the natural order and cosmos, and of the origin of law. This represents another major difference between Chinese and Western laws. First, from the Tang Code:

> Virtue and ritual are the basis of governmental teaching; punishment and chastisements are the instruments of governmental teaching. Like night and day, the *yang* of spring and the *yin* of autumn, they are mutually dependent to bring completeness. (Johnson, 1979, p. 54)

As Bodde and Morris (1973, p. 13, 49) point out, unlike many other major civilizations, where written law was held in honor and often attributed to a divine origin, law in China was viewed in purely secular terms, and its initial appearance was greeted with hostility by many as indicative of a serious moral decline, a violation of human morality, and even a disturbance of the total cosmic order.[25] So, in an important way, the origin of law for China presents a special case in comparison to other cultures that favor the will of a divine creator (MacCormack, 2001). Bodde and Morris (1981, p. 50) believe that Confucianization of Chinese law was paralleled by the "naturalization" of law—that is, law was fitted into the wider doctrine of the oneness of man and nature, which maintained that man should shape his institutions in harmony with the forces of nature.

Furthermore, MacCormack (2001, p. 12) proposes that the fundamental point expressed in classical Chinese texts is that law is part of the immutable pattern of the universe; rulers responsible for its implementation must ensure that it remains true to its nature. Law must follow the way of Heaven, the *Dao* (MacCormack, 2001, p. 12). It is further noted:

> Sometimes, as in the tradition given prominence in the silk manuscripts, law is ascribed to the impersonal entity known as the Way understood loosely as nature or heaven. Another approach, found in chapter 9 of the *Huainanzi,* simply treats law as having arisen spontaneously from social conditions, in particular from the hearts of men responding to a conception of what was right. It is said specifically that law dropped neither from heaven nor earth, but arose from human society itself. A related line of thinking can be detected in the passage from the Legal Treatise of the *Hanshu* that speaks of the sage rulers as conforming to the feelings of the people. It may be misleading to dissociate the approach based on social conditions and people's feelings altogether from that based on the Way. Quite possibly the social conditions and human feelings which gave rise to law were themselves conceived as determined by, or acting in accordance with, the *Dao.*
>
> In sum, we may identify two different kinds of source to which law is ascribed. One is a being described generally as a "sage ruler," or identified more particularly as one of the rulers from the earliest stage of China's recorded history. The other is the impersonal concept of nature described as Heaven or the Way. (MacCormack, 2001, p. 18)[26]

According to MacCormack (2001, p. 19), a way of thinking that prevailed at the end of the Warring States period, expressed in texts such as the *Guanzi* and Huang-Lao school of thought, located the origin of law (*fa*) in the *Dao* (the Way).[27] MacCormack (2001, p. 19) concludes that it is likely that to the ancient Chinese, irrespective of the different schools of thought, *Dao* was considered the origin of law, as the Huang-Lao text *Jingfa* stated in its opening line: "The Way (Dao) gave birth to the law."

Dong Zhongshu (Tung Chung-shu, 179–104 BCE) was a leading Confucian thinker of the Han Dynasty. He adopted and further developed the earlier Confucian idea of *tian ren he yi* (Heaven or nature and humans as one), which is considered the most influential philosophical thought in Chinese philosophy. His ideas and the following words from *Luxuriant Gems of Spring and Autumn (Chunqiu fanlu)*, regarding criminal punishment in traditional Chinese law, have had a long-lasting impact in Chinese law and legal practice:

> Gifts, rewards, penalties, [and] punishments and spring, summer, autumn and winter respond to one another according to kind, like the joining of two halves of a tally. Therefore it is said: "The king is the counterpart to Heaven." This refers to the Way.
>
> Heaven has four seasons;
> the king has four policies.
>
> The four policies resemble the four seasons. They are in the same category; they are what Heaven and the ruler have in common.
>
> Gifts are spring;
> rewards are summer;
> penalties are autumn;
> punishments are winter.
>
> With gifts, rewards, penalties, and punishments, you will never be unprepared, just as with spring, summer, autumn, and winter [Heaven] will never be incomplete.
>
> Gifts, rewards, penalties, and punishments must be promulgated in accordance with the appropriate occasion, just as warmth, heat, coolness, and cold must issue forth in accordance with the appropriate seasons.
> Gifts, rewards, penalties and punishments each have their appropriate occasion, just as spring, summer, autumn and winter each have their appropriate time. These four policies must not interfere with one another, just as the four seasons must not interfere with one another.
> These four policies must not trade places, just as the four seasons must not trade places.
>
> Therefore when there were instances in which gifts, rewards, penalties, and punishments were not implemented on the proper occasion, the *Spring and Autumn* criticized them. [55/58/11019] (Queen and Major, 2015, p. 433)[28]

Dong Zhongshu was credited with securing the acceptance of Confucianism as the official doctrine of the state during the Han Dynasty.[29] Explicit influence of Dong Zhongshu's thought found expressions, both in language and in substance, in the Tang Code.[30] As Johnson (1979, p. 14) notes, the "provisions of the Code attempt to reinforce harmony with the natural world through compliance with the *yin–yang* and five elements theories," and "indeed, the Code itself represents the *yin*—the dark side of social control—in contrast to the *yang* influence of ritual, morality, and education." The primary purpose of law, as Dong Zhongshu states, is to maintain a balance in society and a harmony between the human and the natural worlds (Johnson, 1979, p. 10).

From a different perspective, this may illustrate a kind of thinking—and an influential one—of the ancient Chinese regarding law and punishment and their relationship with the natural order. Everything under the sun and beyond is relative to everything else, complementary to one another in the universe.

It is acknowledged that it is hard to trace the ways in which the concept and practice of punishment in China was shaped by cosmological traditions (Mühlhahn, 2009, p. 21). One example is that during the Han Dynasty, vast tables of correspondence were compiled to identify and organize things in the natural and social world that were thought to provide a meaningful context for one's life. Tables of Five compared the Five Phrases, or elements (wood, fire, earth, metal, and water), the Five Directions (north, east, south, wests, and center), the Five Colors (green, red, yellow, white, and black), and so forth. Such classifications included body parts, psycho-physical and affective states, styles of government, the weather, domestic animals, technological instruments, heavenly bodies, and much more. For our purpose here, there were the Five Punishments, illustrating the influence of cosmological thinking on basic penal concepts (Mühlhahn, 2009, p. 21). A concrete example of such thinking and influence is found in the practice of execution for capital crimes in imperial China. A conspicuous manifestation of this doctrine and way of thinking in the legal sphere was the idea, law, and practice that death sentences should be carried out only during autumn and winter, and should be totally avoided during spring and summer. The cosmologists maintained, and Chinese imperial law upheld, that the execution of punishments was linked to the larger cosmological order:

> They saw crime as a disturbance of the human order, hence punishment was supposed to redress and rectify the damage done to social harmony. The grade and severity of punishment depended on the degree to which the order had been thrown out of balance. The cosmologists believed that without an appropriate effort to remedy the social harm caused by a crime, this disturbance of the human order would affect the larger cosmic order of things. Through negative natural phenomena, such as draughts or floods, disturbances of the cosmos would in terms have a negative impact on the human world. In the cosmological approach, social disruptions that were not properly redressed would provoke complex responses by nature. The act of punishment was thus placed in a wider context: it had a meaning that went far beyond society and extended to the cosmos as a whole. Punitive reactions to crime were understood as an indispensable attempt to resurrect the balance within the world and to smooth any temporary perturbations. (Mühlhahn, 2009, p. 22)

Thus punishments were meted out with the intention not only to correct evil, but also to preserve the harmony and balance that transcend the human world. Such thinking manifests in many aspects of punishment as embodied in the imperial laws. Sentencing for capital crimes and the execution of death sentences were carried out only in late autumn or winter; the Chinese idiom for this is *qiu hou wen zhan* (carrying out execution in autumn). It was believed that in winter, nature was prepared for death, while in spring, nature's vitality increased (Mühlhahn, 2009, pp. 22–23), as Dong Zhongshu says. A criminal process had to be conducted, with consideration given to such seasonable changes in nature (Mühlhahn, 2009, p. 23). To execute prisoners in other seasons would incur the wrath of nature. There were a few high-profile executions that were said to have taken place in summer. For instance, according to Sui Dynasty Historical Records and Chinese legends, a Sui emperor executed a prisoner in summer despite advice from his minister that it was forbidden to execute anyone during that season. However, the emperor was not persuaded. He replied that it was correct that summer was a season for things to grow, but in summer there was thunder, and it meant the heaven was showing its power through thunder when it was at its peak of *yang* power. He said, "I am following the Heaven's example, what is wrong with that?" Another well-known summer execution in a famous Chinese story was Dou E, who was executed in June. This act was said to have resulted in heavy snowfall in the middle of summer and Dou E story has been a powerful symbol of injustice in popular Chinese culture ever since (see chapter 4).

LINGUISTIC AND CULTURAL RELEVANCE: PAST AND PRESENT

What can the foregoing description of the law-related Chinese keywords and their origins tell us about law in China today?

First, it is well known that the Chinese have a long-standing tradition of using history to comment upon contemporary events, known as *yi gu shi jin* (using the past to interpret the present) (Alford, 1984, p. 1180). This is facilitated by the fact that in linguistic continuity, many Chinese characters are still written in much the same way as they originally were, and retain the same essential meanings. None of the key legal words—*xing*, *fa*, and *lü*—has disappeared or lies dormant in modern Chinese. In fact, these are among the frequently used words in today's Chinese vocabulary, used more often than ever before. The Chinese people use the services of *lüshi* (lawyers), and Chinese society and everyday life are increasingly regulated and controlled by a myriad of *falü* and *fagui* (laws and regulations). Furthermore, people are still being deterred and threatened by the omnipresent long arm of *xingfa* (criminal law) and its enforcers—whether they are a street peddler or an ordinary blogger surfing in cyberspace. Obviously, the social and general environment and context in China have changed dramatically over the past two thousand years, especially during the past two centuries. Nevertheless, the keywords discussed in this chapter retain their meaning in the hearts and minds of the

Chinese people. The Chinese language has played a vital role in maintaining continuity and transmitting Chinese cultural values and meanings. These words, along with the ideas they represent, are passed on in formal education, through political and legal hierarchies and via social interactions as a form of cultural transmission.[31] The words, ideas, and practices are inherited, and manifest themselves as part of Chinese culture. Chinese legal culture has always drawn upon a reservoir of tradition derived from Confucianism and its assumptions of authority and hierarchy in social organization (N. He, 2014, p. 21), including the language of Confucius. The Chinese written language has an unbroken history extending for some three thousand years, and has been the single continuous linguistic carrier of Chinese culture during this time. The Chinese written language has contributed significantly to the spread, cohesion, and homogeneity of Chinese civilization, giving China both a cultural continuity in time and a unity in space (Bodde, 1991, p. 28).

Apart from the words, in terms of the Chinese conception of law as represented by those words, one cultural legacy is that the Chinese people throughout history, up to the present time, often associate law with criminal sanction and punishment—law being synonymous with criminal law (Z. Liang, 2004). For the collective Chinese language user, this is a direct result of the meaning that they derive from language, and from the reality and life associated with law in their midst. In traditional Chinese law, the imperial codes mostly consisted of criminal law. Even civil matters such as marriage and inheritance were treated as part of criminal law. We now have more knowledge about civil law-related processes and procedures in ancient China thanks to recent empirical works by various scholars (e.g., Huang, 1996, 2001; L. Liang, 2007). Traditional Chinese law contained civil law elements, not just criminal law, especially during the late Qing Dynasty (1644–1911) toward the end of the imperial era. Nevertheless, overwhelmingly, traditional Chinese law for over a thousand years—especially from the Tang to the Ming (1368–1644) and the early Qing Dynasty—was dominated by criminal law, and people's understanding of and association with law during that time were mostly related to criminal law (Z. Liang, 2004). For most Chinese, until very recently, law has first and foremost been criminal law. Even in modern China, in the lawless period from 1949 to 1976, the laws enacted were mostly criminal, and were very limited in dealing with non-criminal matters. The major legislation during this period included the Marriage Law (1950), the Trade Union Law (1950), the Land Reform Law (1952), the Constitution (1954), the Military Service Law (1955), and tax laws. But the laws, regulations, and rules that were widely promoted and known were related to criminal law, such as the Rules on the Punishment of Counter-revolutionaries (1951), the Rules on the Punishment Concerning Corruption (1952), the Rules on Arrest and Detention (1954), the Organization Rules on the Public Security Bureau and Offices (1954), Rules on People's Police (1957), and Rules on the Management and Punishment Concerning Law and Order (1957). The emphasis on and focus of criminal law in China's laws during those three decades reinforces the previous typical or stereotypical view that the Chinese people had about law in traditional China. The situation has changed in recent years due to the expansion of law and the increasing codification of law, in a wave of "juridification" (to borrow from Habermas) that increasingly pervades all aspects of Chinese life and society, particularly civil and economic areas. Despite the changes, however, the traditional notions of the functions and authority of law has never really disappeared or altered much over the long history of China. In contemporary China, the supreme leaders of the Chinese Communist Party and the state, apart from the ordinary people, still firmly believe in the deterrent philosophy of harsh punishment by criminal law (Liu, 1998, p. 322). Additionally, parallel to the idea of the emperor or the supreme ruler being unquestionably regarded as the source of written imperial laws, for modern and contemporary China, the belief and practice that law is the expression of the ruler's will is not unfamiliar or an ancient fiction:

> As the twenty-first century unfolds, the native Chinese rule by law mentality and rule of man actuality and, the imported Western rule of law ideal have colourful traces on an aging canvas that portrays both the spirit of the Chinese civilization and a renewed image of Chinese legality. (N. He, 2014, p. 3)

Admittedly, the Chinese language has been a powerful agent for conserving and diffusing Chinese cultural values, but traditional Chinese law was not static, and its implementation was not a homogeneous or identical reproduction. Notwithstanding this, it was largely stable and maintained its remarkable longevity and continuity. As mentioned earlier, there was no noticeable significant change in the language of *fa*/law in traditional China, either internally or externally motivated, for well over a thousand years (until the late Qing Dynasty), and the "letter and form" of traditional Chinese law—at least the formal law—remained largely the stable as embodied in the imperial codes.[32] Similarly, due to the dominance of *lü* (codes) in traditional Chinese law, there has been a lack of philosophical study of law in China, both in the past and today. Jurisprudence hardly existed in China, by which it refers to the thinking and inquiry that ask the most fundamental questions about law, about the nature of law, about the authority and legitimacy of law, and the epistemological and ontological probing into law (Cao, 2004). *Faxue*, *falixue*, or *fazhexue* (jurisprudence or legal philosophy) is not just a new word in Chinese, but also a new concept and a new intellectual activity.[33] What imperial China had instead was *lüxue* (the study of imperial codes), the annotation of and commentary on the successive imperial codes, and there were scattered commentaries on some well-known cases, as mentioned earlier. As Liang Zhiping (2004, p. 262) reminds us, *lüxue* is not science or scientific study of law, and it is not the same as *faxue* (jurisprudence or legal science). Self-reflexive questioning about the nature and essence of law has been recessive in Chinese thought. This situation is still largely true today.

Finally, regarding the characterization of traditional Chinese law, the subject of this chapter, when we examine Chinese law and try to generalize its characteristics, it may be advisable not to interpret it in strict black and white terms. For instance, regarding the characterization of Chinese traditional law as Confucianization of law or as a system of punishment, one does not need to see these in absolute terms. As Schwartz (1985, p. 9) states, dominant cultural orientations exist in China, which have their origin in early times. Similarly, for traditional Chinese law, it is naïve to think the dominant orientations were the only features, given the complex subject matter and a long history, vast landscape, and huge population. This is particularly relevant too, given the long-lasting Chinese philosophical and popular ideas of balance, change, the *yin–yang* complementality and a holistic worldview. By the same token, the traditional Chinese conception and practice of law can be seen as a blending of Confucian morality (*li*) and Legalist law (*fa*), although they carry a deeper imprint and watermark of Confucianism, with penal law overwhelming the civil and other concerns. To use today's cliché, it may be a seamless blending. The blending was natural in the Chinese political, cultural, philosophical, and behavioral contexts, like the *yin–yang* dichotomy, incorporating both—or *he*, combining or even harmonizing. To use a Chinese phrase to describe this, *Ru Fa he liu* (Confucianism and Legalism combined into one flow), Confucianism and Legalism were in the same flow or current, even though Confucianism was the main stream while Legalism represented the tributaries.

NOTES

1. From Yan Fu's translation of Montesquieu's *De l'esprit des lois*, and the English translation of Yan Fu's words is taken from Cao (2007, p.1). The original Chinese reads:

> 盖在中文物有是非谓之理，国有禁令谓之法。而西人则通谓之法。故人意遂若理法同物，而人事本无所谓是非，专以法之所许所禁为是非者。此理想之累于文字者也。中国理想之累于文字者最多，独此则较西文有一节 之长。西文法字, 于中文有理礼法制四者之异译。学者审之。

For a discussion of Yan Fu as a translator, see Wright (2001).

2. *Shuo wen jie zi* (*The Origin of Chinese Characters*) is the earliest and the most authoritative classical Chinese etymological dictionary, believed to have been written

around 100 CE by Xu Shen (c.58–147 CE), a Han Dynasty scholar. It uses radicals to classify Chinese characters. Its main text contains 14 volumes, and lists 9,353 characters and a total of 133,441 entries. For a discussion of the dictionary, see Watson (1971 [1962]).

3. The original Chinese reads:

昔者，三王始用肉刑。赭衣难嗣，皇风更远，朴散淳离，伤肌犯骨。尚书大传曰，「夏刑三千条。「周礼」司刑掌五刑」，其属二千五百。穆王度时制法，五刑之属三千。周衰刑重,战国异制,魏文侯师里悝,集诸国刑典,造法经六篇，一盗法，二贼法，三囚法，四捕法，五杂法，六具法。商鞅传授，改法为律。

4. *Lun Yu* (*The Analects of Confucius*) consists of 20 chapters, comprising a collection of sayings by Confucius, including brief statements, short dialogues, and anecdotes. It was believed to have been compiled by two successive generations of Confucius's disciples 75 years after his death, perhaps around 400 BCE. The original Chinese text and the English translation of *Lun Yu* quoted in this book are taken from the *Confucian Analects*, but with modifications, including the use of *pinyin*. The *Confucian Analects* was translated by James Legge, published in 1893 and reprinted in 1970.

5. Lao Tzu or Lao Zi, with his personal name of Li Er (c. 604–531 BCE), was one of the founders of Daoism (Taoism), and he is regarded by most as the author of the Daoist classic, *Dao De Jing* (*Tao Te Ching*). For a discussion of Daoism and also classical Chinese language, see Hansen (1983, 1989, 1992).

6. Han Fei (c. 280–233 BCE), or Han Feizi, was a student of a Confucianist, Xun Zi (c. 313–238 BCE). Han Fei was a prince in the State of Han during the Warring States period. His works are mainly found in *Han Feizi*, a collection of essays. An English translation of selected passages of *Han Feizi* is found in *Han Feizi: Basic Writings*, translated by Watson (2003). For the latest translation and interpretation of Han Feizi in relation to law, see Chang (2016, pp. 354–458).

7. It is commonly known that Shang Yang initiated law reforms and changed the usage from *fa* to *lü*, but there is also some doubt as to whether it was accurate, see Jiang (1985).

8. The English translation is found in *The T'ang Code* by Johnson (1979, 1997).

9. For discussions of traditional Chinese legal thought, see Bodde and Morris (1973), Hulsewė (1955), Ch'ü T'ung-tsu (1965, 1998), Z. Liang (1989, 1991, 1998), Turner (1992), Liu (1998), MacCormack (1996), Li Guilian (1999), and Chang (2016).

10. According to Turner (1992, pp.14–15), the Confucian model, which celebrates the moral man over the law, ritual over legal systems, and the familial over the impersonal model of society, has obscured the importance of other discussions about government in early China that looked toward formal laws and models derived from abstract standards as ways mitigate the influence of particularized, kin-based conceptions of the state; such concerns were not limited to the Warring States Legalists.

11. Due to the linguistic focus of the book, it will not go into an interesting comparison between the provisions on stables and working animals such as horses and

donkeys in the Tang Code and the ancient Roman law. The Tang Code (and the later codes including the Qing Code) had provisions on working animals as official/imperial property, focusing on criminal sanctions for mistreatment or for deviation from official guidelines. In contrast, the ancient Roman law focused on animals as property and on the various rights attached for property owners of animals. For a discussion of the animal provisions in the Tang Code, see Cao (2015b). For a discussion of the legal status of animals and animal-related provisions in the ancient Roman law, see Cao (2015a).

12. For similar views and discussions of traditional Chinese law, see He Qinhua (2004), Zhang Zhongqiu (1999), and Li Guilian (1999).

13. For studies of the civil law features of traditional Chinese law of later dynasties, see Macauley (1998), Z. Liang (1996), Bernhardt and Huang (1994); Huang (2001); and L. Liang (2007).

14. As MacCormack (2001, p. 3) points out, in classical Chinese sources, a number of different terms were used to convey the idea of laws and punishments. Sometimes the emphasis is placed upon the notion of rules that contribute to the good ordering of society, such as those that regulate the behavior of relatives to each other, or define the relationship of superior and inferior, or regulate weights and measures, such as *fa* 法, *dian*典, *zhi* 制, and *du* 度. Such terms (or a combination of them) may include a reference to punishments, but the penal aspect of law is not the principal idea to be conveyed. Where the emphasis is placed upon punishments or penal rules, the term most frequently used is *xing* 刑.

15. It may be true, as Turner (1992) argues, that the Legalists and others such as Guan Zi advocated such ideals as impartiality, consistency, and accountability, but such ideas were hardly realized in law or the practice of law in imperial China.

16. For Legalism on law and Han Feizi's works, see Liao (1959) *The Complete Works of Han Fei Tzu: A Classic of Chinese Political Science*. See also Chang (2016) for his interpretation of Han Feizi in relation to law.

17. *Confucian Analects* was translated by James Legge (1970[1893]). Another translation is found in Simon Leys (1997), *The Analects of Confucius*. For discussions of Confucius and Confucianism, see also Fung Yu-lan (1959), Schwartz (1985), Waley (1939), and Creel (1953). For the latest interpretation of Confucius in relation to law, see Chang (2016).

18. The word used in Chinese here is *zheng* 政 but, as explained in the notes in Legge (1970), *zheng* in contrast to *de* 德 refers to laws and prohibitions, hence its translation as "law."

19. For a discussion of Confucianism and Neo-Confucianism, see also Chung-ying Cheng (1991). For a discussion of Confucianism and law, see Bodde and Morris (1973), MacCormack (1996), Liu (1998), Yu Ronggen (1999), and Chang (2016).

20. *Li* (礼rites, rituals, ritual propriety, rules of proper behavior) is central to Confucius. According to Schwartz (1985, p. 67), the original *li* seems to refer to religious ritual. The character took the shape of a utensil for holding offerings at a place of paying homage to ancestors. *Li*, or rites, are believed to have started as customary practice and to have later been formalized as norms of behavior. Schwartz (1985, pp. 67–75) believes that *li* encompasses all the prescriptions of behavior—whether

involving rites, ceremony, manners, or general conduct—that bind human beings and the spirits together in networks of interacting roles within the family, a human society, and the realm beyond. In other words, it represents the cement of the entire normative sociopolitical order and the whole network of hierarchy and authority on which the order is based, and is at the heart of Confucius's teaching. See also Bodde and Morris (1973) on their discussion of the Confucian *li*; see Ames and Rosemont (1998), Hall and Ames (1987, 1995). For discussion of *li* and law, see de Bary (1998, pp. 3–40), who argues that *li* (rites) affirms and exemplifies the basic norms of human conduct, including governance, and that in Confucianism, *li* represents a basic constitutional order, correlative in importance to both individual and public morality. See also Zeng and Ma (2006) for their analysis of the relationship between *li* and *fa*, and Chang (2016).

21. See also Lee and Lai (1978, pp. 1308–1309), quoting Chang Chin-tien (1960, p. 4).

22. One example in determining guilt by Confucian classic is the principles as embodied in a Confucian classic, *Chun Qiu* (Jiang, 2015, p. 388).

23. For Xun Zi's works in English translation, see *Xunzi,* translated into modern Chinese by Zhang Jue and translated into English by John Knoblock (1999).

24. For a discussion of the ethical foundation of the Chinese imperial law and the Legalist and Confucian perspectives, see MacCormack (1996, pp. 52–68).

25. Bodde and Morris (1973) and Hulsewė (1955) propose the view that acts of moral or ritual impropriety or of criminal violence seem to be violations or disruptions of the total social order; the restoration of social harmony requires that punishments be inflicted to exact retribution from their doer. They argue that, in traditional Chinese thinking, a disturbance of the social order meant a violation of the total cosmic order because the spheres of man and nature were inextricably interwoven to form an unbroken continuum. MacCormack (1990, p. 42) argues that the view that each crime committed by an individual was believed to disturb cosmic harmony and thus entail the malfunctioning of natural punishment may be overdrawn and misleading. However, as MacCormack (1990, pp. 42–43) points out, there is some evidence for the proposition that legal punishment is believed to restore the disruption in the harmony of the universe caused by a crime. MacCormack (1990, p. 43) states that many statements are found in historical and literary sources to the effect that excessive cruelty in punishment, or the failure to punish those responsible for outrageous crimes, will lead to adverse manifestations of nature such as excessive rain or drought. This may reflect the general belief that gross cases of injustice are likely to lead to the visitation of an evil on the part of Heaven (MacCormack 1990, p. 43). It is believed that this view is still widely held by ordinary people in China today. However, as MacCormack (1990, p. 43) says, this should not lead one to conclude that every crime was thought (both by the ordinary people and by those responsible for the administration of justice) to disturb the harmony of nature unless the appropriate punishment was imposed on the offender. As MacCormack (1990, p. 45) suggests, one may accept the possibility that the Chinese did believe that glaring or repeated acts of injustice or maladministration on the part of the ruler or his officials might prompt some manifestations of Heaven's displeasure in the form of a natural disaster or prodigy, but it

would be absurd to accept that the Chinese believed that every criminal act disturbed the harmony of the universe and would be met with an act of requital. Furthermore, MacCormack (1990, p. 45) notes that, regarding the relationship between the doctrine of cosmic harmony and the penal codes, "by and large many people in all dynasties held that the acts of the ruler should accord with the 'will of Heaven.' Among these acts was the promulgation of the penal codes. Just as the 'will of Heaven' determined the course of natural phenomena so it determined the way in which humans should behave. Hence the ruler should ensure that the rules of behavior enforced by means of the penal code accorded with the 'will of Heaven'." For another argument against Bodde and Morris's view regarding disturbances of the cosmic order as a result of crimes, see Dau-Lin Hsu (1970).

26. For a discussion of nature and law in early China, see Turner (1993), Z. Liang (1991), and Chang (2016).

27. The Huang-Lao school of thought is a term for Daoism used by the people of the Han Dynasty. It was an influential school of thought in the early second century. Huang-Lao thought prospered during the late Warring States period and the Han Dynasty. It is named after the two most important deities, the Yellow Emperor, a mythical ruler of antiquity, and Lao Zi of Daoism. For a discussion of Huang-Lao and law, see Peerenboom (1993).

28. *Chunqiu fanlu* (*Luxuriant Gems of Spring and Autumn*) was believed to have been written by Dong Zhongshu, and its latest English version was edited and translated by Queen and Major (2015). The original Chinese text reads:

> 庆赏罚刑,与春夏秋冬,以类相应也,如合符,故曰,王者配天,谓其道。天有四时,王有四政,若四时,通类也,天人所同有也。庆为春,赏为夏,罚为秋,刑为冬。庆赏罚刑之不可不具也,如春夏秋冬不可不备也,庆赏罚刑,当其处不可不发,若暖暑清寒,当其时不可不出也,庆赏罚刑各有正处,如春夏秋冬各有时也,四政者不可以相干也,犹四时不可相干也,四政者不可以易处也,犹四时不可易处也。故庆赏罚刑有不行于其正处者,春秋讥也。

29. For the translation and discussion of Dong Zhongshu, see Fung Yu-lan (1952).

30. See Johnson (1979, pp. 10–11, 14) on the general principles of the Tang Code and his discussion of the harmony of law and nature as expressed in the Code. For discussions of law and nature and Dong Zhongshu's influence, see MacCormack (1989, 1990).

31. For different modes of cultural transmission, see Cavalli-Sforza and Feldman (1981), and Cao (2004).

32. As McKnight (1995, p. 411) says, Qing China did differ in very important ways from Tang China, but China continued to employ laws with relatively little change for a millennium. See also Head and Wang (2005, p. 229), calling the Chinese imperial codes "constitution" rather than ordinary laws.

33. Studies have shown that the phrase *faxue* (jurisprudence) was coined by the Japanese and then borrowed into the Chinese language: see Z. Liang (2004).

Chapter 3

Doing Justice Linguistically

A story was told from the 1940s in China. An American official delegation was visiting China and, to the amazement of the visitors, a Chinese host in conversation asked about the American "Emperor." It turned out that the Chinese host was under the impression that the United States was an empire and had an emperor as the head of state because the word "president" in English had been mistakenly translated into Chinese as "emperor," as the word "president" was believed to be the equivalent to *huangdi* (emperor) and *guojun* (monarch), instead of *zongtong* used today.[1] Similarly, *chaoting* (royal or imperial court/government) was first used to translate the English word "administration."

In the more recent past, in early 2011, Chinese president Hu Jintao was paying a state visit to the United States. In a television reports broadcast on Chinese television, a Chinese reporter asked ordinary Americans what they thought about the visit. One American was stopped by the Chinese reporter on a street in Chicago and asked about his impression of China and Hu Jintao. The African American pedestrian first said that almost everything was made in China these days, including the clothes and scarf he was wearing. He then said that he had heard about the Chinese president's visit. "He is a big man," he told the reporter. This was broadcast on CCTV, the Chinese state television broadcaster, and the report was in Chinese except that the American was speaking in English with Chinese subtitles running across the screen: 他是一个伟大的人（*Ta shi yi ge weida de ren*—He is a great man).

The above two examples illustrate some of the problems associated with words in translation. The first example is a case where wrong translation of seemingly simple institutional words may cause serious misunderstanding. In the second example, an inaccurate message was conveyed due to a deliberately manipulative choice of words in translation, literally putting words into someone's mouth without that someone or the receiving audience realizing it, other than viewers who were bilingual and were paying particular attention to the words spoken and written on the screen—as I was at the time. For people who have some familiarity with modern China, the word *weida* (great) carries significant political connotations. *Weida* is often used to describe the Chinese Communist Party (as in the common official sloganeering *weida guangrong zhengque de gongchandang*—the great, glorious and correct Chinese Communist Party), and is also often used for the top Chinese political leaders or figures. The American was obviously referring to Hu as a very important figure, but the Chinese media literally put into his mouth the kind of political phraseology that the Chinese government and its mouthpiece often employ. It is also obvious that such word choice and deliberate mistranslation were done for a reason.

This chapter focuses on the translation between English and Chinese of legal words or words used in legal contexts, and the manipulation of language in translation between English and Chinese. It first discusses the translation of Chinese institutional terms from imperial China into English, followed by a comparison of "justice" and *yi*, and an investigation of the meanings of the Chinese concept of *yi*. Lastly, it considers some of the implications of cross-cultural legal communication.

ENGLISH TRANSLATION OF CHINESE LAW-RELATED WORDS OF THE PAST

In contrast to the examples given at the beginning of the chapter, we now examine the reverse situation—translating from Chinese into English—as well as the manipulative use of English.

When one reads academic works written in English about traditional Chinese law, one inevitably comes across words and descriptions about Chinese legal institutions and operations. Commonly, for instance, one would read about the Chinese imperial Ministry of Justice, and imperial courts and judges or magistrates administrating justice in criminal trials, invoking laws and other rules in deciding cases, occasionally with lawyers assisting litigants in the process. Such descriptions may give one the impression that the imperial Chinese legal process and legal system operated and functioned in a somewhat similar fashion to Western courts, or that law functioned or played a similar role in traditional Chinese society to the one it plays in Western culture. However, such an assumption would be seriously mistaken. The Chinese courts and legal order never operated in any way that was similar to Western courts—certainly not in the past, and in many ways even today. Language and choice of words sometimes can mislead. Indeed, one may wonder whether the Western and Chinese commentators writing in English (including myself) about traditional Chinese law and courts set out to mislead readers.

The answer is plainly no, but the reasons are not straightforward. The main culprit has to do with language and translation, and the idiosyncrasies and similarities of diverse human experience and human societies.

Legal Institutional Words

In describing the traditional Chinese legal order, words such as courts, judges, and lawyers are often used in English translation. Yet the translation of seemingly simple legal institutional words may not be simple at all, even between closely related languages such as English and French or other European languages. For instance, when translating "court"-related words between English and French, such words may not correspond between the two languages. In the English court hierarchy, there are two words: "court" is the general term, while "tribunal" is a narrower term, referring to panels and bodies that exercise administrative or quasi-judicial functions with limited or special jurisdiction. But in French as it is used in France, there are three words for "courts": *cour, tribunal* and *juridiction. Cours* deliver *arrêts,* while the lower courts, called *tribunaux*, deliver *jugements* (Weston, 1991, p. 66). *Juridiction* is superordinate to *cour* and *tribunal*. Any *cour* or *tribunal* may be described as a *juridiction*, whereas some *juridictions* are *cours* and others are *tribunaux* (see Weston, 1991). In translation, *juridiction* needs to be translated as "court." If it is in plural, as in *les juridictions françaises*, it needs to be translated as "courts and tribunals." However, *juridiction d'instruction* needs to be translated as "judicial authority." The three French terms generally are translated by a single English word because the distinctions between *cour, tribunal*, and *juridiction*, insofar as they correspond at all to distinctions in the English language, are not reflected in the English language system (Weston, 1991, p. 67). There can be confusion when the French terms are translated literally into English.[2] More problems follow when we translate the two English words and three French words into Chinese, as in Chinese there are two generic words for "court"; *fayuan* and *fating. Fating* normally is used to describe specific courts for adjudication set up under the *fayuan* system—for instance, *xingshi fating* (criminal court)—while *fayuan* refers to the court in general; it is the generic term for the judicial institution and is used as part of the name of a court—for instance, *Beijing zhongji renmin fayuan* (Beijing Intermediate People's Court).[3] More complications arise when we translate legal institutional terms from classical Chinese into English, with different challenges.

Xing bu

As alluded to earlier, the Ministry of Justice in imperial China, as often described in English, did not actually exist. The name is the English translation of *Xing bu* (刑部Board of Punishments). *Xing,* as explained in chapter 2, means "punishment," not "justice." For most of imperial China, the Board of Punishments was a branch of the six major central government departments: *Li bu* (Board of Officials), *Hu bu* (Board of Revenue), *Li bu* (Board of Rites), *Bing bu* (Board of War), *Xing bu* (Board of Punishments), and *Gong bu* (Board of Works). The Board of Punishments was responsible for the national judicial and criminal matters. It was titled *Qiu guan* (Autumn Office) for a short time during the Tang Dynasty (618–907 CE).[4] The Board of Punishments was headed by an official called *Da si kou*, which later was changed to *Xingbu shangshu*. Confucius was once a *Da si kou*, a judicial officer. Furthermore, while *Xing bu* was the branch of the imperial government in charge of law and punishment for most of the imperial era, the Qing government gave it a name change in 1906 to become *Fa bu* (Ministry of Law, or Ministry of Legal Affairs) in an effort to distinguish it from its traditional past, to modernize and reform China's traditional legal system, and to introduce elements of Western-style constitutional rule.[5]

In terms of translation, *Xing bu* was uniquely Chinese in its naming, reflective of the philosophical thinking about law and the social reality and historical background of imperial Chinese law focusing on criminal punishments. As discussed in chapter 2, *xing* and *fa* are similar but different, with different symbolic meanings in the Chinese language. If the meaning of *xing* (punishment) in *Xing bu* is not translated into English, this, intentionally or unintentionally, portrays a partial picture of the role of law in imperial China. Besides, the name change in late Qing from *Xing bu* to *Fa bu* by the government was to signal and differentiate the roles of law in China in transition to modernity. If both these Chinese names were translated as Ministry of Justice, something would seem amiss. Given these, and the predominately criminal law focus of traditional Chinese law, it is more accurate to translate *Xing bu* as Board of Punishments. Not to translate *Xing bu* as Board of Punishments because of the absence of such an English term, thus opting for a more familiar term in English, is not a sufficient justification, despite the fact that this inaccurate translation has been used in English over the ages.

Courts

Another translation issue is found in Chinese court-related terms. The "court" as it is often used to describe criminal trials in traditional China does not actually exist as a physical space or as a specially designated law court. It is the general English description for *yamen* trial proceedings held in a *datang* (big hall) within a county *yamen*, which was the local government administrative headquarters in imperial China.[6] Trials of first instance were normally held and adjudicated by the county chief in *datang* within *yamen*.

Yamen 衙门 is unique in its function and role in imperial China; it is not an easily translatable term and has no equivalent in English. Often, *yamen* is used as a transliteration in English. As the *Oxford English Dictionary* explains, *yamen* is the office or residence of a public official in the Chinese Empire. *Yamen* existed at the *xian* (county), *zhou* (prefecture), *fu* (province), and central government levels. Within a local *yamen* at the lowest level of administration of a county, mandarins or officials managed the running of the local county or district under the direction of the chief official (often translated as county or district "magistrate") in charge of such matters as tax collection, local education and cultural matters, everyday civil affairs and law and order, investigating crimes, adjudicating civil and criminal cases, and issuing decrees and rules. *Yamen* did not have any specifically designated law court. *Datang*, the big hall or the main hall, was where the county chief conducted important business matters, including hearings of criminal and other cases as part of the functions of the local government. There was a designated prison within *yamen* for holding prisoners. The officials and their families also resided within the *yamen* compounds. The physical structure of *yamen* is virtually identical throughout ancient China, built on the same or similar architectural plan, all south facing, and some with 300–500 people living and working there at any one time (Meadows, 1847).[7] Interestingly, when a newly created office for dealing with foreign countries was set up by the late Qing government in 1861, it was named *Zongli yamen* (Office in Charge of Foreign Affairs), later changed to *Waiwu bu* (Ministry of Foreign Affairs) in 1901.

In short, neither *yamen* nor *datang* means "court," even though "court" has been used in English to describe where trial proceedings were held in imperial China.

Legal officers

With regard to the county or district "magistrates" in imperial China, as they are often referred to in English, they were not designated judicial officers but rather office holders of *yamen* at the county or district level as administrative officials or bureaucrats.

In imperial China, there were the central and local government administrative branches. There were some differences in the naming and title for these in different dynasties, but generally speaking, they were largely similar. For instance, in Qing Dynasty, for the administrative hierarchy for local government, each province had *zongdu* 总督(governor-general), *xunfu* 巡抚(governor), a lieutenant governor who was concurrently *buzhengshi* 布政使(provincial treasurer), and *anchashi* 按察使 (provincial judge, similar to and evolved from *tixing* 提刑in the Song Dynasty). Below the provincial level were *dao*道(circuits), presided over by daotai 道台(circuit intendants), who formed the intermediate link between the provincial and local functionaries. For the local administration, there were *fu* 府(prefecture) and *zhou* 州(department) or *xian* 县 (district, also translated as county). The chief official for the prefecture was *zhifu* 知府(prefect), literally "overseer of the prefecture." Under prefecture, there were department and district, each headed by a *zhizhou* 知州and *zhixian*知县, literally "overseer" of the department or district. The department or district head, the "overseer," has been translated as "the magistrate" (Djang, 1985, pp. 16–17).

For judicial officials, parallel to the Board of Punishments in terms of central government departments related to judicial matters, there was *Da li si* 大理寺, translated as the Court of Judicature, the highest court in the land; for most of the imperial reign, it was in charge of the review of major criminal cases and court matters. For instance, during the Ming and Qing Dynasties, *Da li si*, *Xing bu*, and *Duchayuan huishen* were the three official departments in charge of national judicial matters. In 1898, during the Hundred Days Reform, *Da li si* was merged with *Xing bu*, but in 1906 *Da li si* was separated again and changed to *Da li yuan* (Supreme Court). *Da li yuan* was used until 1927 when the government of the Republic of China changed it to *Zui gao fayuan* (Supreme Court). *Zui gao fayuan* has been used since for the supreme court in China. *Li* 理,the classical word for judges, is no longer used in this sense in modern Chinese. In some dynasties, such as the Song Dynasty (960–1279 CE), there was a judicial office, *Tidian xingyu si*, at the provincial level. The head official of the office was called *Tidian xingyu gongshi* (shortened to *tixing*, judicial intendant), a judge-cum-prosecutor whose responsibilities included holding circuit court hearings around different places in the province, and reviewing and investigating cases decided by different trial officials at county and prefecture levels (see below). The most famous official holding such a position was Song Ci (1186–1249 CE) of the Song Dynasty, who wrote the world first book on forensic medicine based on his experience as *tixing* (judicial intendant) (see also chapter 4).

The county chief, *zhixian*, also called *xianling* and *zhishi* at various times, was the head of a county within the county *yamen*. He was the county chief administrator or so to speak,[8] often colloquially referred to by ordinary Chinese as *xian tai ye* (county great-grandfather). As for the translated term "magistrate," this official title has invariably been used, either county or "district magistrate" or just "magistrate," for the Chinese county chief. It is unclear who was the first person to translate it into English this way, and when it occurred. "Magistrate" has been the standard English translation for the last couple of centuries. A more appropriate translation could be "county chief," or "head of county," although judicial duties were part of his portfolio.

As for the accuracy of the translations, we now review the issues in terms of the official functions, powers, and status of the office of the county chief, and from the perspective of the people under his governance, and in view of the status of law in ancient Chinese governance as a body politic. First, the imperial Chinese county chiefs—or "magistrates," as they are called in English—were classically trained scholars who had to pass vigorous imperial exams in order to became appointed officials.[9] They were sometimes referred to as "mandarin" in English. As the head of a county, they were in charge of and administered all aspects of governance at the lowest level of government on behalf of the emperor. Their power and functions were diverse and multiple:

> To the common people the magistrate was the government. He was the representative of the emperor, who was remote and whose power was awesome. The magistrate was the person to whom their taxes and labor-service imposes were due. He presided over the court of the first instance when they were in the clutches of the law. As head of the *pao-chia* system, he was responsible for keeping public order. He represented everyone when he prayed to the city god to avert catastrophe. He was the dispenser of imperial law and largess, and the arbiter of morals. It was also his responsibility to encourage agriculture, provide famine relief, supervise students, build and repair public works, and interpret imperial edicts to the public. The department or district *yamen* was the point where government and people met. The magistrate was, therefore, called *qinmin zhiguan*, the "official who was close to the people." In the paternalistic society of China, he was aptly addressed as *fumu guan*, "father and mother official." (Djang, 1984, pp. 21–22, with modification)[10]

In short, a magistrate would take charge of the government of a district—settling legal cases, meting out punishment, encouraging agriculture, extending charity to the poor, wiping out the wicked and the unlawful, promoting livelihood, fostering education, recommending scholars, reading and elucidating the law and imperial edicts, caring for the aged, and offering sacrifices to the gods (Chü, 1969; Watt, 1972). Such a "magistrate" was in charge of everything within the territory under his jurisdiction. His position was located at the very bottom of officialdom, and he managed complex relations with the constituency within his jurisdiction and with his superiors in the imperial bureaucracy (N. He, 2014, p. 27). It was commonly believed that the management of judicial and fiscal affairs was the principal role of the magistrate (L. Liang, 2007, p. 18). This is perhaps the reason why *xianling* and its variants were translated as "magistrate."

Another issue in translation is that the term "magistrate" does not accurately reflect the official functions and powers of this role; nor does it reflect the meanings of the Chinese word and how such an official was regarded by the Chinese people. As quoted above, from the Chinese perspective, such local government officials were the government and were *fumu guan*

(父母官father and mother officials, or parental officials). Correspondingly, the people governed by the officials were called *zimin* (children-people, or ordinary people), or commonly known as *laobaixing* (one hundred household names, ordinary folk) or *chenmin* (subjects). The term *fumu guan* (parental official) can help illuminate for English readers the Chinese perspective and mentality regarding the role of officials as parental officials. This is more than just a figurative expression.

First, the term *fumu guan* is believed to have into usage influenced by a Confucian classic, the Great Learning:

> In the Book of Poetry, it is said: "How much to be rejoiced in are these princes, the parents of the people!" When a prince loves what the people love, and hates what the people hate, then is he what is called the parent of the people. (Legge, 1970, p. 374)

Second, in imperial China, parents were in total control of their children and their life. Parents' absolute authority and guardianship lasted the entire lives of their children right up until the passing of the parents. Officials with total authority and control of the people under their charge were also regarded as having a guardianship role over the people, in the manner of a father dealing benevolently and often intrusively with his children. Such power and authority could determine a person's life and death, as one's parents would in traditional China. Corresponding expressions are *ai min ru zi* (loving the people as one's own children) and *shi min ru zi* (regarding the people as one's own children). From such a standpoint, *fumu guan* was used as a complimentary affirmation of a local official who was deemed as caring and paternal as one's parents; this was the model and ideal that local officials strived to achieve. The phrase has been used in China over the last two thousand years with positive connotations. Only in recent times has the Chinese government started to change tones in declaring that such a description is anachronistic and no longer appropriate. It says that officials should not regard themselves as parents of the people; it should be the other way around—that is, officials should regard the people as parents and serve them.[11]

Third, specific to the county chief's judicial role, a legal secretary working for a county head in the Qing Dynasty once wrote that whenever he was assisting on a case—great or small—he always sat quietly for a while, put himself in the position of the criminal, and reflected about it as if he were his "father and mother" (Watt, 1972, p. 230). The Chinese description of the job title of the county chief was the "overseer" and "head" of a locality—just as the father, as the head of a family, decided matters affecting people's life, for the county chief, adjudicating matters of all kinds, including legal matters, was only a part of the role. These officials were the highest local officials closest to the lives of the ordinary people at the local level, and their role combined both authority and power (Watt, 1972). *Xianling*'s position made him both the highest official in close contact with the lives of the people and the only local official whose power was of any immediate concern to them, as well as the dominant symbol of political power (Watt, 1972, p. 11). He was the sole "father and mother official" (Watt, 1972, p. 17).

The English translation "magistrate" fails to capture and represent the political and parental symbolic power of the head official in imperial China. Instead, it gives an unwarranted emphasis to the judicial and legal role of the position while omitting the dominant meaning of the original Chinese. In the Chinese language, and for the Chinese people, this official position was first and foremost a government official position, a position with power and control over people's lives and the government business of a locality. This position was that of an imperial delegate, and represented the local symbol of the unitary power of the emperor and the legitimate source of authority.

Fourth, generally speaking, in most dynasties the head at each level of government had executive and military as well as judicial responsibilities, and the first two of these were generally considered to be more important (Chang, 2016, p. 501). This conformed to, and was reflective of, the prevailing philosophical ideas in traditional China as well (as described in chapter 2)—that is, law was not a first-order norm in the governance of Chinese society or the main regulator of social relationships. Thus the emphasis on the judicial role in the title of "magistrate" in English is unwarranted and misleading.

In short, "magistrate" does not reflect the multifunctional roles and multilayered meanings of the county chief as the local *fumu* official in imperial China. "Magistrate" in the English translation highlights the judicial responsibility of the Chinese official position, likely miscommunicating the pragmatic, literal, and symbolic meanings of the Chinese title. The Chinese saw the job of county chief as encompassing all sorts of duties, including legal matters, as a parent figure of an official, rather than the judicial and legal role. In this connection, a similar example is the inaccurate translation of the title of the historical figure Bao Gong (see chapter 4), reflecting the different perspectives of the Chinese and non-Chinese, respectively. Judge Bao—or Justice Bao as he is known in English—is the most renowned detective judge from Chinese history (Hayden, 1974, p. 205), but his title and name in Chinese say nothing about him being a judge. In Chinese, he is called Bao Gong (Sir Bao) and Bao Qingtian (Clear Sky Bao). For most of his civil service during his life, Bao Gong was not a judge, and he is not called a judge in Chinese. But at various times, he held the position of a county head and prefect, prosecuting criminal cases, and was also a fiscal commissioner, deputy head of the Board of Punishments, and deputy commissioner of the Board of Revenue, among other positions. Bao Gong is best known to the Chinese as a *qingguan* (clean official), a competent, impartial, incorruptible, and upright official, not yielding to the rich and powerful and acting in the people's and country's interest, rather than seeking personal gain. Admittedly, he is also known as an official who upholds justice and makes just decisions—an embodiment of justice. It is not entirely wrong to call him a judge, but by calling him Judge Bao in English, the emphasis is on his judicial role, while in Chinese and to the Chinese people, he is much more than a judge: he is a highly respected and much admired official. Like the translation of "magistrate," the title Judge Bao is not accurate—although nor is it entirely wrong. The English words convey partial meanings in the original Chinese, focusing on the legal aspect. This accentuation of law is not justified, given the low priority and status of law in traditional China and, very importantly, in the minds and eyes of the Chinese people.

Lawyers

As for lawyers, there were lawyers of sorts in traditional China, not throughout all of imperial times, but mainly during the late imperial period in the Ming and Qing Dynasties. They were unlike modern lawyers in China or elsewhere. They gave people advice on legal matters and helped people to draft complaints and other legal documents, such as contracts or deeds, as most ordinary Chinese in imperial times were illiterate. They were called *songshi*, litigation masters, or more commonly known as *songgun*, literally litigation hooligans or tricksters, among other derogatory names.[12] They enjoyed very low prestige, were regarded as malicious and greedy pettifoggers, and some were persecuted for performing legal services.[13] They operated outside the law, not sanctioned by the state, had a very low social status, and were despised widely—partly due to Confucian influence to downplay and minimize litigation as a dispute-resolution avenue. Their activities were viewed as being inconsistent with Confucian teaching:

> Litigation masters, often called "litigation hooligans" (*songgun* 讼棍), had an unsavoury reputation. They were associated with a variety of questionable legal behavior, which epithets to describe them reflect: inciting litigation (*jiaosuo cisong* 教唆词讼), proxy litigation (*baolan cisong* 包揽词讼), reversing right and wrong (*diandao shifei* 顛倒是非), calling black white (*bianluan heibai* 变乱黑白), habitual erasers (*guanlong daobi* 惯弄刀笔), falsifying and passing appeals (*jiaci yuegao* 架词越告), bribing yamen officials (*dadian yamen* 打点衙门), colluding with corrupt officials (*chuantong yadu* 串通衙蠹), ensnaring country bumpkins (*youxian xiangyu* 诱陷乡愚), cheating good people (*qiya liangmin* 欺压良民), stealing commissions (*congzhong quli* 从中取利), and extorting and swindling (*kongxia qicai* 恐吓欺财). Thus, according to public perception at least, litigation masters encouraged unnecessary litigation,

> protected the guilty, employed tricky means to secure success, embellished litigation documents, colluded with *yamen* functionaries such as clerks and runners, and robbed good people of their money. In short, they were ruffians who committed every evil deed imaginable. *Songshi* has often been translated into English as "pettifogger," but this term is inadequate to describe the extent to which the authorities loathed litigation masters, nor does it reveal, conversely, how important a role litigation masters played in society. (Fuma, 2007 [1993], p. 80, Chinese in the original with modifications)

In imperial China, there was no legal profession. Those litigation masters were very different from the modern lawyer (Fuma, 2007 [1993], p. 80). Although litigation masters had legal skills and knowledge, they were not allowed to represent clients in court proceedings, and defence assistance by third parties was largely prohibited throughout the imperial period, as such practices were regarded as inciting the populace to challenge the small elitist establishment and represented rebelliousness and disrespect for the paternalistic bureaucracy (Lu and Miethe, 2007, p. 35). Despite this, it does not mean that imperial China was lawless. There was a large body of laws consisting of imperial codes, and detailed laws and procedural requirements, in all the imperial dynasties. Nevertheless, as pointed out already, the basic functional needs of the prevailing rulers to maintain and enhance their hierarchical authority resulted in a criminal process that was highly disciplinary and repressive throughout imperial history (Lu and Miethe, 2007, pp. 35–36).

In short, the translation of law-related institutional words from ancient China is not an easy task, due to the idiosyncrasy of the Chinese system and substantive differences between Chinese and Western legal orders and the two linguistic systems.

CONCEPTUAL TRANSLATABILITY BETWEEN *YI* AND "JUSTICE"

Now let us examine the word "justice" in English and its Chinese counterpart *zhengyi/yi* 正义/义. This is more complex than translating institutional terms because justice is a legal concept, and there are substantive and substantial conceptual gaps between Chinese and English, posing challenges in translation.

As I questioned the translation of *Xing bu* as Ministry of Justice earlier, and pointed out that *xing* means "punishment," not "justice," nevertheless this linguistic fact alone does not necessarily exclude a possibility of translating *Xing bu* as Ministry of Justice. Sometimes seemingly different words may denote the same or similar realities when used in translation. By the same token, sometimes identical or similar words used in law may not mean the same thing due to the fundamental differences found in the background culture and legal order of different societies. Apart from the semantic and general linguistic differences or similarities, we need to look more deeply, and consider the relative status of the linguistic signs in their cultural and behavioral contexts of use and the respective philosophical traditions and legal cultures.

The English Concept of Justice

First, let us have a brief look at the meaning of "justice" in English, without going into the theories or history of justice in Western legal philosophy. In terms of linguistic meanings, according to the *Oxford English Dictionary*, online,[14] "justice" means, among other things:

- Administration of law or equity: maintenance of what is just or right by the exercise of authority or power; punishment of an offender; administration of law and due legal process; and justice personified.
- Agent of the administration of law or equity: judicial officers.
- The quality of being just or right.

The word "justice" comes from the Latin *jus*, meaning "right" or "law." As pointed out, it may be necessary to get beyond etymology and dictionary definitions to consider, for example, the nature of justice as both a moral virtue of character and a desirable quality of political society, as well as how it applies to ethical and social decision-making (Pomerleau, n.d.). Justice is one of the most important moral and political concepts, and Western philosophers generally regard justice as the most fundamental of all virtues for ordering interpersonal relations and establishing and maintaining a stable political society (Pomerleau, n.d.). I may add that it is also the most fundamental in the Western conception and practice of law. In Western thought about justice, although institutions varied dramatically in history, the idea of dualistic justice was a regulator in the historical evolution from ancient to modern law (Deng, n.d., p. 5). Linking law with justice also has a long history, as evidenced in ancient Greek philosophy, including Plato and Aristotle, as well as ancient Roman laws and English legal philosophers such as Blackstone and Bentham. The Justinian law declares: "Justice is the constant and perpetual desire to give everyone that to which he is entitled," and "Jurisprudence is the knowledge of matters divine and human, and the comprehension of what is just and what is unjust" (*Justinian's Institutes*, 1987, 1.1.10). According to Aristotle, the word "just" or "justice" has two meanings: first, it is used to describe a conduct in agreement with the law, "a moral disposition which renders men apt to do just things and which causes them to act justly and to wish what is just"—that is, the application or observance of the law; and second, justice signifies equality (Chroust and Osborn, 1942, pp. 129–130). In modern times, as Hart (1994 [1961]) explains, there is a certain complexity in the structure of the idea of justice, consisting of two parts: a uniform or constant feature, summarized in the precept "Treat like cases alike"; and a shifting or varying criterion used in determining when cases are alike or different. In other words, treating like cases alike and treating different cases differently is essentially a restatement of Aristotle's distributive and retributive justice—justice is equality for equals and inequality for those who are unequal (Aristotle, 1997, Chroust and Osborn, 1942). More specifically in the practice and implementation of law in Euro-American legal systems, distributive justice concerns the division of shares in social benefits and burdens—fairness in the distribution of rights or resources; retributive or corrective justice involves the rectification of injustice—fairness in the correction of wrongs, including criminal law, torts and contracts, and procedural justice concerns the fairness and the transparency of the processes by which decisions are made. Therefore, justice is more than settling disputes or deciding whether a person is guilty of a crime. It may be true that the word "justice" is language dependent and may differ semantically in major European languages (Wiezbicka, 2006, pp. 155–156); nevertheless, the concept of "justice" is largely understood in a similar sense in Western legal philosophy, and it entails the meanings of respecting persons as free, rational agents at its core (Pomerleau, n.d.). The concept of justice, including Aristotle's dualistic justice, is the foundation of the law and legal culture of the Greco-Roman civilization. This is the case despite different views and philosophies and conceptions of justice in both the ancient and modern West. Justice has been a keyword and key concept in Western law, and has been the goal of Western law and legal process or as Lon Fuller (1969) sums up, law is the means and justice is the end, and let justice be done, though the heaven may fall. If law is a system of rules, the idea of justice would be its architecture. In contrast, I suggest that the Chinese concept of *yi* has different meanings, status, and application in relation to Chinese law and legal tradition.

The Chinese Concept of Yi 义

As discussed earlier, despite the fact that *Xing bu* is often translated as Ministry of Justice, *xing* does not mean "justice." The linguistic equivalent of "justice" is *zhengyi* in modern Chinese.

In terms of meaning, *zhengyi* has a long etymological history, like its counterpart "justice." *Zhengyi* is believed to have first been used in *Xunzi* over two thousand years ago; however, unlike the Greek origin of "justice" associated with the meaning of law and rights, *zhengyi* was not connected with law, much less with rights, which did not exist in the classical Chinese vocabulary (see chapter 5). According to Chinese dictionaries, *zhengyi* in classical Chinese is used as two words, *zheng* and *yi*, and there are two broad separate and unconnected meanings. For the first meaning of *zheng* and *yi*, *zheng* means "correct" and *yi* has the sense of "meaning," as used in the book title *Wujing Zhengyi* (*the Correct Meanings of the Five Classics*). For the second broad meaning, *zhengyi* is associated with the meaning of fair, just, and righteous. Here, *zheng* means "straight and upright," and *yi* means "righteous." So *yi* carries the two broad senses: "meaning" or "significance," and "righteous" or "righteousness," "rightness," "principle," "integrity," "duty," "just" or "justice." It has another unrelated sense of adopted or adoptive, as in *yizi* (adopted son). *Zhengyi* and *yi* were not used in any of the official titles or institutional names, or in the imperial codes in traditional China in the sense of "righteousness" or "justice." In classical Chinese, *yi* was not used in the sense of "justice" or "righteousness" in the legal process or in law,[15] unlike the word "justice" in English and its variations in different Western languages in relation to Western law and legal order.

In addition, in the modern usage of *zhengyi*, according to the *Chinese Xinhua Dictionary* (online), *zheng* means straight, and *yi* means fair and appropriate reasons or acts. The dictionary says that *zhengyi* as one word means the affirmative judgment regarding right and wrong, and good and evil, in the political, legal, and moral spheres; it is a synonym of *gongzheng* in moral discourse, referring to the conducts that conform to certain social and moral norms. It also says that conformation of people's conduct to the historical development norms and the fundamental interests of the overwhelming majority of the people is the objective criteria for judging whether people's conduct conforms to *zhengyi*/justice. In another Chinese dictionary, *zhengyi* is defined as meaning "justice in the sense of fair and just reasons," "just and correct," and "the affirmative assessment of good and evil and right and wrong in political, legal and moral arenas, as part of morality."[16] It is noted that the contemporary legal usage and meaning of *zhengyi* in China is very much influenced by, or largely direct imported from, Western justice theories. There is little systematic explication or indigenous theories of the concept of *zhengyi* in Chinese jurisprudence. *Zhengyi* has become an important word over the last decade or so in China, mainly due to Western influence in contemporary Chinese law. Accordingly, the modern philosophical or legal meaning of *zhengyi* in China today will not be discussed further here. Instead, we focus on the meaning and usage of *yi* in classical Chinese.

Yi is a keyword in Confucian philosophy, a central concept in Confucianism. It is one of the Confucian five constant virtues (*wuchang*) that constitute the foundation of Confucianism. The constant virtues were first formulated in Confucius's teaching as *ren* (仁benevolence or humaneness), *yi* (义righteousness or rightness), and *li* (礼propriety or rites), expanded to *ren, yi, li,* and *zhi* (智wisdom or knowledge) in Mencius, and further expanded in Dong Zhongshu to *ren, yi, li, zhi, xin* (仁, 义, 礼, 智, 信, benevolence, righteousness, rites, wisdom, and sincerity or trustworthiness). The five virtues have been part of the moral teaching for the Chinese for the last two thousand years (except the chaotic decades of the PRC). They are often called *meide* (beautiful virtues) for an exemplary or virtuous person in modern parlance.

In the Confucius Analects (as cited in Ames and Rosemont 1998), *yi* is explained in this way: "The Master said, 'Exemplary persons (*junzi*) understand what is *yi* (appropriate); petty persons understand what is of personal advantage (*li*)'." *Yi* is used 24 times in *The Analects*, and it generally refers to rectitude, justice, or simply right, correct (Chang, 2016, p. 50). There was no definition for *yi* or for what is right, correct or just. It was said that to Confucius, there was a right principle governing every relationship and a right way for a person to follow in his dealings with the world (Chang, 2016, p. 50). As Confucius believed in the basic feelings and aspirations common to humans, what was in agreement with common human feelings and aspirations was considered right and correct, and people should know this innately, although this argument is not on particularly firm ground (Chang, 2016, p. 50). In this regard, another important explanation found in *The Analects* relates *ren* (benevolence), *yi* and *li* (rites or propriety), the three most important concepts in Confucianism:

> Benevolence [*ren*] is the characteristic element of humanity, and the great exercise of it is in loving relatives. *Righteousness* [*yi*] is the accordance of actions with what is right, and the great exercise of it is in honoring the worthy. The decreasing measures of the love due to relatives, and the steps in the honor due to the worthy, are produced by the principle of propriety [*li*]. (Legge, 1970, pp. 404–405)

Here, *yi* (righteousness) is explained by another Chinese word homonym, *yi* 宜, with the same pronunciation but different writing. This second *yi* means "fitting," "suitable," or "appropriate," that is, fitting or appropriate for a situation or context. *Yi* is the ethical set of moral principles that underlies Confucianism. *Yi* represents the perfection of morality, and *li* (rites) is the expression of *yi*.

Confucianism highly values the notion of *yi* or righteousness in a person's moral compass as the highest state of morality. In another classical Confucian text, Mencius, *yi* is also used frequently, referring generally to being ethical. To Mencius, *yi* is said to have evolved from the sense of shame. It is rooted in human nature and amounts to a natural human propensity, focusing on the inherent dignity of a person among his peers and in social relationships. To be able to foster yi in this sense is to be able to preserve the intrinsic dignity and social responsibility of a person and as a specific virtue (Cheng, 1997, p. 186). *Yi* involves acts importing significance into the world through optimizing appropriateness in relations with others (Hall and Ames, 1987, p. 94). Such acts of *yi* contribute to the cultivation of an exalted self that is not an atomistic individual constantly in competition or at war with others, but a person-in-context for whom social relations are constitutive of their sense of self (Hall and Ames, 1987, p. 94). In this connection, Mencius developed and explained the dichotomy of *yi li* (righteousness vs. interest or profit), the same phrase mentioned in chapter 1, recycled by the Chinese leadership today. *Yili* (righteousness vs. interest, benefit, or profit) are often used together as a phrase, as a contrast, the *yili* dichotomy. The positive *yi* and negative *li* and their relationships have been part of the intellectual debates in China since the pre-imperial times, as Confucius contrasts *yi* for the exemplary person and *li* for the petty person, discussed above. Mencius thought there was almost an inherent conflict between the two (Chang, 2016, p. 50). Hence, in Chinese, there are a few idioms contrasting *yi* and *li*—for instance, *jian li wang yi* (见利忘义 forget honor at the prospect of profits or gains, disregard moral principles in pursuit of self-interest), *jian li si yi* (见利思义 remember what is right at the sight of profits or gains). It is noted that none of these meanings are law or justice related.

A word of caution here regarding definition of classical Chinese concepts. As pointed out, Chinese are good at concrete thinking while abstract thinking only transitorily existed among the logicians prior to Qin Dynasty (221–206 BCE), and became lost in Chinese philosophical tradition; the Chinese incorporated abstract logical thinking into concrete profound theories and seldom separately study it in an abstract way (Mou, 1983, cited in Zeng and Ma, 2006; for further discussion, see Zeng and Ma, 2006). One illustration of this is the way in which many key concepts of Confucianism found in *The Analects* and other Chinese classics are discussed. Each time a concept is elaborated, it has different illustrations with different specific focus and concrete examples. This is also true for ancient Chinese statements of law and law-related concepts. Ancient Chinese philosophers and scholars held their own opinions about law and its functions, but there was no complete or rigorous representation of key legal concepts such as *fa* formulated by ancient Chinese (Zeng and Ma, 2006, pp. 36–37). Generally speaking, "no diligent building of accurate and strict definitions and concepts and no conscious system construction are the features of traditional Chinese learning" (Zeng and Ma, 2006, p. 36). This is also true of the word and notion of *yi*.

Yi is an essential concept in Confucianism, a complex concept, and it has many meanings, connotations, and dimensions that can be interpreted and understood in multiple ways. For instance, as described, "*yi* is the standard by which all acts must be judged while there is no further standard by which *yi* itself can be judged," and the object of all learning is *yi*, and all rites, and rules of conduct are based on *yi* (Lau, 1979, p. 3). The *yi* principles represent right action, duty, and righteousness. It has also been proposed that *yi* is a characteristic of acts (Lau, 1979, p. 27, cited in Tan, 2014, p. 492), and is both external and internal—about agent as well as action (Tan, 2014, p. 492). Moreover, it is said that there is a concept of justice in Confucianism, since *yi* sometimes behaves like the word "just," meaning "to treat cases that belong to the same kind alike and cases that belong to different kinds differently" (Xiao, 1997). Ch'en Ta-ch'i (cited in Xiao, 1997) classifies the use of *yi* in Mencius into four categories: (1) self-regarding morality; (2) others-regarding morality; (3) norms or values; and (4) principles of human affairs (Ch'en, cited in Xiao, 1997, p. 535).[17] Another explanation of *yi* goes like this:

> Confucian notion of justice *(yi)* has different meanings, the most primary of which refers to a person's righteousness or the appropriateness of one's action. To act in accordance with *yi* is to act according to the ethical norms associated with one's social role—for example, a son's *yi* is to be filial to his parents. Most analyses of *yi* in contemporary scholarly literature focus on this primary meaning. However, "social justice" means the justice of distribution of resources (or, more generally, benefits or burdens). Social justice, or *distributive* justice, is not a prominent concept in Confucianism, as it receives little systematic, explicit treatment in Confucian texts. It is difficult to tell whether Confucianism has a theory of social justice. The reasons are partly *conceptual*—what "social justice" means is not very clear; partly *interpretive*—traditional Confucian concepts are quite different from modern social and political concepts and hence difficult to be interpreted in modern languages; and partly *historical*—the historical conditions in which Confucianism evolved are very different from those in present times. (Chan, 1994a)

As we have seen, *yi* does not have a definite or clear-cut meaning. Given its complexity, *yi* does not have a one-to-one equivalent in English. Nevertheless, it is regarded as a word having resemblance to "justice" in English, or the only classical Chinese word that has meanings close to "justice."

Yi versus Justice

In view of the foregoing discussion of *yi* as a counterpart to "justice," in both Western and Chinese cultures, moral values are built into the meanings of justice and *yi*. However, the Western concept of justice and the Chinese concept of *yi* are distinct and display different characteristics in their usage and status. The basic meanings of *yi* are different from "justice." "Justice" in English, as described earlier, is associated with the general meaning of the administration of law, with an etymological origin in the meaning of law and rights. Justice is not merely the sum of all virtues, but the source of all virtues (Cheng, 1997, p. 183). In contrast, in Chinese traditional culture and philosophy, *yi* is a comprehensive, concrete, practical, and personal concept. It more signifies a virtue or a character trait for a good person, or *junzi*—a gentleman, a moral person. *Yi* is one of the moral dispositions of such a cultivated person. It is about right or appropriate thinking and acting from one's own viewpoint, with rational action, self-restraint to resist temptation, and the fortitude to do one's duty in one's social relations and interactions, and preserving one's integrity. *Yi* means living and behaving according to Confucian moral standards and virtues, instead of seeking personal gains or pursuing self-interest. The practice and cultivation of such virtues are essential to becoming a good person in guiding individual ethical actions and decision-making. As such, *yi* is one of the basic virtues and character traits of a humane and virtuous person that must be cultivated.

Furthermore, and for our purpose, justice in Western culture and civilization is a legal concept, a keyword in Western law and legal culture. In Western civilization, the concept of justice was integrated into law early in the development of Western law (that is, the legal system and legal culture originated in the Greco-Roman tradition), and it has become essential and fundamental to it. Justice plays a significant role in Western philosophical, political, and legal thought, and the concept of justice shapes the political and legal system. The concept of justice is a keyword and foundational concept in Western law. In contrast, *yi* in the Chinese tradition is not a legal word or a key concept in Chinese law, although in its many different shapes and forms, it carries the sense of righteousness, just and fair and sometimes the meaning of justice. We are reminded that Confucianism and its basic tenets were incorporated into traditional Chinese law and individual life and Chinese society as a whole. Nevertheless, *yi* as a concept and practice was not a goal or guiding principle for law and legal process because it was not conceived in that way. Here, we try to avoid the trap of comparing *yi* in Confucianism to the modern Western concept of justice. A juxtaposition of justice in Aristotle and *yi* in Confucian classics as shown in the foregoing amply demonstrates this. This is not a value judgment or criticism of one or the other. Such recognition is necessary and relevant to our discussion. One of the most important characteristics of Chinese philosophy is said to be the conspicuous lack of a term for "justice." There is not a term for "justice" in the classical lexicon of Confucius (Peerenboom, 1990). *Yi* has been translated in terms associated with justice—righteousness, duty, principle, obligation—but never consistently as justice (Peerenboom, 1990). However, it is also true and correct to say:

> we cannot presuppose that there must be *one* word or term in Chinese that corresponds to the English word "justice," and there might be a complex relationship between the English word "justice" and a set of Chinese words, not just one Chinese word. Or, if there is a corresponding relationship between "justice" and a Chinese word, it may be that only some uses of this Chinese word, not necessarily the other uses of the word, can be said to mean "justice." (Xiao, 1997, p. 524)

It is acknowledged that the reluctance of translating *yi* as justice has to with do with the extremely diverse uses of *yi* in Confucian ethics (Xiao, 1997, p. 524). I would argue that, first, this points to the fact that *yi* does not always carry the meaning or a close meaning of "justice." In fact, in most cases it does not mean "justice" or "just" in a more general sense, and does not carry the sense of justice associated with law. Its meanings are mostly unrelated to law as we have in the earlier discussions. Even within the imperial codes, none of the varied meanings of *yi* is related to "righteousness" or "justice" (Cao, 2018, forthcoming). Second, there was no other alternative word or concept for the equivalent of "justice" in classical Chinese legal discourse and traditional Chinese law. Third, it is commonly agreed that in traditional Confucian ethics, there is no modern liberal conception of justice in terms of equal liberties and inalienable individual rights (Xiao, 1997), and this is hardly surprising. Our interest here is that there was no equivalent word or conception in classical Chinese for the old meaning of "justice" expounded in old Western philosophies and legal jurisprudence such as Plato, Aristotle, Blackstone, and Bentham, which were fundamental to and closely intertwined with the concept and practice of law in Western civilization. Fourth, if one accepts that *yi* in Confucian ethics contains the meaning of justice in the sense of "treating like cases alike and treat different cases differently," as Xiao (1997) argues, the fact remains that *yi* in this sense was not considered fundamental or central, or as a guiding principle or goal in the thinking and practice of traditional Chinese law. This is because that law was regarded predominantly as a tool of punishments and rewards to carry out the state's or emperor's will against the broad backdrop of a culture dominated by Confucian doctrines that lacked comparable ideas of law in the Western style (Deng, n.d., p. 15). *Yi* in the sense of justice was not advocated as a pillar or foundation for the legal order in traditional China.

My proposition is not to deny that *yi* can and sometimes does mean "justice," nor to claim that the sense of justice was absent from traditional Chinese culture and philosophy. Indeed, *yi* can be understood to have meanings of justice and *yi* was a concept of justice in the Chinese way and in the Chinese context (see Xiao, 1997). However, the concept and word of *yi* was not fundamental or central to Chinese imperial law and the legal system in the same or similar way as the conception of "justice" has been to Western law and civilization. Such a deficit in Chinese legal culture also finds an echo in the word *yuan* (injustice) as a keyword in traditional Chinese law, legal order, and legal culture as I have argued (see chapter 4). This Chinese phenomenon is not often commented on in the literature on Chinese law, but only occasionally, as noted in Wan (2015), was the word "justice" used in the Chinese court-case drum ballads she studied: "From the way the plots are constructed—a crime is exposed and the judge resolves it by punishing the wrongdoer—one could say that justice is a central concept in these court-case drum ballads. Intriguingly, there is no one term that clearly means 'justice' in these stories" (Wan, 2015, p. 289). As said, "whatever the cause, many Western scholars have found little to suggest that the Chinese populace viewed the formal criminal justice process as a means through which individual justice might be secured" (Alford, 1984, pp. 1995–1196).

As a linguistic exercise, I compared the idiomatic expressions containing the word "justice" in English and idioms containing *yi* in Chinese as a pointer to their respective linguistic manifestation in relation to law (Cao, 2018, forthcoming). For "justice" in English, there are many common phrases and expressions associated with law—for instance, "to bring someone to justice"; "miscarriage of justice"; "travesty of justice"; "poetic justice"; "rough justice"; "social justice"; "justice is blind"; "justice is served"; "natural justice"; and "justice has long arms," among many others. Most of these expressions tend to be used in relation to law or the legal process. In contrast, for *chengyu* (idioms) containing *yi*, there are over one hundred such expressions. *Chengyu*, or set phrases or idioms, are traditional idiomatic expressions, usually consisting of four characters, and most have ancient origin and derived from classical works. They are part of the classical Chinese developed over the centuries, and are commonly used today as part of the modern Chinese language. None of the over one hundred Chinese idioms containing *yi*, as far as I can ascertain, is associated with law or the administration of justice. The meanings of *yi* in these expressions belong to two broad categories: the sense of "meaning" in a small number of cases (for instance, *duan zhang qu yi* 断章取义to interpret out of context, to make a deliberate misinterpretation out of context), and the sense of appropriate, righteousness, duty, or related meanings in most other cases (for instance, *bei xin qi yi*背信弃义 treachery, or breach of trust), *bu yi zhi cai*不义之财 ill-gotten gains; obtained by inappropriate or dubious means, *jia ren jia yi* 假仁假义pretend to be the a paragon of virtue; sham benevolence and righteousness, *li yi lian chi* 礼义廉耻the sense of propriety, integrity or honor; and the sense of shame, and *zhong xiao jie yi* 忠孝节义loyalty, filial piety, chastity, and righteousness. Many of these idioms are associated with or derived from Confucian teaching. None is associated with law (with the only one possible exception being *da yi mie* *qin* 大义灭亲which can be used to refer to the sense of justice or doing the right thing, unlike the counterpart English "justice" (for a detailed discussion, see Cao, 2018, forthcoming). This linguistic evidence may be regarded as another indication that *yi* is not a legal word in Chinese. Interestingly, the English expression "justice has long arms" is often translated into Chinese as *tian wang hui hui, shu er bu lou* 天网恢恢, 疏而不漏—literally, "the net of Heaven has large meshes, but it lets nothing through," a saying from Laozi of Daoism. It refers to people who commit criminal acts, who will not be able to escape unpunished and will get caught. Both idioms carry similar meanings, but the Chinese expression does not use *yi* or other similar words, instead, using a totally different metaphor.

In short, *yi* and justice are dissimilar in their semantics and meaning associations in Chinese and English legal culture and law, respectively. Justice is a keyword in Western law such as English, but *yi* is not a legal word or concept in traditional China. Besides this, and more importantly, there is a conspicuous absence of a keyword or a set of keywords in traditional Chinese law corresponding to the English keyword and concept of "justice" in a similar status or relationship with Western law, legal order, and legal culture. There was no such a keyword, linguistically or conceptually, in classical Chinese and traditional Chinese law.

TRANSLATION ISSUES IN CROSS-JURISDICTIONAL COMMUNICATION

In view of the foregoing discussion of the translation of legal institutional terms and the legal concept of justice and *yi*, a few words about legal translation across different jurisdictions are warranted.

There are two general translation strategies in dealing with foreign words, concepts, and texts regarding the degree to which the translator makes a text conform to the target culture. One is foreignization—that is, the form of translation deliberately foregrounds the cultural other, so that the translated text can never be presumed to have originated in the target language; the final product may seem strange and unfamiliar (Bielsa and Bassnett, 2009, p. 9). In contrast, domestication or acculturation is the strategy of making the translated text closely conform to the culture of the target language, which may involve the loss of information from the source text (Venuti, 1995). In domestication, the translated text is adapted to suit the norms of the target culture, since the signs of its original foreignness are erased (Bielsa and Bassnett, 2009, p. 9). The domesticating strategy is said to "violently" erase the cultural values, and thus create a text that appears as if had been written in the target language and that follows the cultural norms of the target reader (Venuti,

1995). Furthermore, Venuti (1992, 1995) is of the view that the dichotomy between domestication and foreignization is an ideological one. According to Venuti (1995), every translator should look at the translation process through the prism of culture, which refracts the source language cultural norms. It is the translator's task to convey them, preserving their meaning and their foreignness, to the target language text. There is a tendency in English translation of foreign texts of over-domestication, the tendency to minimize the foreignness of the target text and reduce the foreign cultural norms to English language and cultural values.

For legal translation, there is no strict rule about which approach is preferable, although it seems appropriate that the translation of legal concepts should try to preserve as much as possible the original tenor and style. Such translation should be source language and culture oriented, especially in terms of translating legal concepts and institutional terms. For translating legal terms from Chinese into English—particularly from classical Chinese into English, generally speaking—there is a tendency to domesticate, making the Chinese legal processes and practices sound like familiar English, as illustrated by the use of words such as "magistrate," "court," and "Ministry of Justice," losing some of the meanings in the process.

For translation of Chinese law, an early case of domestication and acculturation is Staunton's (1966 [1810]) translation of the Great Qing Code, where the translator bends over backward to make the translation of the imperial Chinese law comprehensible to the English reader (André, 2004). Staunton omits, adds, and changes negative Chinese words into affirmative English legal terms, and makes imperial Chinese law sound "logically organized, well-reasoned, universal in scope, non-contradictory, best adapted for Chinese culture, changing over time to meet the needs of a changing society, and esteemed and honoured by the population because it is just"; his translation tries to present an alien legal order in a familiar frame, where the law is efficaciously applied in the society, decisions are reached through precedent as well as the application of the code, applied to people of all ranks, and it produces just solutions to real problems (André, 2004, p. 23). He adds words such as "precedent" into Chinese imperial law where they do not exist, and also "just," "justice," "flagrant injustice," and "impartiality," among others, into his translation where the original says none, and omits words such as "concubine" (André, 2004); he also introduces a distinction between civil and criminal law that does not exist in the Chinese code, and even writes extremely long sentences in his translation to reproduce the legal style of nineteenth-century England, transforming the Chinese text into a form in English that would be familiar, intelligible, and acceptable to English readers through the process of translation (André, 2004, p. 23). It has been suggested that Staunton's translation of the imperial code can and should be read as a work of literature, which was meant to persuade its readers that the Chinese had a concept of justice, while William C. Jones, the contemporary translator who produced the now authoritative translation of the Great Qing Code, dismisses Staunton's work as "essentially useless since it was so free as to be inaccurate" (Jones, 1994, p. v). Nevertheless, Staunton's 1810 translation was the only published English translation of the Qing Code until 1994.

The problem of intercultural understanding and misunderstanding is quite pervasive in Western studies of China and Chinese philosophic ideas, often related to the presumption of equivalence. As we have seen, *yi* and "justice" are not substantively equivalent, even though they are sometimes used as semantic equivalents. The next example, although not a legal term, may help to remind us of the complexity and dilemma in translating between Chinese and English, and of the fact that words in writings about Chinese law written in English do not make them identical or similar to words used in English or Western law, just as words such as "rule of law" and "democracy" used in China do not mean the same as they do in English. We need to be constantly aware of the issues of understanding and interpretation of translated language for both legal and general texts. The difficulty of intercultural translation between Chinese and Western languages was vividly illustrated by Hall and Ames in the duck/rabbit analogy as first used by Wittgenstein. Hall and Ames (1995) propose that it may be that the Chinese have drawn a duck in instances where Westerners should expect to see a rabbit, and the problem may become even more perplexing if the Chinese and Western interlocutors have learned of one another's worlds:

> For example, when Western students of Chinese culture see *tian* translated as "Heaven," they may naturally assume that connotations of transcendence and spirituality attaching to the notion of "heaven" in their tradition apply to *tian*. And when Chinese students of Western culture see "God" translated as *tianzhu*, "the Master of *tian*," or as *shangdi*, "the ancestral lord," they contextualize this term by appealing to an ancestral continuum analogous to our family structure. In instances such as this, the Westerner is inclined to believe that the Chinese, too, see a rabbit, just as the Chinese individual is persuaded that we are all looking at a duck. (Hall and Ames, 1995, p. xvi)

To further illustrate this point with a recent real-life example, in 2014 an opinion survey conducted by Pew Research Center's Global Attitudes Project provided an interesting case study for misunderstanding caused in translation.[18] The survey asked people in 40 countries whether belief in God was necessary for morality. The results from China showed that 14 percent of those surveyed affirmed the need for belief in God. According to the Pew data, a full 75 percent of Chinese people said it was not necessary to believe in God to be moral. The results struck *New York Times* reporter, Ian Johnson, as odd. He further investigated and found out that the question in the survey was translated into Chinese and used *shangdi*, a term for "God" that is applicable in modern China almost only to Protestant Christianity. Johnson later writes:

> In Chinese, the questions were: "不信仰上帝, 也能有良好的道德和价值" and "为了有良好的道德和价值观, 信仰上帝是必要的." I would translate these questions back into English as, "Even without believing in (the Protestant) God, one can still have good virtues or values" and "In order to have good virtues and values, one must believe in (the Protestant) God."
>
> *Shangdi* has a pre-Christian meaning—referring to a supreme deity—but it was appropriated by Jesuit missionaries in the sixteenth century and since then has come to be synonymous with the monotheistic God of the Abrahamic religions, especially Protestant Christianity. (Johnson, 2014)[19]

As Johnson (2014) points out, *Shangdi* is an accurate translation of "God" in the Protestant tradition, but it excludes the religious experience of the vast majority of the Chinese, who do believe in higher spiritual forces, and very often link belief in such forces to morality. The problem is that the Chinese use the word *tian*, literally "sky" or "heaven," to refer to the idea of a supreme deity or force. It also includes *fo* or Buddha, while *shangdi* as used in the Pew poll translation refers to an Abrahamic paradigm, the Christianity God. So the question put to the Chinese in the survey was understood by the Chinese participants as meaning whether morality is linked to a Christian-like God (Johnson, 2014). After Johnson's article was published, Pew undertook an internal review of the translation of the word "God" in its Chinese questionnaire, and then announced that the Chinese results had been excised from the final report, the reason being that the term for God or a higher power was "mistranslated on the China questionnaire, rendering the results incomparable to the remaining 39 countries."[20]

As the case illustrates, despite the fact that Western religion and Chinese religion share certain similarities in the sense that they are human-created religions, they are different in terms of beliefs and practices regarding the creators and supernatural beings. The confusion may be similar to, although admittedly also different from, the example cited at the beginning of the chapter in the mistranslation of U.S. president as *huangdi*. For our interest in law, the inaccurate translations of the administrative county chief as magistrate and of other Chinese legal terms are yet to be corrected and may well perpetuate into the future.

Finally, as a note to the discussion in this chapter, around 2013 Chinese government media outlets started to promote *yili guan* (义利观 the notion of *yili*) of Xi Jinping, the current Chinese president. According to the Chinese government mouthpiece, Xi Jinping's *yili* approach to China's foreign policy was first mentioned in 2013 by Xi during his visit to Africa; since then, he has repeatedly used and explicated his views on the "correct notion of *yili*" in China's foreign policy.[21] Xi also used the term in his speech to the 2015 United Nations Climate Change Conference in Paris that China upholds the correct approach to *yili*, and takes an active part in international cooperation on climate change, and this was rendered as "China upholds the values of friendship, justice and shared interests" in the Chinese official English translation.[22] This new application of the *yili* dichotomy has been hailed by the Chinese government as a major ideological advancement by the Chinese leader on the foreign policy front,[23] and a major "new banner" of China's diplomacy.[24] For linguistic interest, the translation of this new application of *yili* in China's diplomacy varies. *Yi* once again poses a challenge. It has been translated into English in the Chinese media as "justice," "friendship and justice,"[25] "greater good,"[26] and "morality."[27] As we have seen in this chapter, the *yili* dichotomy came from early Chinese philosophers. *Li* simply means "interest" or "benefit," which can be either positive or negative, but the meanings of *yi* are still hard to pin down, still uncertain, fluid, ambiguous, and polysemous as it was some two thousand years ago when the concept was first debated. Its meaning varies according to contexts of use. It nevertheless is familiar and understandable to Chinese people both intuitively and intellectually, but very hard to translate it exactly into English. One thing certain about *yi* is that it is a keyword in Chinese culture, but not a keyword in Chinese law, in a way analogous to the concept of justice in Western law and legal culture.

NOTES

1. In the late 1800s and early 1900s, "president" was translated into Chinese as *touren* (leader), *zongli* (superintendent), *guozhu* (lord of the state), *qiuzhang* (chief of a tribe), *bangzhang* (leader of the country), *tongling* (commander), *huangdi* (emperor), *guojun* (monarch), *guohuang* (emperor of the state), *minzhu* (lord or head of the people), *bolegesi, bolixidun*, and *bolixitiande* (the last three were transliterations); none of these terms is used now. For discussions of the translation of political terms into Chinese, see Xiong (2001). In 2014, a Chinese translation of a news report carried in the *New York Times* erroneously used *zongtong* to describe Chinese president Xi Jinping, whose title in Chinese is *zhuxi*, not *zongtong*. The latter term is used for the presidents of other countries such as the U.S. president. For discussion of the Chinese translation and introduction of new legal terms around the late 1800s and early 1900s, see Qu (2011).

2. See Cao (2007) for a further discussion of translating legal terms between English and French and how courts deal with and interpret such translations when ambiguity arises.

3. Similarly, only one phrase is available in Chinese for the translation of both Minister of Justice and Attorney General: *Sifa buzhang*.

4. For that name, according to *The Rites of Zhou (Zhou Li)*, six main government offices were called Heaven, Earth, Spring, Summer, Autumn, and Winter Offices. The Office of Autumn was in charge of criminal law and prisons.

5. Taiwan today uses the *Fawu bu* (a variation of *Fa bu*) for the name for Ministry of Legal Affairs or Ministry of Justice.

6. Some scholars believe that the character衙 (*ya*) in 衙门(*yamen*) was originally 牙(*ya* for teeth) before the Tang Dynasty. The two characters have the same pronunciation. *Ya* (teeth) referred to animal fangs, and *yamen* refers to gates that have menacing animals with big fangs carved on them, to give a fearsome image. However, it was said that some officials thought *ya* (teeth) was not refined or dignified enough for an official title, and it was substituted with a different *ya* 衙. The fearsome-looking animal head and teeth remained on the *yamen* gates, though. See http://xbxsf.nwupl.cn/Article/flxy/201402/15841.html.

7. As described by Thomas Meadows (1847), a British diplomat serving in China in the mid-nineteenth century. See also N. He (2014).

8. Today, *xianling, zhixian*, and *zhishi* are no longer used in China, but in Japan, 知事(*zhishi*), using the exact Chinese characters, is the official title for the chief executive of a prefecture, and it is translated as "governor." This Japanese title is believed to have been borrowed from China during the Tang Dynasty.

9. See Watt (1972) and Djang (1984) for discussions of the office, as well as the qualifications, appointment of county officials, and other details about their work in imperial China.

10. For the roles and functions of local officials in the Qing Dynasty, see *A Complete Book Concerning Happiness and Benevolence,* written by a seventeenth-century Chinese local official by the name of Huang Liuhong, translated by Djang (1984). It is a step-by-step instruction manual for officials covering official selection and appointment, tax collection, administration of justice involving criminal trials, legal processes and laws, rites and ceremonies, education and economic matters, famine relief, courier service, and other administrative affairs.

11. See http://zqb.cyol.com/html/2013-12/17/nw.D110000zgqnb_20131217_5-02.htm.

12. According to Zhiping Liang (2004, pp. 275–276), "in Chinese traditional society, *songshi* (litigation masters) were always looked down upon. People's impression of them included being greedy, cold, sly, treacherous, and best at sowing discord, turning white into black, fabricating things and taking advantage of others." See also Macauley (1998) for discussions of lawyers in imperial China.

13. In recent times, largely due to the arrests and persecution of rights lawyers by the Chinese authorities, the word *songgun* is being revived among some Chinese to refer to lawyers in a derogatory sense.

14. http://www.oed.com/view/Entry/102198

15. See Cao (2018, forthcoming) for a discussion of the various meanings of *yi* used in the Great Qing Code, and why *yi* in the sense of "righteousness" is not a legal term and concept in classical Chinese.

16. See http://cidian.xpcha.com/f7966na8o3z.html.

17. Ch'en's other classification consists of: (1) the *yi* of respecting the elderly and obeying elder brothers; (2) the *yi* between the ruler and the ministers; (3) the *yi* that has to do with taking and giving; (4) the *yi* of the heart/mind of shame; (5) the *yi* that is said to be the human path or way; (6) the *yi* that conflicts with profits (*li*); (7) the *yi* that is said to be internal; (8) the *yi* that is said to be common *yi* of the world, and so on (Ch'en, cited in Xiao, 1997, p. 535). No original reference of the work by Ch'en was given in Xiao (1997). Ch'en Ta-chi'i (Chen Daqi, 1886–1983) was a well-known Chinese philosopher and psychologist working in China and later in his life in Taiwan. He wrote about Mencius and other ancient Chinese philosophers in the Chinese language.

18. See http://www.nybooks.com/daily/2014/03/24/chinese-atheists-pew-gets-wrong.

19. http://www.nybooks.com/daily/2014/03/24/chinese-atheists-pew-gets-wrong/

20. http://www.nybooks.com/daily/2014/03/24/chinese-atheists-pew-gets-wrong/

21. See http://cn.chinadaily.com.cn/2016xivisiteeu/2016-06/19/content_25762023.htm.

22. See http://www.china.org.cn/chinese/2015-12/01/content_37207254.htm.

23. See http://cn.chinadaily.com.cn/2016xivisiteeu/2016-06/19/content_25762023.htm.

24. See http://au.china-embassy.org/eng/xw/t1119520.htm.

25. See http://www.chinadaily.com.cn/world/XiattendsParisclimateconference/2015-12/01/content_22592469.htm.

26. See http://china.org.cn/chinese/china_key_words/2014-11/18/content_34085512.htm.

27. See http://au.china-embassy.org/eng/xw/t1119520.htm.

Chapter 4

Yuan

Injustice as a Keyword

In April 2016, a deeply sad and disturbing photo was posted on Chinese social media. In it, a person was seen dead, hanged by some ropes, with his or her head sunken facing inwards and the body dangling in the air in front of a building. The Chinese lawyer who posted the photo wrote in Chinese, "This morning, at the entrance of Shanghai Second Intermediate People's Court, an aggrieved person [*yuanmin*冤民] dangling in the air, has gone to *Yanwangye* [Yama, or the wrathful King of Hell] to plead grievances [*gaoyuan* 告冤]."

Equally striking is the big character 冤 (*yuan*) that is written in red ink on the back of the person's large white tunic. The person is dressed in black top, pants and shoes. A picture is worth a thousand words, and additionally, in this case, the character is worth many tens of thousands of words to the Chinese eyes.

Yuan 冤, the topic of this chapter, is intimately familiar to the Chinese but largely unnoticed in the study of Chinese law, both in China and elsewhere. It is proposed that *yuan* is a keyword that has been associated with law and justice—or, more precisely, injustice—for centuries. It essentially means "unjustly treated" or "wrongful accusation," with no exact one-to-one translation in English. It is a unique word with illocutionary force that has resonated with the Chinese over the ages. It is a word that can be heard in court and seen in defendants' statements, on placards in bold type or heavy calligraphy and on T-shirts when people feel wronged by the criminal justice system, literally making their grievances and associated injustice stand out in sharp relief.

For various reasons, this important word *yuan* has somehow escaped the attention of scholars, and is not discussed in either Chinese or English. One possible reason could be that most scholars commenting on Chinese law are not linguistics specialists and Chinese linguists writing about language matters are not particularly familiar with the law, but more importantly, in both the domestic and overseas academic discussions of Chinese law, there is a tendency to talk about Chinese law with reference to Western keywords and legal concepts and English terminology, such as *lüshi*, *fa* or *falü, fazhi, gongzheng*, and *quanli*, corresponding to "lawyer," "law," "rule of law," "justice," and "rights," among others, and language associated with black-letter law. English does not have a word similar to *yuan*. As discussed in chapter 2, Chinese keywords associated with law include *fa/xing/lü*, and they correspond—albeit not exactly—to "law" in English; yet these Chinese words do not implicitly or explicitly carry any meaning of justice or rights, unlike the *jus* or *droit* or *recht* in European languages (see chapter 2). The sense of justice was not prominently significant in traditional Chinese law or its administration. This is where *yuan* comes in, not in the sense of justice, but rather the opposite of justice—that is, the injustice and unjust treatment that the aggrieved feel and experience due to the enforcement of law. The absence of justice in law is highlighted by the felt presence of injustice. In many ways, *yuan* represents an antithesis to the famous and often-quoted aphorism and legal precedence and principle in English law, "Not only must justice be done; it must also be seen to be done" (*R v Sussex Justices, Ex parte McCarthy* ([1924] 1 KB 256; [1923] All ER Rep 233). The Chinese situation can be described as follows: when injustice is done, it must be heard in order to be undone. Or more precisely, *yuan* is the very word that must be seen and heard as a first step toward undoing the injustice a person endures—real or alleged.

This chapter focuses on *yuan*, a word with a long history in Chinese culture that can give us a glimpse of some of the largely hidden aspects of the criminal justice system in China. The linguistic meanings of *yuan* and its classical and modern usage and associated words are discussed first, followed an examination of the possible reasons why *yuan* should be considered a keyword in Chinese law against the backdrop of the imperial Chinese criminal system and its modern counterpart. It is proposed that *yuan* has both ordinary and legal usages, with different meanings and functions, and importantly, that *yuan* is a keyword in Chinese law, used as speech acts with illocutionary forces in the Chinese legal process (for discussions of speech acts, see chapter 6).

CORE MEANINGS OF *YUAN*

According to Chinese dictionaries, *yuan* 冤 has the basic meaning of being innocent but wrongly accused of a crime, and the meaning of not at fault but wrongly blamed. According to the authoritative classical Chinese dictionary, *Shuo wen jie zi* (this and the following examples have been numbered for easy reference):

(1)冤, 屈也。从兔,在冂下不得走,益屈折也。

Yuan means *qu* (being bent). It denotes the meaning of *tu* (rabbit) unable to walk under the door, and being bent and twisted. (Xu Chen, 2007)

It says that the character *yuan* consists of two parts, the top radical 冖, which represents a door frame or a door of a room or enclosed space, denoting "to cover" or "to enclose," and the bottom character 兔, for rabbit. The whole character carries the sense of a rabbit being enclosed and trapped inside a room, unable to move or stretch, signifying a sense of being trapped beyond one's control, meaning "injustice" and "wrongs."[1]

In modern Chinese, according to the *Chinese Xinhua Dictionary*, *yuan* means *yuanwang* 冤枉—that is, *yuan* and *yuanwang* are synonyms. The *Online Chinese Xinhua Dictionary* says that *yuanwang* means not guilty but wrongfully accused of a crime; not at fault but being blamed; to give someone a bad name without any factual basis; and not worthwhile and wasting one's efforts (as in *yuanwang qian*, money not worth spending; and *yuanwang lu*, walk or journey that one should have not walked or traveled, wasting one's efforts). *Wang* in *yuanwang* means "being bent"—for instance, *wang fa* (枉法 to bend or break the law).

Both *yuan* and *yuanwang* are used in classical and modern Chinese, and have been used for at least two thousand years. *Yuan* sometimes is short form for *yuanwang*. They are similar in many ways in both usage and meaning. Both can be used as a noun and adjective or modifier, but *yuanwang* is often used as a verb "to wrongfully accuse someone," while *yuan* cannot be used as a verb for this meaning. In many instances, the two words can be used interchangeably. Another difference is that *yuan* can be used by itself and also in combination with other characters (see below).

The core meaning of *yuan* and *yuanwang*, first and foremost, is wrongs, grievances, injustice, or miscarriage of justice. They are used to refer to both ordinary wrongs and legal wrongs, and are used as colloquial words in everyday speech as well as in a formal legal context. The most famous phrase containing *yuan* is found in the title of an old play, *Dou E Yuan* 窦娥冤, written by Guan Hanqing (1241–1320 CE) during the Yuan Dynasty (1271–1368 CE). *Dou E Yuan*—literally Dou E's Grievances—commonly is translated as *Injustice to Dou E.* The full Chinese title of the play is *Gan Tian Dong Di Dou E Yuan*, literally *Injustice to Dou E that Touched Heaven and Earth*, also known as *Snow in Midsummer, Injustice Done to Dou E,* and *Dou E was Wronged.* It remains one of Guan Hanqing's and China's most popular plays from ancient times. It is one of the best-known Chinese classic tragedies, with Guan Hanqing being considered a Chinese Shakespeare. The story of the play is believed to have been taken from folklore of the Eastern Han Dynasty (25–220 CE) and its plot runs as follows:[2]

A young girl, Dou Duanyun is sold by her father, a poor scholar, to the Cai family as a child bride to the son of the Cai family because her father had to pay off his debts. She is renamed Dou E. The Cai family's son dies soon after the wedding, so Dou E is widowed at the age of 20. Once, Dou E and her mother-in-law, Mrs Cai, are threatened by others and they are rescued by another man, Zhang Lü'er, who lives with his father. Zhang, who has ulterior motives, then tries to force Mrs Cai to marry his father and Dou E to marry him. These proposals are rejected. Zhang plots to kill Mrs Cai so that he can forcefully marry Dou E, but he poisons his own father by mistake. Zhang subsequently accuses Dou E of the murder.

Dou E at first rejects the charges but under torture by the interrogating officials and the threat of her mother-in-law being tortured, she falsely admits to the crime, as described in the words of the play: 打的我肉都飞，血淋漓，腹中冤枉有谁知! (I was beaten so badly that my flesh was tearing apart and blood dripping all over. Who would know about the wrongs that I know in my heart?) As a result, she is sentenced to death. As she is led to her execution, Dou E condemns the corrupt local trial officials at the execution ground, vowing to extract revenge for the injustice. She prophesizes and makes three predictions—before her death: snowfall in June, her blood spilling on a piece of one-meter white silk and a three-year drought in Chuzhou. All three predictions are realized in due course. After her death, Dou E turns into a ghost and continues to fight to clear her name. Eventually, her father, once a poor scholar, but now a high official, returns. Guided by the ghost of his daughter, he reviews the case, uncovers the truth and sentences Zhang to death; he also orders the corporal punishment of the official. Finally, Dou E is exonerated and the injustice to her redressed.[3]

Dou E Yuan is a Chinese cultural icon, a symbol of injustice done to an innocent person. It is a popular classic work, with which the Chinese people are intimately familiar. Consequently, Dou E Yuan has become a metaphor for extreme injustice in Chinese. Most Chinese associate the word *yuan* with Dou E Yuan. Now a common and colloquial expression is *bi Dou E hai yuan* (比窦娥冤 suffering more wrongs and injustice than Dou E—see Example 30 below). A real-life example was a modern day re-enactment of the play, staged in August 2015 in the city of Hangzhou in Zhejiang province. About 100 actresses dressed as Dou E knelt down on the ground and cried that they had been framed, while a fictional animal, supposedly a symbol of justice, was killed with fake snow flying in the air. The publicity stunt was organized by a tourism and entertainment company in Hangzhou, which had issued a petition to the CCP Central Commission for Discipline Inspection against the president of Zhejiang court alleging malfeasance and perversion of the course of justice by the court president.[4]

For our purpose here, apart from the title, *yuan* and *yuanwang* are used extensively in the play. Dou E Yuan, for instance, says:

(2) 这都是我做窦娥的没时没运, 不明不暗, 负屈衔冤。

This is because I am unfortunate, with things distorted and murky, carrying wrongs and grievances with me.

The phrase *fu qu xian yuan* 负屈衔冤 is a common idiom, literally meaning carrying grievances on one's back and holding grievances in one's mouth, having enormous grievances. Here *qu* and *yuan* have a similar meaning of grievances and wrongs.

(3) 大人，如今是三伏天道，若窦娥委实冤枉，身死之后，天降三尺瑞雪，遮掩了窦娥尸首。

Your honor, now it is the hottest days in the middle of summer. If I am truly wronged, then, after my death, three *chi* [or one meter] of snow will fall from heaven, covering my corpse.

(4) 大人, 我窦娥死的委实冤枉, 从今以后, 着这楚州亢旱三年。

Your honor, I am about to die from truly being wronged. From now on, Chuzhou will have draught for three years.

Examples 3 and 4 are the two of the three prophecies Dou E made, as mentioned above.

As noted previously, *yuan* and *yuanwang* have two different usages and functions, one ordinary and one legal. To put it in an overly simplified way, *yuan* and *yuanwang* in ordinary usage means "wrongly blamed" and "to wrongly blame," while *yuan* and *yuanwang* in legal usage mean "wrongfully blamed or accused" and "to wrongfully blame or accuse." One major difference is also found in legal usage of *yuan* and *yuanwang* that can carry illocutionary forces. They are speech acts as opposed to ordinary usage, as discussed further below.

ORDINARY USAGE OF *YUAN* IN A NONLEGAL CONTEXT

The examples of *yuan* and *yuanwang* in the following sections are taken from a major Chinese corpus (unless otherwise indicated) called National Broadcast Media Language Corpus (http://ling.cuc.edu.cn). It was built and maintained by China Communication University, and consists of texts collected from broadcast and TV programs from all major Chinese radio and

TV stations, aired from 2008 to 2013, with 34,039 broadcast and TV shows, transcribed into 200,071,896 characters. It is a significant collection of real-life modern Chinese language use, both formal and colloquial, from speakers of Mandarin Chinese in mainland China and, to a lesser extent, Taiwan and Hong Kong. The actual examples of the linguistic usage and meanings of *yuan* and *yuanwang* are necessary, as these two important words have not previously been discussed elsewhere—especially regarding their legal usage and significance. This may help to achieve a better understanding of Chinese legal language and law as a whole.

First, as already stated, *yuan* and *yuanwang* have the essential meaning of being wronged. They can be used as a noun and adjective or modifier. *Yuanwang* can also be used as a verb. When translated into English, there is no exact or fixed translation. They sometimes can be translated as "crying foul," "wrongly blamed," "feeling aggrieved," or "unjustly treated," depending on the actual use and context. For instance:

(5) 最后这老教授挺冤的, 因为周围同学反应, 这个教授还真是不错, 讲课的时候总是满满当当的。

In the end, because the students reacted, the old professor was unfairly treated. He is actually a really good professor, and his lectures always had full house.

(6) 我是今天早晨才来, 我觉得挺冤的, 因为我不去它景点, 只是去城里转一转, 为什么进城就要收费呢?

I only came here this morning. I feel it was unfair because I did not go to visit any scenic spots, but only walked around the city. So why should I be charged for entering the city?

(7) 从我的角度我觉得冤枉, 我们在为全世界做贡献。

From my perspective, I feel I am being wronged. After all we are making contributions to the world.

(8) 我觉得这个理解是不对的, 也就是说, 我们让微软受了点委屈, 冤枉了它。

I think it is incorrect to understand it this way. That is to say, we caused Microsoft some grievances, and wronged them.

In Examples 6–8, *yuan* is used as an adjective to mean "to feel aggrieved or wrongly blamed." As ordinary usage, *yuan* and *yuanwang* have a number of synonyms including *weiqu* 委屈, but *yuan* and *yuanwang* are much more emphatic, stressing being wrongly blamed.

(9) 医学专家就说, 猪流感有冤枉猪的嫌疑, 这种病毒其实和猪没有关系。

Medical experts said, to call it swine flu is to blame pigs unfairly. Swine virus actually does not have anything to do with pigs.

(10) 这段日子刚开始是非常难过的, 非常低落, 觉得被冤枉, 被委屈, 但是很快的我就找到了自己的方向。

During this period, I was very sad, very depressed in the beginning. I felt wronged and aggrieved, but quickly I found my own direction.

In Example 9, *yuanwang* is used as a verb, "to wrongly blame someone," and in Example 10, it is used in the passive structure, *bei yuanwang*, "being blamed wrongly."

(11) 政治斗争与家族冤仇纠缠在一起, 使得两人水火不相容。

Political struggle and family feud were intertwined. As a result, the two persons were like water and fire, not able to live with each other.

(12) 任贤齐在现场被质疑近年电影作品较少, 对此他只能以一个字回应: 冤!

Ren Xianqi was challenged at the scene that he made very few films in recent years, to which he could only respond with one word: unfair!

In Examples 11 and 12, *yuan* is used as a noun, to mean resentment, unfairness, or wrong.

To sum up, in the above examples, *yuan* and *yuanwang* are used in ordinary nonlegal contexts, carrying the ordinary meaning of being unfairly or wrongly blamed or treated, and they can carry different degrees of such meanings, depending on the contexts.

LEGAL USAGE OF *YUAN* IN A LAW-RELATED CONTEXT

The legal usage of *yuan* goes back in history. For instance, *yuan* was found in the Yuan Code from the Yuan Dynasty:

(13) 诸所在重刑, 皆当该官司, 公厅圆坐, 取讫服辨, 移牒肃政廉访司, 审复无冤, 结案待报。若犯人翻异, 家属称冤, 听牒本路移推。其赃验已明, 及不能指论, 抑屈情由者, 不在移推之例。

With regard to a serious offense in any locality, the government authorities shall hold at the public office a joint conference to decide the case. When the affidavit of accepting the decision shall have been obtained [from the offender], the case shall be transferred to the *Su zheng lian fang si* for review. If no grievance is found, the case shall be concluded to await a [routine] report. On the other hand, if the offender shall retract his statement or his family shall plead a grievance, the case shall be permitted to be transferred to the governing *lu* for rehearing. However, if evidence shall have been clear and the family cannot indicate in argument the details of their grievance, [the case] shall not be within [the scope of] the provision concerning transferring and rehearing. (Ch'en, 1979, pp. 154–155, with modifications)

(14) 诸见禁罪囚,各处正官,每月分轮检事。凡禁系不廉,淹滞不决,病患不治,并合给囚粮,依时不给者,并须随事究问。肃政廉访司官所在之处,依上审察。其在都罪囚,中书刑部、御史台扎鲁火赤,各须委官,季一审理,冤者辨明,迟者催问,轻者断遣,不致冤滞。

As to the offenders imprisoned in the capital, the Board of Punishments of the Zhongshu sheng, the Censorate, and the *Zhalu huochi* [*jarynci*] shall appoint respectively an official once a quarter to review and deal with [their cases] so that the grievance may be clarified and the delay may be pressed for action and trivial mattes may be [immediately] decided and discharged so as to prevent any grievance or hindrance. (Ch'en, 1979, p. 155, with modifications)

Here *yuan* refers to legal grievances and legal wrongs. In the Great Qing Code, *yuan* (injustice) and *yuanwang* (injustice and misapplication of law) are used. For instance:

(15)辩明冤枉–凡内外问刑衙门辩明冤枉须要开具本囚,所枉事迹实封奏闻,委官追问其冤情,得实被诬之人,依律改正所枉之罪,坐原告诬告,原问官吏,以故失入罪论。

Article 410. Exposing Injustices and Misapplication of the Law.
1. Every reviewing yamen, whether within the capital or outside, which is exposing injustices and misapplication of the law must write down all of the traces [evidence] of wrong suffered (by the prisoner). The facts must be reported by memorial under seal to the Emperor. If the official delegated to do so pursues the investigation (of the injustices) and finds them to have occurred, the one who was wrongfully accused will have his sentence rectified. (the Erroneous) punishment will be inflicted on the complainant (the one who made the false accusation [that resulted in the erroneous sentence]) and the original investigating official and clerk (will be punished on the basis of intentionally or mistakenly increasing [a penalty]). (Jones, 1994, p. 392)

The expressions *hu yuan* 呼冤, *cheng yuan* 称冤, *jiaosu yuanwang* 叫诉冤枉, and *ming yuan* 鸣冤 are also used in the Great Qing Code, all meaning "to call out, to shout or complain of injustice when one felt aggrieved or wrongly accused."

This usage continues to this day. For instance, in Taiwan, *yuan* was used in the title of the law *Yuanyu buchang fa* (冤狱补偿法 False Imprisonment

Compensation Law [1959]), but the word *yuanyu* was dropped and the name of the law was changed to刑事补偿法 (*xingshi buchang fa*) in 2011. In China, *yuan* was not used in the formal wording of the State Compensation Law (国家赔偿法 [1995]), but in the interpretations and discussions of the law in relation to wrongful conviction, *yuan* is often used, as in *yuan an* (冤案 wrongful cases).

As the examples indicate, *yuan* and *yuanwang* have been used for legal grievances since ancient time. It is fair to say that whenever someone feels they have been wrongfully accused and protests against injustice and pleads their innocence (real or alleged), *yuan* or *yuanwang* would be used. *Yuan* and *yuanwang* can be used as nouns, adjectives, or modifiers, and *yuanwang* can also be used as a verb. In the following, the various meanings and usages of *yuan* and *yuanwang* associated with legal meanings are presented.

Yuan 冤 and *yuanwang* 冤枉

When one feels wronged by the legal process, wrongfully accused, or wrongfully convicted, *yuan* or *yuanwang* is used as an adjective. In this sense, it is very common to hear the Chinese say:

我很冤啊! *Wo hen yuan ah*!
冤啊! *Yuan ah!*
我很冤枉啊! *Wo hen yuanwang ah!*
冤枉啊! *Yuanwang ah!*
我是冤枉的! *Wo shi yuanwang de*

All these mean "I am wronged!" "I am wrongfully accused!" or "I am wrongly treated." It can be for legal and ordinary situations, depending on the context. In the legal context, it means "I am wrongfully accused." It can be put in the third person to describe how a person is wrongfully accused in the legal process—for instance:

(16) 檀先生就觉得冤呀, 于是提出了上诉。

Mr. Tan felt being very wronged, so he appealed.

(17) 女子说她与郑先生无怨无仇, 莫名被抓到派出所很冤枉。

The woman says she had no hard feelings or hatred toward Mr. Zheng, so she felt she was very much wronged when she was arrested and sent to the police for no reason.

(18)我知道我儿子没有杀人,我也知道我儿子是冤枉的,我经常去看我儿子, 我儿子实在太冤枉了, 那个判决书前后矛盾。

I know my son did not kill anyone, and I also know my son was wrongfully accused. I often go to see my son. He is truly wronged. The verdict was full of contradictions.

As we can see, Examples 16–18 are specifically related to legal matters. Either *yuan* or *yuanwang* can be used, but it seems that the *shi . . . de* sentence structure for emphasis is only used with *yuanwang*, not *yuan*. Normally one cannot say: *wo shi yuan de*, but *wo shi yuanwang de*.

Yuanwang as a verb

When used as a verb, *yuanwang* in its legal usage means to wrongfully accuse someone, to do injustice to someone, or to inflict legal injustice. In contrast, *yuan* cannot be used as a verb for such meaning. For instance:

(19) 最高院以往往往说不冤枉一个好人, 不放过一个坏人。

The Supreme Court in the past often said, not to wrongfully accuse a good person, and not to let a bad person go free.

(20) 到底是宁可错杀一千, 还是绝不冤枉一个无辜者?

In the end, is it the case that you would rather wrongfully kill a thousand persons, or is it a case of never wrongfully accusing an innocent person?

In both these examples, one cannot substitute *yuanwang* with *yuan*.

One of the most popular legal slogans and guiding principles in Chinese criminal justice system is embodied in the catchphrase and popular saying *Juebu yuanwang yige haoren, ye juebu fangguo yige huairen* (决不冤枉一个好人, 也决不放过一个坏人 never wrongly accuse a good person and never let a bad person go free, as used in Example 19). It is a succinct and easily understood slogan that almost every Chinese knows. It uses simple and colloquial words such as *haoren* (good person), *huairen* (bad person), and *fangguo* (let go) instead of formal words such as "innocent persons" (*wuguzhe*), as in Example 20. It is one of the conventional linguistic formulas that Chinese often employ using short and slogan type of words that are easy to say and to remember, a tradition that began with Confucius (see Cao, 2004, p. 11).

Yuanwang is often used in the passive structure, as being wronged by others:

(21) 比如, 犯罪嫌疑人在侦查阶段因刑讯逼供屈打成招而被冤枉入狱, 直至真凶出现, 冤情才得到昭雪的。

For example, in the investigation stage, the suspect suffered from torture to obtain his confessions and was sent to jail and it was not until the murderer appeared that grievances were redressed.

(22) 但是孙中界坚持说自己是被钓鱼执法给冤枉了, 为证清白, 竟然自断一根小手指。

But Sun Zhongjie insisted that he had been wrongly accused due to entrapment in law enforcement, and to prove his innocence, he even cut off his own little finger.

(23) 法律援助的范围和途径， 延伸到侦查阶段， 减少犯罪嫌疑人或者被告人被冤枉的可能。

The scope and means of legal aid, extending to the investigation stage, reduces the chance of suspects or defendants being wrongfully accused.

In Examples 21–23, the common *bei* passive structure is used with *yuanwang*, meaning "being wronged" or "being wrongfully accused." In this usage, *yuan* cannot substitute *yuanwang* either.

Yuan'an 冤案

After a case is decided and verdict rendered and if it is believed to be wrongful, it is called *yuan'an* (冤案 wrongful case). There are a number of words available for this, including *yuan jia cuo an* 冤假错案, *yuan cuo jia an*冤错假案, and *yuan cuo an* 冤错案, all meaning "wrongful cases." For instance:

(24) 1994 年湖北农民佘祥林因杀害妻子的罪名， 被判有期徒刑15年，在狱中度过11个春秋， 就在他即将刑满释放的时候， 被杀的妻子突然活着出现了， 随后佘祥林也和今天的赵作海一样， 被判无罪，11年的冤案终于昭雪。

In 1994, Peasant She Xianglin was convicted of killing his wife and was sentenced to 15 years in prison where he spent 11 years. Just when he was about to be released, his wife, who had supposedly been dead, suddenly appeared alive. Subsequently, like Zhao Zuohai today, She Xianglin was acquitted of the crime, so the wrongful case was finally corrected after eleven years.

(25) 这起冤案是一记沉重的警钟，相关办案人员应该吸取教训，好好总结。

This wrongful case is a serious warning that the investigators involved in this case should learn a good lesson and reflect on it.

(26) 对，这是整个司法荒谬所在，其实我们看到，根据目前台湾的法律，如果是冤狱赔偿的话，一天法院要赔给冤错假案的当事人，一天是新台币一千块钱。

Yes, this is where the judicial absurdity lies. In fact, we have seen that, based on the current Taiwan law, the compensation that the court must pay to the person in a wrongfully convicted case is one thousand New Taiwan dollars a day.

(27) 实践证明，导致冤假错案发生的原因是多方面的，但是刑讯逼供、非法取证是主要原因。

Practice has demonstrated that the causes of miscarriage of justice are many, but forced confession through torture and illegally obtaining evidence are the main reasons.

(28) 佘祥林案、赵作海案等冤错案让人们对刑讯逼供深恶痛绝。这次刑诉法修订的一个重要方面就是防止和遏制刑讯。刑诉法修正案草案在原有严禁刑讯逼供规定的基础上, 增加不得强迫任何人证实自己有罪的规定。

For the She Xianglin and Zhao Zuohai case and other wrongful cases, the injustice made people detest forced confession through torture. An important aspect of the amended Criminal Procedure Law is to prevent and stop such torture. The draft amendment to the Criminal Procedure Law added the provision that no one may be forced to prove their guilt on top of the original provision strictly prohibiting forced confession through torture.

Yuan'an is the commonly used phrase referring to wrongful cases as shown in the examples above. Another phrase is *yuanyu* 冤狱 as used in Example 26. The measure word for *yuan'an* and *yuanyu* is *qi* 起 as used in Example 25. *Yuanyu* is used more often in Taiwan than on the mainland. The most significant phrase in China is *yuan jia cuo an* (冤假错案 wrongful, fabricated and false cases) as used in Example 27. It is a phrase that strikes to the hearts of literally many millions of Chinese in contemporary China. The largest number of *yuan jia cuo an* was created in the decades from the 1950s to the 1970s, especially during the calamitous Cultural Revolution (1966–1976), when many millions of such cases were produced. After the Cultural Revolution ended in 1981, the Communist Party Central Committee adopted the Resolution on Certain Questions in the History of Our Party Since the Founding of the People's Republic of China, providing an official assessment of major historical events since 1949 and formally admitting the grave errors of the Cultural Revolution and Mao, and acknowledging the serious disaster and turmoil brought to the Chinese people. Following that, attempts were made at rehabilitating victims of the political persecution and other crimes committed during the Cultural Revolution, exonerating people involved in those *yuan jia cuo an*, which amounted to hundreds of thousands in that period.[5] *Yuan jia cuo an* reversed during this period included especially those committed during the so-called Anti-Rightists Campaign in the 1950s, the Cultural Revolution, and also earlier wrongful cases from the 1930s and 1940s within the Communist Party. According to the official statements, by 1985 most of the verdicts of the wrongful persecutions during the Cultural Revolution were reversed, including over 30 cases of major significance and about three million cases involving wrongful persecution of party officials. Party memberships were restored for over 470,000 former party members, and tens of millions of people who had been wrongfully treated and persecuted were exonerated—and this is the official account. The phrase *yuan jia cuo an* has a very special place in modern Chinese history, and in the Chinese collective consciousness, as well as the individual memories of millions of Chinese people.

Today, when the phrases *yuan jia cuo an* (wrongful, fabricated, and false cases) and *yuan cuo an* (wrongful and false cases), or more commonly *yuan an*, are used, they mostly refer to new legal cases that have been wrongfully prosecuted in the past two to three decades since the Cultural Revolution. These *yuan'an* are criminal cases that went through the formal legal processes, but they were either wrongfully convicted or people were framed for certain crimes. The crimes related to these cases may be violent crimes such as homicide or robbery, but they may also be politically motivated crimes. In recent years, a considerable number of high-profile criminal cases of people convicted of capital crimes in China have resulted in exoneration.[6]

Yuan si le 冤死了

There are a few commonly used expressions to describe how bad or how serious a wrongful case is. For instance:

(29) 田亚葵之所以可以沉冤昭雪，第一，他的确是问心无愧的，第二，他相信司法的公正。

The reason why Tian Yakui can be exonerated for his old wrongful case is because, first, he indeed has a clear conscience; second, he believed in judicial justice.

(30) 但是,喊冤归喊冤,像栾某这样当庭失控、大闹公堂的现象却十分罕见,莫非这位栾大官人真的蒙受不白之冤了吗?

However, one can cry *yuan* and protest one's innocence, but it is very rare to have someone like Luan losing control and creating havoc in court. Would it be possible that this certain official Mr. Luan is really being wrongfully accused?

Chenyuan in Example 29 literally means "old wrongful cases," and *bu bai zhi yuanin* in Example 30 means a "wrongful case that has not been corrected." Both are common expressions. Similarly, another expression *yuan si le* is also commonly used both metaphorically and literally:

(31) 这冤死了,我这叫躺着也中枪了。

I was very much wrongly blamed. This is like kind of collateral damage, getting hit in the process.

This *yuan si le* 冤死了 literally means "died as a result of being wronged," and it is used for emphasis, with the actual meaning of "very much wronged," or "terribly unfair" used in ordinary nonlegal situations. In contrast, *yuan si le* can also be used to describe someone who has died due to wrongful treatment in a legal context, as in the next two examples:

(32) 他说他的外婆舅舅等家人，只要提到赣州的事，无不表露出对母亲冤死的悲痛和气愤。

He said that for his grandmother, uncle and other family members, whenever the matter concerning Ganzhou was mentioned, all of them were very sad and indignant regarding his mother's death due to wrongful treatment.

(33) 老赵太冤了，幸亏没被冤死，妻离子散而且11年。

Old Zhao suffered too much injustice. Fortunately, he did not die as a result of the wrongful treatment, but his wife and child left him, and the injustice lasted 11 years.

Yuan si as used in Examples 32 and 33 is a commonly used word for people who die after being wrongfully convicted or treated. This usage is not metaphorical.

Another common expression for stressing how wrongfully a person is treated comes from the play *Dou E Yuan*:

(34) 话说北京一位大姐，最近感觉就一个字：冤！比窦娥还冤。但是法律不这么认为。

I'm telling you, what an older sister in Beijing recently felt can be said in one word: *Yuan*! More wrong than what Dou E suffered. But the law does not think so.

In this sentence, *bi dou er hai yuan* 比窦娥还冤 can literally mean that someone is wronged by the legal process, or it can mean metaphorically that someone is wrongly blamed or treated.

There are other common compound phrases containing *yuan* that are associated with wrongful cases:

(35) 这些就是说，冤魂到现在在空中飘荡，他们的后代不能心安，这是一个感情的东西。

This means that the ghosts of the dead who were wrongly accused are now flying in the sky. Their offspring cannot have a peace of mind. It is a matter of emotions.

(36) 去信访的大多数是有冤情。

Most of those who lodge complaints and petitions have grievances.

Yuanhun in Example 35 and *yuanqing* in Example 36 are words from classical Chinese. They are still commonly used today. *Yuanhun* (soul or ghost from the dead as a result of wrongful conviction) is used in the play *Dou E Yuan* to describe Dou E's ghost after her wrongful death. *Yuangui* is another phrase for ghosts of the dead who were wronged, but this phrase has a more negative connotation. *Yuanqing* in Example 36 refers to the details of a wrongful case, also used in *Dou E Yuan*.

Apart from the examples here, there are other popular idioms containing *yuan* to describe how wrong a wrongful case is and how bad an injustice or miscarriage of justice is, for instance, *yuan yuan xiang bao* 冤冤相报, *huai yuan bao qu* 怀冤抱屈, *han yuan fu qu* 含冤负屈, *han qu xian yuan*负屈衔冤, *chen yuan mo bai* 沉冤莫白, *chen yuan mo xue* 沉冤莫雪, *qian qu qi yuan* 千古奇冤, and *yuan chen hai di* 冤沉海底. All these idioms carry the essential meaning of "being gravely wronged and terrible wrong and injustice being done."

Hanyuan 喊冤

When one believes that one is wronged and wrongfully accused or convicted, one would normally want to seek redress or correct injustice. Two expressions to that effect are *shenyuan* and *xiyuan*:

(37) 有执法人员打死打伤无辜者的粗暴执法事件, 有见死不救的社会冷漠, 有开胸验肺、断指申冤的民怨。

There were cases where the enforcement personnel brutally killed or injured innocent people; there were cases where people were indifferent and refused to assist when another's life was in danger; and there were popular resentments as there are cases where lung disease sufferers had to literally cut open their chests to prove their occupational lung illnesses and those who physically cut their own fingers to swear on their innocence in order to redress injustice.

(38) 但是整个来看, 我们看到整个案子发展到现在, 陈致中似乎对洗刷他冤屈证明他清白的这些证据似乎好像都不太愿意提供给检方。

But looking as a whole, we can see in the whole case up to the present, Chen Chih-Chung seemed unwilling to provide evidence to the prosecution to wash away the wrongs done to him and to prove his innocence.

In Example 38, *xishua yuanqu* 洗刷冤屈 literally means "to wash away wrongs," and it has a short form *xiyuan* 洗冤 which is more commonly used. The phrase *xiyuan* is an important phrase with a long history. Its most famous use is found in the title of the book, *Xiyuan Jilu* (洗冤集录 *The Washing Away of Wrongs)*, believed to be the first ever written account of using forensic medicine to solve crimes in the world, written by Song Ci (Song Tz'u, 1186–1249) around 1247 during the Song Dynasty (960–1279 CE) as a handbook for coroners. Song Ci was a Judicial Intendant (*tidian xingyu*) in charge of the criminal investigation of death-related cases, similar to a coroner (see McKnight, 1981). He combined many historical cases of forensic investigation with his own experience, and wrote the book as a guide for officials assigned to the tasks of holding inquests on homicide and other deaths. The book had a profound influence on the administration of Chinese justice from the time of its initial publication, and that continued into the twentieth century (McKnight, 1981, p. 17; for further discussion of Song Ci and the legal processes of inquests in ancient China, see McKnight, 1981). Song Ci's book is not about wrongful cases, but about how to avoid assigning wrongs to innocent people and wrongful convictions. In 2005, Song Ci's story was made into a popular television drama series titled 大宋提刑官 (*Da Song Tixing Guan*). Today, *xiyuan* is commonly used to mean "to correct legal wrongs or injustice," or "to exonerate people who are wrongfully convicted." For instance, a Chinese website is called Xiyuan wang 洗冤网, similar to the U.S. Innocence Project. Some have also translated the American "Innocence Project" into Chinese as *Xiyuan jihua* (Project of Washing Away Wrongs), although others have translated it directly as *Wuguzhe jihua* (Innocence Project).

The most important phrase for seeking justice and redressing a legal wrong is *hanyuan* 喊冤 or *han yuanwang* 喊冤枉, crying *yuan* or *yuanwang*. This means literally that a person who believes they have been wrongfully accused or convicted, or who is a relative of someone who has legal grievances for wrongful conviction, shouts and utters the word *yuan* or *yuanwang* in court to the authorities or high officials when they get a chance. This practice goes far back in history.

In imperial China, a common practice was that when a guilty verdict was handed down or before execution of a condemned prisoner, if the prisoner called out *yuan* or *yuanwang* before execution, the execution must be halted and the case must be reexamined. This was written into the imperial code (for instance, Art. 410 of the Qing Code). Another related practice was that during imperial times, at the entrance to the local *yamen*'s office, there was a huge drum for ordinary people to beat if they had legal grievances relating to wrongful accusation or conviction. The wrongly accused person could beat the drum to signal that they had grievances requiring official attention. This was mentioned in the imperial code (for instance, the Qing Code)—hence the idiom *ji gu ming yuan* (击鼓鸣冤 beating drum and crying injustice). Another channel to voice one's legal grievances and wrongs in imperial China was to present petitions to the high officials and ultimately to the emperor. Since ancient times, ordinary Chinese with legal grievances involving the death penalty would, as a last resort, attempt to petition to the emperor on the road of his royal inspections around the country, as that was one of the very rare chances for ordinary folk to force their way to see the emperor. When they did so, they would cry "*Yuan ah!*" or "*Yuanwang ah!*" to draw the attention of the official entourage or the emperor himself.

This tradition continues in contemporary China. It is still common for people with grievances against the government or officials to *hanyuan* before higher officials. For instance, in 2015 it was reported that a woman was heard shouting, inaudibly on the video, in an attempt of direct appeal to Xi Jinping, the current Chinese president, when he was visiting Zunyi in southern China.[7] The Chinese description of the video posted on YouTube was *Hanyuan*.

In short, the word and practice of *hanyuan* have been a significant part of the legal process in China throughout the ages. This is unique.

Now we will look at the linguistic usage of *hanyuan*:

(39) 庭审当天两人的弟弟也来旁听此案, 他替姐姐孔祥敏喊冤, 并承认当初确实存在借名买房。

On the day of the trial, the brother of the two also came to attend the hearing. He cried injustice on behalf of his sister Kong Xiangmin, and admitted having bought a home using another's name.

(40) 6月25日, 死者母亲受人唆使到街上喊冤, 引来上千群众围观, 眼看一起群体性事件就要发生, 德江县公安局迅速启动应急预案,局长带领70多名民警赶赴现场, 开展疏导、劝说工作, 围观群众很快被疏散, 死者母亲也被劝至公安局。

On June 25, the mother of the deceased, after being instigated by others, took to the street, crying injustice, and attracting more than a thousand onlookers. As a mass incident was about to happen, Dejiang County Public Security Bureau quickly activated a contingency plan. The bureau chief led more than 70 police to the scene to manage the crowd and quickly managed to disperse the onlookers. The mother of the deceased was also persuaded to leave and go to the police station.

(41) 那时候我脑子里一片空白,我想他们都没什么证据,他们就判我死刑了, 我想这就是口供人家逼我的, 刑讯逼供的, 我在庭上喊冤嘛, 哭着喊冤嘛, 但是他们没有理我。

At that time, my mind went blank. I believed that they had no evidence. Even if they sentenced me to death, that would be due to forced confession they got from me—confession by torture. I shouted and cried injustice in court, but they paid no attention to me.

(42) 《法制日报》说, 贪官喊冤的事情并不少见。比如, 广东珠海市人大常委会原副主任冼文曾经这样对司法人员喊冤: 我是珠海改革开放的拓荒牛, 多吃一点多拿一点算什么?

Legal Daily said that it was not uncommon for corrupt officials to cry injustice. For example, in Zhuhai City, the former deputy director of Guangdong People's

> Congress, Xian Wen, once cried injustice to the judiciary, "I am the pioneering working bull in Zhuhai's reform and opening up. So what if I ate a little bit more and took a little bit more?"

In the examples above, *hanyuan*, basically means "shout injustice" or "cry injustice," that is, to protest that one's wrongfully accused or convicted, and here it is all used in a legal context. In the next examples, variations of the expression are used, but they all carry the same meaning—in Example 43, it is *gaohu yuanwang* (shout injustice in a loud voice); in Example 44, *han le shi ji nian yuanwang* (cry injustice for over ten years), and *han yuanwang* (cry injustice).

> (43) 当法官宣读判决时，张治安将话筒打翻在地，并三次高呼冤枉，一同受审的汪成也当庭表示将要上诉。
>
> When the judge read the verdict, Zhang Zhi'an knocked the microphone to the ground, and shouted injustice three times. Wang Cheng, who was tried at the same time, also said in court that he would appeal.
>
> (44) 如今, 徐浩仍在监狱服刑, 喊了十几年冤枉的他, 一直等待张文华有一天落网, 还自己一个清白。
>
> Today, Xu Hao is still serving time in prison. He has been crying injustice for a dozen years. He has been waiting for the day when Zhang Wenhua would be arrested, thus clearing his name.
>
> (45) 后来，贞观十六年有300多死刑犯人，没有一个人喊冤枉，都认为自己应该是死罪。
>
> Later, in the year of the 16th year of the reign of Emperor Zhenguan, more than 300 people were given the death penalty, but no one cried injustice, and they all believed they deserved capital punishment.

As the examples indicate, *hanyuan* or *han yuanwang* mean that a person utters the words *yuan* or *yuanwang* aloud, often in court or elsewhere. *Hanyuan* and *han yuanwang* (crying injustice) are used to describe the act of crying injustice, and it is an illocutionary act, a speech act.

Yuan/Yuanwang *as Speech Acts*

Yuan and *yuanwang* are unique in Chinese legal discourse and legal culture. In their legal usage, it is proposed here that these two words can also perform speech acts carrying illocutionary forces.

As noted earlier, when Chinese people feel that they have been wrongfully accused or wrongfully convicted, or otherwise suffer a legal wrong, they will cry out, *yuan!* or *Wo yuan ah/Wo yuanwang ah* (I am being wronged!), either in court—especially after a guilty verdict—or afterwards. Some would write the character *yuan* in large font in heavy calligraphy or in their own blood. These days, some would also print the large character on a T-shirt. This is common among petitioners in China today when people feel they are being treated wrongfully by the authorities or officials. This is unique—similar to but also different from people protesting their innocence in English. In English, one may say: I am innocent! In Chinese, one occasionally also says: *Wo shi qingbai de* (我是清白的 I am innocent) and this is a description, but much more commonly one says: *yuan!* (I am being wronged!) So, in English, one protests one's innocence, stressing innocence, while in Chinese, one stresses *yuan* being wronged by others—that is, by institutional actors that are important for the performance of the speech act. They include the state and the court as represented by judges, prosecutors, and lawyers. *Yuan* also carries the sense of something beyond one's control—as the Chinese character suggests, being trapped and bent—that the English word "innocence" does not have. In these situations, *yuan* and *yuanwang* perform legal speech acts.

In this connection, a speech act, as the term suggests, refers to speech that acts. Speech is not just words, which is what people normally associate it with, but is also actions. A speech act is based on the notion that words are something we use not only to say things; but also to do things, as first proposed by J.L. Austin (see chapter 7). We do something, rather than merely say that something is or is not the case. Uttering a performative utterance is to constitute the performing of a further act in addition to the linguistic act itself. To say, "I promise that *p* (propositional content) . . . " is performing the very act of promising that can only be accomplished by saying the right words. These words do not describe the fact that a person is promising; they are the act itself. Such types of performative acts are illocutionary acts that carry illocutionary forces.[8] Law relies heavily on performative utterances. Legal effects and legal consequences are commonly obtained by merely uttering certain words—for instance, "You are sentenced to ten years' imprisonment," as regularly pronounced by judges. By uttering words, people may accept public and private legal responsibilities, and assume legal roles and qualities; they can also transfer legal rights and impose or discharge obligations (Jori, 1994, p. 2092). Thus legal performatives are said to be constitutive of their effects (see chapter 7).

It is proposed that the legal usage of *yuan* and *yuanwang* in the first person (both singular and plural) can be a speech act. It is more than just saying something, more than just stating that one is wronged. It may be classified as a representative in speech acts theory (see Danet, 1980, pp. 457–461)—that is, utterances that commit the speaker to something being the case or assert the truth of a proposition, including testifying, swearing, asserting, claiming, and stating. When *yuan* and *yuanwang* used in the first person—for instance, *wo yuan ah, wo yuanwang ah* (see above)—it is more than just saying something. It is asserting the truth of a proposition that the person is claiming they are innocent. *Yuan* and *yuanwang* are used to perform a number of extra-linguistic functions, including to proclaim one's innocence, to draw attention to one's case, to draw sufficient attention to one's case so that the case could be reviewed or retried, and ultimately to get redress if the case is indeed a wrongful case.

YUAN AS A KEYWORD IN CHINESE LAW

As mentioned earlier, there is little discussion of the word *yuan* (and *yuanwang*) in relation to Chinese law, in either Chinese or English. Nevertheless, it is believed that it is an important word associated with Chinese law, especially the criminal justice system—a keyword that reveals much about the Chinese sense of justice—or, more accurately, injustice—in both the past and present.

Yuan is a concrete word, an experiential and emotive word, unlike abstract or conceptual words such as law or justice; it is a three-dimensional word that ordinary Chinese can feel, sense, and empathize with when they see or hear it. People can literally see a creature being trapped in the Chinese character. Above all, it is a unique Chinese legal word. It does not have a one-to-one translation in English. As explained in the first part of the chapter, it can be translated as "wrongful accusation," "wrongful conviction," or "being wronged and aggrieved," but the translations cannot convey the history and often painful stories the word represents to the Chinese people. The ideographic and iconic image that this Chinese character presents visually to the Chinese eyes cannot be translated into other languages either. Notwithstanding this, people do not normally say, for instance, that "injustice" and "unfairness" are keywords of English law or the American legal system. So how can a word associated with injustice and legal wrongs be considered a keyword in Chinese law? To understand *yuan*, it is constructive and useful to reflect on the history of the imperial Chinese criminal justice system, in order to provide the context and cultural background that give and produce the meaning and illocutionary force of *yuan* for the Chinese. It is rightly pointed out that it is virtually impossible to understand criminal justice in twentieth-century China without taking into account the ramifications of premodern legal language, practice, and theory (Mühlhahn, 2009, p. 14). As a general proposition, it is suggested in this book that *yuan* is a keyword in Chinese law, and it is also a word literally filled with the enormous pain that people who were wrongly convicted often felt, both physically and emotionally. This has to do with the harsh punishment of the criminal law, and the forced confessions and torture that were often employed or required in the legal process, and the disconnect between justice and law in traditional China.

CRIMINAL PUNISHMENT-DOMINATED LAW

Chinese law is one of the oldest legal traditions in the world. Traditional Chinese law as discussed in this book refers to the laws, legal rules, and legal cultures of imperial China up to 1911, when the last imperial dynasty ended. As we know, Chinese legal culture and the Chinese legal order are different from the common law and civil law traditions of the West. A number of general features of this legal tradition are worth mentioning to assist our understanding of *yuan*.

The criminal trial portrayed in the play *Dou E Yuan* described earlier was indicative of the criminal trials in imperial China that remained largely unchanged until the end of the nineteenth century (N. He, 2014, p. 33). It may not be coincidence that in Chinese, *xíngfǎ* (刑法 criminal law) and *xíngfá* (刑罚 criminal punishment) are homonyms with the same pronunciation except for the tones. While it is not correct to say that traditional Chinese law only contained criminal law, it nevertheless was predominately penal law, since any human act recognized in the law was linked with a punishment (Mühlhahn, 2009, p. 15), and criminal punishments were the most prominent features of the law for over two thousand years. The imperial penal law was regarded as an indispensable part of governance and social order, and the law codes of each dynasty prescribe what behaviors were punishable, and the specific penalties for such acts. Moreover, it is believed that Confucianism, Legalism, and the cosmological school exerted a major influence on penal philosophy and the conception of justice (see Mühlhahn, 2009; see also chapter 2). In addition, the Confucian notions of law and order were incorporated and reflected in the punishments prescribed by the imperial law against behaviors deemed immoral by Confucian moral standards. A synthesis of the various schools and philosophical thoughts on punishment occurred during the Han Dynasty (206 BCE–200 CE), providing a basic rationale for the administration of justice and punishment that continued to influence the way criminal justice operated in imperial China up to the twentieth century (Mühlhahn, 2009, p. 5). In 550 CE, the Northern Qi State (550–577 CE) of the Northern Dynasty started to formally classified crimes into ten categories, also known as ten categories of heinous crimes or ten abominations (*shi e* 十恶), punishable by severe penalties. The five punishments (*wu xing* 五刑) established by the Tang Code during the Tang Dynasty (618–907 CE) were, in descending order of severity, death, life exile, penal servitude, beating with a heavy stick, and beating with a light stick (for details, see Mühlhahn, 2009, pp. 31–33). These were part of the law throughout the imperial era (Ren, 1997, p. 37). Imprisonment and fines were not forms of criminal sanction. The previous five punishments that *wu xing* replaced, as they were practiced and recorded in *Lü xing* of the Classic of Documents *(Shujing)* during the Zhou Dynasty (112–256 BCE), were tattooing, amputation of the nose, amputation of one or both legs, castration, and the death penalty (see Mühlhahn, 2009, p. 29). In short, in the long history of imperial China from 221 BCE to 1911 CE, the public image of law was mostly that of penal law and fearful sanctions, and almost without exception, the threat of physical punishment was attached to any normal criminal trial (N. He, 2014, p. 25).

In the Chinese imperial era, application of harsh laws was partly responsible for numerous popular uprisings resulting in the change of dynasties. The death penalty (*sixing* 死刑, also called *jixing* 极刑, extreme punishment) has been used since the first ancient Chinese law code, *Fajing*. For most of the imperial era, there were different methods of execution and different degrees of severity, including strangulation with or without delay and beheading with or without delay, and tormented death such as *lingchi* 凌迟—the executioner made a number of cuts with a knife upon the victim, with the final cut severing the head (Mühlhahn, 2009, p. 33).[9] The Confucian aversion to law's premise and the brutal rule by law campaigns waged by the Legalists in China's first imperial dynasty created a legacy that left a genuine feeling of distaste and fear of law in the hearts and minds of the Chines people for more than 2,000 years (N. He, 2014, p. 13).[10]

The underlying assumption of the penal system was that punishment would achieve their greatest effect when the severity of the penalty corresponded as closely as possible to the seriousness of the crime (Mühlhahn, 2009, p. 36). It is commonly acknowledged by Chinese scholars and ordinary folk alike that the criminal punishments meted out during imperial times in China were harsh, designed to inflict the maximum degree of physical and mental pain on the offenders, and sometimes their families (through *zhulian*, joint punishment of family members).[11] It was not just "the right degree of pain" as has been described by Mühlhahn (2009); rather it was maximum pain.

As for the moral justification for harsh punishment in traditional Chinese law, punishment was thought to serve two ends: it was a complement to moral conformity; and it was also the physical and spiritual elimination of malignity (Ren, 1997, p. 38). The human body of the offender was believed to possess evil spirits and to be instrumental in substantiating the malicious spirit. Corporal punishment, such as cutting off the hands of a thief or castrating a rapist, was aimed at incapacitating the evil spirits by removing the instruments through which they worked. Although the punishment was violent, its end justified the means because it was seen as less evil than the violence and disruption of social order brought about by the crime. Punishment was morally justifiable and a fairly reciprocal penalty for the commission of a crime, and it was retributive (Ren, 1997, p. 38). The two main functions of law were that harsh punishment through criminal law was used as a deterrent, and to instruct and reform a person for self-renewal—as it is still the case today. As pointed out, punishment was employed as a "motivational technique" with its key purpose being to deter the populace from engaging in activities that would violate the dominate value system, and the notion of punishment as a deterrent was widespread and relatively undisputed in imperial China (Mühlhahn, 2009, p. 26).

EXCESSIVE MENTAL AND PHYSICAL PAIN IN THE LEGAL PROCESS

Needless to say, traditional Chinese criminal trials did not resemble those in the modern courts of the West. Chinese traditional law was punitive, and people were treated in a humiliating manner before the courts. There was no lawyer or defender representing or defending the accused. The criminal procedure was an inquisitorial system (as it still is), and the accused bore the burden of being presumed guilty until or unless found innocent by the trial official. Furthermore, the law was concerned primarily with status-relationship and the corresponding obligations, paying little attention to individual rights (Ch'ü, 1965, p. 284). The emphasis on status gave rise to the unequal treatment of individuals in the legal process according to their status—e.g., eight categories of persons *(ba yi)* were exempt from criminal prosecution. The status of the parties involved in legal cases became the main consideration in the administration of justice; right or wrong was not an absolute standard, but relative to one's status (Ch'ü, 1965, p. 284).[12] This was a direct manifestation of Confucian ethics and values, or *liyi* 礼义, ritualized morality in Chinese traditional law.

Regarding the criminal procedures that were directly relevant to the word *yuan*, in traditional China, in terms of judicial personnel (as described in chapter 3), the basic office holder was the "county chief" (commonly translated as county or district magistrate), who administered all aspects of governance on behalf of the emperor at the lowest level of government, including investigating crimes and conducting trials, and performing dual administrative and judicial functions (see chapter 3). In terms of legal process and procedure, imperial Chinese governance was marked by a fusion of administrative and judicial power (Minzner, 2011, p. 80). Local officials were in charge of all local government matters, including tax collection and law enforcement. They were directly involved in legal dispute resolution and criminal prosecution at the basic level (see chapter 3). As described:

> During the Qing (as in earlier dynasties) no independent judiciary existed in China; officials who handled judicial matters were essentially regular members of the administrative bureaucracy, appointed and controlled by the central government in Beijing. At the first level of the judicial system, the district, the magistrate heard all cases, both civil and criminal, from his area of jurisdiction. The magistrate's role was a broad one: he not only presided at trials, he was also responsible for investigating crimes, conducting inquests and preliminary hearings, and apprehending criminals in his jurisdictions. In the courtroom as well he played a more active role than a common law judge. Since juries were never used in Chinese trials, the magistrate acted as trier of fact and of law in all cases before him. It was his responsibility to obtain the facts of cases and the necessary depositions; he therefore conducted the interrogation of all parties, including witnesses as well as the plaintiff and defendant, none of whom was represented by an attorney. (Conner, 2000, p. 134)

The county chief (or magistrate, as he would have been called in English) conducted investigations of crimes and decided cases and punishments. He was not allowed arbitrary decisions or to rely on local customary law, but rather was constrained by imperial edicts and the law codes. The imperial codes described offenses in detail. Typically, as in the Ming Dynasty (1368–1644 CE), the criminal trial process consisted of a first trial by the county chief, a second trial by a prefect, then a review by the provincial governor; if it was a capital offense, the final ruling would be by the emperor. Local trial officials bore responsibility for applying the law in particular cases, but ultimate judicial authority rested in the hands of the emperor, who made the final decision (Minzner, 2011, pp. 80–81).

In terms of conducting trials, generally speaking the accused had no rights and relied on the mercy of the trial official, and was not allowed legal or other representatives. During the entire imperial period, presumption of innocence did not exist, and the accused bore the presumption of guilt. It is believed that the presumption of guilt grew out of a respect for and obedience to the office of official investigators. If they suspected someone of a crime, that person was presumed to be guilty (Belkin, 2011, p. 296). It is telling that suspects in a criminal proceeding were referred to as *fan* (犯 offenders), suggesting that they were considered to be guilty of something even though they had not yet been convicted of anything (Park, 2008, p. 61). The trial official directed the gathering of evidence and witnesses, and conducted the trial. He decided the guilt or innocence of the accused and imposed the punishment according to the law.

In the trial process, one important principle of traditional Chinese law was that a person could not be convicted of a crime without a confession. Confession was rooted in Confucian ideology. It served two purposes: to establish an objective truth, which the trial official had to uncover in the course of his investigation; and for the offender to show through confession that they had started to understand their crime and were on the way to repenting (Mühlhahn, 2009, p.49). The attitude of the accused was institutionalized in the penal codes throughout Chinese history, including today. Confession of the accused is believed to have first been recognized in the Qin Code, and it continued to be recognized throughout the imperial era. For most of the imperial period, the trial official (county chief) relied on interrogation of the accused during the trial, and the complainant, witnesses, and anyone connected with the case could be questioned. One of the most important tasks of trials was to get at the truth of a case. As it was believed that only the accused could know the truth, the emphasis was put on obtaining the truth from the accused by all means possible. Forensic methods were also applied where available, as documented in Song Ci's book (see earlier), so the trial official could announce his verdict and punishment when all the facts were known to him.

Another important and relevant aspect of trials was that trial officials could use torture to obtain confessions. A confession was ordinarily required before a case could be closed, irrespective of the strength of evidence otherwise available to the trial official. Until the offender confessed, the trial official was unable to pronounce a sentence (Mühlhahn, 2009, p. 49). As pointed out, the law of confession was the law of torture (Conner, 2000, p. 137). The atmosphere of the courtroom was described by a well-known Chinese writer:

> A salt convoy passing through [the] district had been robbed, and the helmsman and salt clerk were advised by scholars traveling with the convoy to take the case to the local magistrate. When they did so, the magistrate rejected their story . . . and had the helmsman given twenty strokes with the bamboo "till his flesh was torn to shreds." The young clerk, "terrified" to see the magistrate pointing at him and reaching for another bamboo chip, immediately volunteered whatever the magistrate wanted to hear. "Kowtowing as quickly as a pestle pounding onions," he begged that his life be spared. (Watt, 1972, pp. 12–13, quoting Wu Jingzi's *The Scholars*)[13]

Commonly uttered words by the trial official (as often portrayed in Chinese dramas) were *dadan diaomin* (大胆刁民devious person), *rushi zhaolai* (如实招来confess the truth), and *fouze daxing cihou* (否则大刑伺候otherwise torture will be meted out). In a typical trial, the county chief (or, as he was known, *xiantaiye*, county great-grandfather, see chapter 3) acted as the trial judge, sitting high above in the courtroom looking down, with the prisoner kneeling down before him. The county chief would hit the table with a gavel, then say to the accused, "You unruly and devious person, I dare you, truthfully confess, or torture awaits you!"[14] Here, with *rushi zhaolai*, *zhao* 招means "to confess," and *da xing*大刑means "serious corporal punishment or torture." As explained in chapter 2, *xing* is another word for law—that is, legal punishment—and also means legally authorized torture. *Xing* or *shangxing* (上刑to use torture) in a way highlights the meaning of law and its relationship with torture and punishment in the criminal process, with the meaning of *xing* "evolved to include all forms of legally sanctioned torture and punishment" (Park, 2008, p. 38). The use of torture as a tool for the extraction of information or confession existed at least as far back as the Han Dynasty (206 BCE–220 CE), and continued to be a legally sanctioned feature of the judicial process for all but the last six years of imperial Chinese history (Park, 2008, p. 37). Torture was used as an interrogative tool in the course of a legal proceeding and as punishment meted out to convicted wrongdoers in the aftermath of a trial (Park, 2008, p. 37):

> As explained by Lu Longqi (1630–93), a magistrate who was renowned for his incorruptibility, *xing* had two purposes, the "lesser" of which was investigative (*xun*) and the "greater" of which was adjudicative (*jue*). Used as an aid to investigation, *xing* was seen as an effective technique for determining the "true facts" (*shiqing*) of a case and extracting a confession from the guilty parties. Used as a tool of punishment, *xing* was viewed as a just retribution for past wrongs and a useful deterrent against future misconduct. The shared terminology for torture and punishment reflects the essential similarity of these practices in the eyes of Chinese jurists, who viewed them as regrettable but necessary tools in the pursuit of justice. The conception of torture and punishment, properly applied, as efficient and effective instruments of justice, was propounded by countless writers throughout China's history and forms the philosophical backdrop against which Chinese judicial torture must be understood. (Park, 2008, p. 38, footnote omitted)

Like other legal punishments, torture was a legally sanctioned form of state violence (Mühlhahn, 2009, p. 49). The accused, witnesses, and complainants could all be tortured if they were suspected of giving false evidence. This was written into the law. For instance, the Ming Code has provisions to that effect:

> First have the complainant state his case, then question the accused. If he does not admit his guilt, question the witnesses. If they support the complainant, question the accused again. If each sticks to his story, question the accused and the witnesses in the presence of each other, listening to their voices and watching their demeanors. Whoever speaks firmly and without any change of facial expression must be telling the truth. Whoever stammers and is evasive must be speaking without conviction. When a person is obviously telling falsehoods, have him beaten with a bamboo. If he still refuses to tell the truth, have him beaten with a wooden staff. Question him closely and extract the facts. (cited in Shapiro, 1990, p. 22)

A Western eyewitness account graphically describes a late Qing Dynasty criminal trial:

> The almost unceasing flail-like sounds of beating with the bamboo, either as a punishment for ascertained guilt, or to extort confessions and evidence; the cries of the sufferers; the voices of the examining mandarins questioning, bullying, and wheedling; and the frequent appearance of criminals and witnesses being escorted to and from the prisons and rooms for examination, are sounds and sights that bewilder and agitate those who have not been accustomed to them, and serve to heighten that dread which all private Chinese entertain of entering a *yamen.* (Meadows, 1847, p. 115)

Today, numerous Chinese period television dramas portray this even more shockingly on the big screen, to the horror of many Chinese people. So the above description was not just a Western-biased and partial view unaccustomed to the Chinese way of doing things. As pointed out, "Legal punishments in imperial China were carefully orchestrated public spectacles of physical suffering. The public production of pain was believed to serve as a clear message, as a lesson to others and to prevent further transgressions by the convicts themselves" (Mühlhahn, 2009, p. 28). Beatings were legal and commonplace as a means of compelling confessions and eliciting testimony, and were legally sanctioned throughout China's imperial period, going back to the Zhou Dynasty and extending to the end of the Qing Dynasty. As pointed out, in imperial China, "a criminal case was not considered satisfactorily solved without an admission of guilt by the accused. If he would not confess voluntarily, it was standard practice for the court to have him beaten until he did" (Shapiro, 1990, p. 22). It seems that suspects were regularly beaten during interrogation, and they were only spared during mid-spring each year, for reasons that remain unknown (Shapiro, 1990, p. 22). Other types of torture included twisting of ears, slapping or beating, pressing sticks to the shins, ankles, or fingers; making the accused kneel on an iron chain; and head-squeezing bands (Mühlhahn, 2009, p. 49). As pointed out:

> The legal acceptability of torture reflects the relative emphasis of Chinese criminal law on substantive rather than procedural justice in the sense that it placed greater importance on the judicial goals of finding the "truth," punishing the guilty, and absolving the innocent than it did on the mechanics of the legal process. This does not mean that there were no standards for prosecution and punishment or that these standards were arbitrarily applied, but that judicial fairness was not measured in terms of the predictability and impartiality of the legal process. Instead, it was measured in terms of the perceived quality of the result, which was construed as the frequency with which criminals were made to pay for their misdeeds and the extent to which punishments were made to fit the crime. (Park, 2008, p. 60)

Despite the limited empirical evidence from the ancient past, the very public display of judicial torture in plays and folk stories is more than enough to leave an indelible impression of judicial torture—not only of its existence but also of its absolute tyranny (N. He, 2014, p. 34. For a historical analysis of criminal interrogation and torture from the pre-Han period to the post-Mao era, see Wu and Vander Beken, 2012).

According to MacCormack (1990), complex rules on confession, mutual concealment, and accusation are found in all the Chinese dynastic codes. As torture was legally sanctioned, it was done according to the prescribed rules (Conner, 2000; Mühlhahn, 2009, p. 50; Park, 2008; see also Alford (1984) for discussions of Qing criminal procedure). For instance, the instruments used for beating were bamboos, rods, and staves, and their shape, thickness, and length were prescribed. So were their size and description, the number of blows, which parts of the body should be struck, the intervals between beatings, and who could or could not be beaten. These were all detailed in the imperial codes. The law also exempted some from torture, including the eight categories of the specially privileged, people aged 70 years and older, or fifteen years and younger, those who were ill and pregnant women out of sympathy, mercy and social status considerations (Park, 2003, pp. 49–52). There were also rules designed to provide fairness. For instance, in the Tang Dynasty, the law was that whoever gave false testimony—whether claiming guilt for the innocent, or innocence for the guilty—should be punished as if guilty of the same crime, but in two degrees less severity. Confessions elicited by torture were generally deemed conclusive, even though there may have been strong evidence to the contrary (Shapiro, 1990). Some officials avoided the use of torture because they feared that it would produce false confessions. The officials could be punished if they invoked the wrong law or imposed a sentence that was either too harsh or too lenient. Nevertheless, given that the law allowed forced confession and torture for admissions of guilt, wrongful convictions were legion (Shapiro, 1990, p. 29). A commonly used phrase is *qu da cheng zhao* (屈打成招beaten into making confession) as used in Example 21. The most vivid description of such forced confession and torture was found in the Yuan play *Dou E Yuan*, described earlier in the chapter. It can be said that "Chinese history is replete with examples of injustice that are tied to the actions that transpired inside the magistrate's courts" (N. He, 2014, p. 26).

CRYING INJUSTICE

Throughout the ages, many wrongful cases and wrongful convictions occurred, partly due to forced confession and torture. A story was told of a case from the Sui Dynasty (581–618 CE). The emperor Sui Yang Di ordered a wide sweep of suspects due to extensive banditry. More than two thousand people were arrested. They were so severely beaten during interrogation that every one of them confessed. The emperor ordered their deaths by decapitation. His chancellor, suspicious of the mass admissions of guilt, conducted his own investigation. He found that only five of the condemned were bandits, while the rest were innocent. But since they had confessed, and because he dared not go against the wishes of the emperor, all of them were executed (Shapiro, 1990, p. 26).

In traditional China, life and death were regarded as the most important matter, often described as *renming guantian* (human life is the most serious) or *renming da yu tian* (human life is bigger or more important than heaven). So the killing of an individual, either by an individual or by the state in the case of death penalty, was taken most seriously. Starting from the Tang Dynasty, all death sentences were reviewed by the emperor. Similarly, the aggrieved and the accused who believed they had been wrongfully accused could appeal to the emperor. Likewise, serious cases of any nature could be appealed or reviewed, ultimately to the emperor. The responsible official could be reprimanded for not investigating thoroughly, for not following correct procedure, or for any other abnormality. Although the local trial official was given wide leeway in the conduct of cases, he had the authority to pronounce final sentence only for ordinary cases. All serious cases had to be forwarded to his superior officials for approval. Cases involving a charge of homicide had to be retried by the provincial chief and reported to the central government Board of Punishments. Finally, all cases involving the death sentence had to be reviewed by the board and were eventually forwarded to the emperor for ratification (Conner, 2000, p. 134).

This is where *yuan* and *yuanwang*, and the expression *hanyuan*, play a major part in the appeal and review process for wrongful decisions. As described earlier, in imperial China when a guilty verdict was handed down or before execution of a condemned prisoner, if the prisoner called out *yuan* or *yuanwang* just before execution, it was common practice for the execution to halt and the case to be reexamined. Similarly, at the entrance of the *yamen* compound, there was a drum to beat for ordinary people who may have legal grievances relating to wrongful cases, as described earlier and written in the Qing Code. Another channel during imperial times to voice one's legal grievances and wrongs was to present petitions to the high officials and ultimately to the emperor. After all, the emperor acted as the final appeal judge, and was the final adjudicator of capital crimes. Only the emperor could review and reverse cases of capital punishment.

Needless to say, in relation to contemporary China and the modern usage of *yuan*, Chinese criminal law is very different from its ancient counterpart, but many aspects remain the same—albeit some in different forms, including confession and torture to obtain confession. The word *yuan* and the practice of *hanyuan* also endured time; they never went away, and remain very much part of the Chinese people, culture and language, although their legal status has long disappeared.[15]

To summarize, the language of *yuan* and *hanyuan* became part of the Chinese legal tradition over a thousand years ago. It was part of the Chinese legal vocabulary and usage. Today, there is no formalized *hanyuan* procedure as in the past, and it is no longer part of the law, but the practice of *hanyuan* continues among the aggrieved Chinese, in and outside court, and often in the form of appeals to higher authorities.

LACK OF JUSTICE SYMBOLS

As we have seen, forced confession was an important part of traditional Chinese law and the judicial process. This unfortunately is also true in modern China. Thus *yuan* and *hanyuan* have also continued as accompaniments to the criminal law, with crying injustice as a public channel and means to seek justice. Separately but relevantly, it is interesting to observe that in traditional China, there was no equivalent to the Western symbols of justice. There was no similar goddess of justice in China—or even a god of justice, given the male-dominated nature of Chinese society. In contrast, in Western culture there was in Iustitia/Justitia, or Lady Justice, the Roman goddess of Justice, or the Greek goddess Themis, an allegorical personification of the moral force in judicial systems. The distinguishing features of the Goddess of Justice are a blindfold, a balance, and a sword. As Rudolph von Jhering states:

> And hence it is that Justice which, in one hand, holds the scales, in which she weighs the right, carries in the other the sword with which she executes it. The sword without the scales is brute force, the scales without the sword is the impotence of law. The scales and the sword belong together, and the state of the law is perfect only where the power with which Justice carries the sword is equalled by the skill with which she holds the scales. (von Jhering, 1915, p. 2)

There was no scale in traditional Chinese law—just brute force. And there was no such popular figure or symbol either—real or imagined. Instead, China has had a popular cultural symbol of injustice in Dou E, as described earlier. This lack of symbols of justice makes *yuan* even more portent and more prominent in the Chinese legal tradition, as a channel for both venting grievances and redressing legal wrongs.

This does not mean, though, that there was a complete absence of symbols of justice in traditional Chinese culture, or an absence of a sense of justice.

One rare symbol of justice in Chinese culture is Bao Gong (his actual name is Bao Zheng, 999–1062 CE, see also chapter 3). During his civil service as an official and judge, his fearless and upright conduct made him a legendary figure, and he acquired the honorific title Bao Qingtian (Clear Sky Bao) due to his ability to help ordinary people overcome corruption and seek justice. Today, Bao Gong is honored as a symbol of justice in Chinese culture (see Hanan, 2008, and Wilt, 2009). His largely fictionalized stories have appeared in a variety of different literary and dramatic mediums, and have enjoyed sustained popularity. He is often portrayed wearing a judge miter hat and a crescent moon on his forehead. Some Chinese provinces have deified Judge Bao. However, in Chinese, Judge Bao is not called "Judge." He is known as Bao Gong, Sir Bao, or the Reverent Bao. Bao Gong is best known to the Chinese first as a *qingguan* (clean official), his name became synonymous with the idealized "honest and upright official," and he is known as a competent, impartial, incorruptible, and upright official, not yielding to the rich and powerful, and as acting in the people's and country's interest, rather than seeking personal gain. His images and reputation consist of multiple dimensions: intolerance of injustice and corruption, filial piety and stern demeanor, iron-faced judge, and Clear Sky fearless official. Bao Gong and his stories, like the story of Dou E, have been household legends in China for over a thousand years. They have been fictionalized and dramatized through the ages. In these fictionalized works, there is always a symbolic triumph of justice at the end of the story or play, and this is largely to compensate for its absence in the real world of Chinese life, symbolizing "a longing for true justice that remains elusive in Chinese reality since antiquity" (N. He, 2014, p. 33).

In recent times, the icon of the Western goddess of justice has been introduced to China, and it is now familiar to educated Chinese. A goddess of justice statue recently was erected outside the Chengdu City Intermediate People's Court/Procuratorate in Sichuan Province. Nevertheless, many Chinese are still puzzled by such symbolism, especially the blindfold of the goddess. To the Chinese mind, a judge seeing what happens in court—importantly, seeing the emotions, gestures and body language, and verbal language of the accused, witnesses, and so on—is very much part of the theatrics and adjudication of the legal process. Importantly, to many Chinese, the notion of a judicial officer being impartial and balanced is too good to be true in real life. In imperial China, outside courthouses were a pair of fierce looking lions, a symbol of intimidation and power, of "shock and awe," to the ordinary people and those who came before the court. Such lions can be seen outside many Chinese courthouses today, as part of the new construction boom of courthouses in China in recent years. The lions are often described as *zhang ya wu zhao* (baring fangs and brandishing or opening claws), in the sense of making threatening gestures, ferocious looking, representing power and force:

> *Yamen* stone lions, originally a Chinese traditional architecture, is a symbol of "guardian, spelling away evil spirits, and servitude," and, therefore, stone lions stand outside government office in feudal era and the mansion of emperors and high officials and ministers, as well as on the front of the countryside rich man. Two stone lions, bearing their fangs with twisted open mouths, staring eyes with eyebrows straightened up, putting people in awe and also engender hatred. Thus, as a top priority of the people who rebelled, the first thing they did was to smash the stone lions as a symbol of power and tyranny that they stood for (Anonymous).[16]

Another relevant comment is noted in the recent study of Chinese court case-related drum ballads (*guci*) from the Qing Dynasty:

> From the way the plots are constructed—a crime is exposed and the judge resolves it by punishing the wrongdoer—one could say that justice is a central concept in these court-case drum ballads. Intriguingly, there is no one term that clearly means "justice" in these stories. Martial arts novels use the terms "justice" (*zhengyi*), but in the court case drum ballads, the emphasis seems to be on the injustice (*yuan*). The solutions to injustice are varied; they involve Heavenly Principle (*tianli*), the King's Law (*wangfa*), retribution (*baoying*), truth (*zhen qingshi*), fairness (*gongdao*), and reasons or common sense (*li*). The three major terms relating to Qing justice—*qing* (compassion or feeling), *li* (principle or reasons), and *fa* (law)—all appear in the ballads, but often lend themselves to different interpretations than in "orthodox" understandings of the law and morality. (Wan, 2015, p. 289)

To conclude, as described by many Chinese and other legal scholars, the legacy of Chinese traditional law includes law used as a political tool to maintain social order and social stability; law administrated through administrative bureaucracy; and law as a secondary tool for regulating state affairs, after the guidance of Confucianism became the state orthodoxy (Chen, 2008; N. He, 2014, p. 15). Historically, Chinese law was known for its emphasis on penal law. Traditional Chinese penal law is a set of rules emanating from the emperor, which imposes punishments on officials or ordinary people who behave, or fail to behave, in certain ways; it is not concerned with the establishment of the rights of the individual or with the protection of individual freedom (MacCormack, 1990, p. 48). Generally speaking, law in traditional China was never perceived as a means of preserving rights, freedom, and justice (Z. Liang, 1989, p. 89). Despite the more recent studies of civil litigation and related history in the late imperial time, law first and foremost represents punishment. Given such an instrumental approach, law was a personified tool of governing, dependent on and confined by its function with limited use

(Z. Liang, 1989, p. 89).[17] It has been likened to military disciplines or parents handling children and imposing discipline on them (Stephens, 1992). Law as a system of punishment was indeed a legal system with Chinese characteristics in imperial China. As described, punishment and pain, not rights and procedural justice, symbolize the Chinese criminal process as a whole, and this realization is deeply ingrained in a Chinese psyche and culture that was true in the imperial times and may still be true today (N. He, 2014, p. 35). Consequently, with regard to this legal process and culture, there is a lack of popular symbols of justice throughout Chinese history— including today. Instead, it has an enduring cultural icon of injustice or seeking to redress injustice, as represented by the play *Dou E Yuan*. The word *yuan* has been very much part of this cultural tradition and law, although it does not often appear in the formal or official law or in legal texts today. It is the language of the object of Chinese law—that is, ordinary people—mainly used by ordinary Chinese, for both legal wrongs and ordinary grievances, over the centuries. Its usage and currency have continued to this day.

NOTES

1. *Chinese Xinhua Dictionary* online: http://xh.5156edu.com/html3/2676.html.

2. The full text of the play can be found at http://www.gushiwen.org/GuShiWen_2164b0b8c4.aspx; http://so.gushiwen.org/view_69605.aspx.

3. For discussion of the play, see N. He (2014, pp. 32–33).

4. See http://www.nanzao.com/sc/gallery/14f1c304fb954e5/song-cheng-zong-cai-ju-bao-zhe-gao-yuan-yuan-chang-qi-qi-hang-zhou-fei-xue-dou-e-ming-yuan-.

5. Estimates of the death toll during the Cultural Revolution vary according to different sources. These ranged upwards to several millions, but an estimate of around 400,000 deaths is a widely accepted minimum figure. MacFarquhar and Schoenhals (2006) state that in rural China alone, some 36 million people were persecuted, of whom between 750,000 and 1.5 million were killed, with roughly the same number permanently injured. The true figure of those who were persecuted or died during the Cultural Revolution may never be known, however, since many deaths went unreported or were covered up by the police or local authorities. None of them actually went through any proper legal process.

6. For a discussion of wrongful convictions in contemporary China, see J. He (2016a, b).

7. See http://cn.nytimes.com/china/20150619/c19sinosphere-rare-direct-appeal-to-xi-jinping-appears-then-disap/en-us.

8. Austin (1962) distinguishes two kinds of utterances. The first is the "constatives," which are statements or assertions and which describe or report things and events; and utterances that perform actions merely by virtue of the utterances being made. The second type of utterances is called "performatives," to recognize the actional nature of what they do as opposed to constative utterances of what they say.

Austin calls performative utterances "illocutionary" and constative utterances "locutionary"—see chapter 6.

9. *Lingchi* was the most extreme form of bodily punishment that could be imposed under the imperial law in China. It involved the methodical slitting and cutting a part of the body of the condemned in a stipulated number of cuts performed in a prescribed sequence (Brook, Bourgon and Blue, 2008, p. 55). As Brook, Bourgon and Blue (2008) explain, *lingchi* was first acknowledged in the Yuan Code of the Yuan Dynasty, and was used for the very worst political and moral offenses in the Ming Dynasty, and continued in force during the Qing Dynasty, becoming known in the nineteenth century the quintessential "Chinese torture" in the West. For a comprehensive and detailed study of *lingchi*, see Brook, Bourgon and Blue (2008), which focuses on a reconstruction of the execution of a convicted offender by the name of Wang Weiqin in a popular market in downtown Beijing in the autumn of 1904:

> The execution of Wang Weiqin unfolded in the middle of a crowd of soldiers and onlookers who had gathered to watch the most severe legal penalty the Qing state could impose. Two soldiers brought forward the basket holding the knives that the procedures required. Others stripped the victim and bound him by his queue to a tripod in such a way that the front of his body was fully exposed to the state executioner and his assistant. The executioner began by slicing off pieces of flesh from the convict's breasts, his biceps, and his upper thighs. Before the slicing went any further, the executioner punctured Wang's heart with a swift stab, putting the man to death. Thereafter he proceeded to methodically sever the limbs, first at the wrists and ankles, then at the elbows and knees, lastly at the shoulders and hips. His final cut severed the head from the body. A practiced executioner made roughly three dozen cuts to reduce his victim to an incoherent scattering of body parts, though this number could vary. His work completed, he turned toward the officials and called out, "*Sha ren le*! The person has been killed!" (Brook, Bourgon and Blue, 2008, p.1).

Lingchi has variously been translated as "death by a thousand cuts," "death by slicing," and "the lingering death." The procedure that Wang underwent was not exceptional within the context of late imperial Chinese criminal law, and such executions were supervised by officials from the Board of Punishments. For a photograph of the execution, see Brook, Bourgon and Blue (2008, p. 4). Ironically, some scholars in the West may see this as an indication of the existence and observance of law in imperial China, as such execution was indeed carried out according to the law.

10. According to Guy (2000, pp. 88–89), in China, law was an instrument, itself amoral, used by the state to preserve an essentially moral order. Chinese law was the creation of the sovereign, a tool used by Chinese rulers dating back to the sixth century BCE to protect the public order and preserve the state. Far from reflecting any sort of natural law, the Chinese statutes had no particular moral legitimacy; if anything, the need for such a tool as law was a sad commentary on the failure of the natural human propensity for goodness to prevail in the world. Law itself, and those who invoked it, were legitimate only as long as the tools of the government were used

to secure moral political ends. Chinese statutes were fashioned—perhaps more transparently than in the West—to serve moral and political purposes, and prosecutions undertaken under such statutes must be read in this context (see Guy, 2000).

11. *Zhulian, zuzhu*, or *lianzuo* (joint death penalty or criminal punishment of one's family or tribe, also called *zhulian jiuzu*, nine kinship or familial extermination) was part of the traditional Chinese criminal law from pre-imperial China to the Qing Dynasty (1616–1911 CE). Under such law, if one was found guilty of a crime, one's family members, relatives, associates, and even neighbors would also be punished. This was believed to have been started by Shang Yang (c. 390–338 BCE) of the Legalist School. In his days, every ten families were classified as one group, and if one family committed a crime, the other nine would also collectively be held responsible and punished accordingly as a means of deterrence. It was also related to the Confucian idea that family members—particularly parents—were responsible for the wrong-doings of other family members. A similar practice of *zhulian*, although not in formalized legal form, was widely used by the Chinese government from the 1950s to the 1970s for political and other crimes. For provisions on confession and joint punishment in traditional Chinese law, see *The T'ang Code* (Tang Code), translated by Wallace Johnson (1979). The Tang Code, on which all the successive imperial codes were based, was enacted in 653 CE. See also *The Great Qing Code*, translated by W.C. Jones (1994).

12. Although the Legalists advocated punishment for all criminal acts, regardless of status of the perpetrators, both Legalism and Confucianism adhered to the inherent inequality of individuals before the law and morality. Inequality and differential treatment of individual offenders were the ethically prescribed norms in traditional China—for instance, the practice of differential punishment in accordance with the offender's social status and relation to the offender (Ren, 1997, p. 39).

13. Wu Jingzi (1701–1754) wrote *Ruilin wanshi*, translated as *The Scholars*, a novel completed in 1750 during the Qing Dynasty, which describes and satirizes Chinese scholars in vernacular language.

14. There are many Chinese derogatory phrases to refer to ordinary people—for instance, *diaomin* (devious people), *jianmin* (cheap people), and *yumin* (foolish people).

15. In modern China, *zhaogong* or *tanbai*, both meaning "confession of crimes," have been and still are used and promoted in political campaigns and criminal law. Confession is written and practiced in the current criminal law, where it is stipulated that possible lighter sentences will be given for voluntary confession. It is expressed as part of modern Chinese criminal law in the popular slogan *tanbai congkuan, kangju congyan* (confession will be met with leniency and resistance will be met with severe punishment). This is the opposite of the right to remain silent. Under the Chinese law, non-confession or remaining silent was often regarded as "resistance." In recent times, the so-called "zero confession" (*ling kougong*)—that is, no confession—has been promoted and instituted in some instances. Nevertheless, over the past few years, public confessions by suspects on television have become much more frequent. This has led to calls to cease the practice of "putting on trial" criminal suspects in the "court of public opinion" by broadcasting their confessions on state television.

Televised confessions are said to violate both Chinese law and international human rights norms, including China's Criminal Procedure Law (1997), which stipulates that suspects cannot be pronounced guilty without having been judged as such by a court (CPL, Article 12). See Jiahong He's comprehensive study (2016a, b) of forced confession in wrongful convictions in recent years.

16. Taken from http://iask.sina.com.cn/b/5715330.html.

17. For similar views and discussions of traditional Chinese law, see He Qinhua (2004), Zhang Zhongqiu (1999), Li Guilian (1999), L. Liang (2007), and Chang (2016).

Chapter 5

Linguistic and Cultural Meanings of "Rights" in Chinese

The American Declaration of Independence proclaims: "We hold these truths to be self-evident, that all men are created equal; that they are endowed by their Creator with certain unalienable rights." However, within the Chinese cultural and philosophical milieu, it is far from self-evident that everyone is endowed with rights that even the good of society as a whole cannot override (Peerenboom, 1993, p. 37). There has been considerable amount of writings on the issue of rights in legal and other studies, but no so much in linguistics. A prominent linguist proposes that "rights" is a universal concept whether any particular language does or does not have a word for it and that "rights" as a concept is largely innate to all humans (Jackendoff, 2007a, p. 355; 2007b, p. 413). This chapter wishes to provide a counterpoint with the Chinese language and culture as an example to illustrate that, first, classical Chinese language did not have an equivalent word for the English word "rights"; second, classical Chinese culture did not have an equivalent concept of "rights"; and third, after the word and concept of "rights" were introduced into Chinese from the West in the second half of the nineteenth century, the new word *quanli* (rights) has since taken on Chinese shades of meaning, not entirely the same as its English counterpart. Its meaning is still evolving, reflecting the culture, society, and thinking of the indigenous Chinese and the Chinese language users, and the Chinese people are still learning and acquiring it as a word, a concept, and part of existence today. It is proposed here that the claim of the innate or universal nature of the word "rights" is not tenable, or it would have to exclude traditional Chinese culture and classical Chinese language, one of the largest speech communities in the world and one of the longest continuous human civilizations.

LINGUISTIC ABSENCE OF "RIGHTS" AND ITS CREATION IN CHINESE

In English, "right" means a lawful and just entitlement. As Oxford Dictionary defines it, a right means a moral or legal entitlement to have or do something. Another definition is that rights are entitlements (not) to perform certain actions, or (not) to be in certain states; or entitlements that others (not) perform certain actions or (not) be in certain states.[1] There are moral rights as well as legal rights. The notion of legal rights of a person was first found in the ancient Roman law (although the word used was *jus*, not exactly the same as "rights"). In more recent history, the idea of moral rights was traceable to John Locke and his theory of natural rights and other early European thinkers. And of course, there is also the famous description of natural rights by English legal philosopher Jeremy Bentham (1839)—"natural and imperceptible rights," "rhetorical nonsense," "nonsense on stilts."

In the case of China, it has had plenty of stilts as part of traditional folk culture, but there was an absence of a linguistic sign for "rights" in classical Chinese for either legal rights or moral rights, that is, no word or equivalent concept existed in classical Chinese close to the Western idea of "rights." There were no equivalent intellectual discussions and debates about natural rights in early Chinese history. The idea of "rights" was imported to China from the West around the mid-nineteenth century with the introduction and translation of Western social and political science. "Rights" together with other ideas such as democracy, freedom, and constitution were brought to China from the West at a time of great social, political, and cultural turmoil and transformation in China. New words were coined for these concepts and many Japanese words were borrowed that had earlier been translated from European languages (see Cao, 2004). W.A.P. Martin (1817–1916) was credited with being the person who created the word *quanli* for "rights."[2] Martin first used *quanli* in 1864 in *Wanguo gongfa*, his Chinese translation of Wheaton's *Elements of International Law* (Wheaton, 1836–1878. For discussions of Martin's translation of "rights," see Angle, 2002; Liu, 1999; G. Wang, 1991; Svarverud, 2001). Martin translated "independent sovereignty" as *zizhu zili zhi quan* (自主自立之权利self-autonomous and self-determinative right) and "rights" as *quanli* 权利.

Quanli, prior to Martin's usage, had been used since ancient times in China, but it meant something totally different. *Quan* and *li* were mostly used separately, with *quan* meaning "power" and *li* meaning "profit," "interest," or "benefit." *Quan* and *li* were occasionally used together in philosophical texts to mean "power" and "interest or benefit." For instance, in the philosophical work *Xunzi* written by a major Chinese philosopher Xun Zi (313–238 BCE.), it says:

> 是故权利不能倾也，群众不能移也，天下不能荡也。
> Therefore, the exigencies of time and place and consideration of personal profit cannot influence him, cliques and coteries cannot sway him, and the whole world cannot deter him. (Xunzi, 1999, p. 22–23)[3]

Here, *quan* and *li* are two separate words in classical Chinese.

When *quanli* was first used in the new Western sense of rights, Martin described it this way:[4]

> [International] law is a separate field of study and thus a specific vocabulary should be devised for this purpose. Therefore, when there are occasional passages in the original text which are difficult to render comprehensively in Chinese, then the translation may sometimes seem strained. Take for instance the character *quan*. In this book it carries not only the meaning of someone being in power but also the meaning of the share ordinary people ought to obtain (rights). Sometimes a character *li* is added to this meaning, such as in the passage "the rights enjoyed by the common people," etc. Passages and terms like this may seem awkward at first but when one has encountered them several times one comes to realize that there is no other way than to use such an expression.[5] (Martin et al., 1878)

Various historical studies in recent years of Martin's works did not document or identify the sources or inspirations for his choice of *quanli* for "rights." At the time, a few other Chinese phrases were used for the translation of "rights" by various translators, including *liquan* 利权 (which is the reversed form of *quanli*), *daoli* 道理, *gongdao* 公道, *zhengdang* 正当, *lisuodangran* 利所当然, *heli* 合礼, *gewai zhi quan* 格外之权, and *quan* 权 (see Yu, 2001, p. 44). A major Chinese thinker and translator at the time, Yan Fu, questioned the use of *quanli* for rights, and he used *minzhi* for rights instead, but for some reasons, he switched to *quanli*, using *quanli* for his translation of "inalienable rights" (L. Wang, 2005). In short, Martin's *quanli* prevailed. *Quanli* has been used as a semantic equivalent to "rights" in Chinese ever since.

LINGUISTIC USAGE AND MEANING OF *QUANLI*

As we know, seemingly identical words in different languages are not always the same, often carrying meanings or connotations indigenous to the language and culture of a particular society. As there was no linguistic equivalent for the word "rights" in classical Chinese, the word we have now in modern Chinese for "rights" was introduced. However, this new word uses the old Chinese characters, thus its new meaning of rights naturally and inevitably is mixed with and influenced by the old meaning unrelated to rights. *Quanli,* despite its Western origin, now a common Chinese word, has had a complicated history of usage and meaning and user acquisition in China since its inception. Not only *quanli* seemed awkward linguistically as Martin indicated, but it has since been awkwardly ambiguous in Chinese culture, due to linguistic, cultural, political and other reasons.

First of all, the conceptual ambiguity of *quanli* (rights) arises from the meaning of *quan*. In classical Chinese, *quan* originally refers to a type of weight measuring instrument, for instance, the phrase *quanheng* meaning "to weigh," "to deliberate," and "to balance" in a political context. But the more common and the dominant meaning of *quan* is "power," "authority," and "privilege," most often "political power."

Secondly, *quanli* 权利 has a homophone *quanli* 权力, but the latter means "power" or "authority." They are indistinguishable in speech in modern Chinese,[6] except by context. In writing, they are distinguishable by the second character *li.* The two *li* are written differently and carry different meanings. *Li* 力 in *quanli* (权力power) means "strength" and "power," while *li* 利in *quanli* (权利rights) means "benefits," "interests," and "wealth." In the actual use of the two words, even today, many Chinese use them incorrectly, including well-educated ones. When they mean *quanli* (权利rights), they would write *quanli* (权力 power) by mistake, and vice versa. *Quanli* for individual rights virtually disappeared from the Chinese vocabulary in Mao's China before its revival in recent times, while *quanli* (power) has always dominated in Chinese political discourse. The unfamiliarity with *quanli* (rights) among Chinese language users is the result of lack of practice, linguistic and mental, not helped by the linguistic ambiguity.

Thirdly, *quan* with the basic and essential meaning of "power" is a short form for both *quanli* (权力power) and *quanli* (权利rights). This linguistic ambiguity, as noted, may indicate a perspective ambivalence in the Chinese thinking as the two terms may not be conceptually very different to the Chinese, and not as mutually incompatible as they are generally understood in Western languages (Svarverud, 2001, p. 126). In this regard, a usage of *quan* is *you quan* 有权, "to have the right or power to do something." It is ambiguous, distinguishable only by context. For instance, *wo you quan jueding* can be either "I have the power to decide" or "I have the right to decide," depending on the context as illustrated in the following examples taken from a Chinese corpus:[7]

按照规定,森林公安局有权制止这种违法行为。

According to regulations, the Forest Police have the power/authority to stop such illegal acts.

现在选择公开这些证据,是因为公众有权知道真相。

The evidence is now made public because the public have the right to know the truth. But in the next two examples, *you quan* is ambiguous. It could mean either "to have the right" or "to have the power or authority":

> 虽然他们有权来做这件事情, 但是并不代表大家对他们都很放心。
>
> They have the right/the authority to do this, but that does not mean that the people have not concerns about them.
>
> 因为他有权处置这个。
>
> Because he has the right/the authority to deal with this.

Thus, *quan* is ambiguous when used referring to rights due to its connotation of power and authority. Historically, the essential meaning of "power" in *quan* was retained in *quanli* (rights) since it was first used by Martin, and this meaning remains dominant till this day as *quan* has mostly meant "power" in Chinese. This can be illustrated by the way of the Chinese absorption and internalization of the Western rights idea against the historical and cultural background and by the linguistic usage. Following Martin's use of *quanli* for rights, along with the introduction and translation of other Western works in political science, the notion of *quanli* (rights) was fiercely debated among leading intellectuals in China toward the end of the nineteenth century. *Quanli* then came into common usage. Among the intelligentsia then, there was a growing consciousness of the Western idea of rights. However, such an understanding was gained from within the Chinese meaning (G. Wang, 1991, p. 167). One such preexisting Chinese meaning was, power and authority: the total dependence on power for anyone to have rights at all (G. Wang, 1991, p. 178). In imperial China, *quan*, that is, political power and authority, belonged exclusively to the ruler, the most important power of the four dominant powers in Chinese society. The four powers were *junquan* (the power of the emperor), *zuquan* (the power of the family clan), *shenquan* (divine power), and *fuquan* (power of the husband) that Chinese women were subject to (and as indicated earlier, rights for a wife in a marriage would be an alien concept in traditional China).[8] Power and authority in premodern China was pervasive in all spheres of life and often absolute.

Against such background, in introducing and translating the rights notion from the West, particularly from the ideas of Western liberal philosophers such as Kant and Locke, the Chinese rejected the traditional Kantian belief that rights were of intrinsic value to the individual. They instead opted for the more instrumentalist view of rights as a means to the nation-building goals of the Chinese state (Weatherley, 1999). Similarly, the Chinese came to see rights as a way of augmenting power, enhancing the omnipotence of the state in its quest to unite and strengthen the Chinese nation, rather than a necessary restraint on state power, as Locke envisaged (Weatherley, 1999, p. 150). Such

Chinese conceptualization was reinforced by the fact that *quanli* (rights) was first translated into Chinese in the context of sovereign or state rights in international law as described earlier. Thus, as observed, the blurred distinction of *quan* as "rights" and as "power" may not be very apparent to the Chinese intellectuals in the late 1800s because *quan* retained its early meaning of "power" while gaining the new meaning of "rights" (Svarverud, 2001, p. 134).

The meaning of *quanli* (rights) with the sense of power can be illustrated with the concept of *minquan* (民权people's power or popular empowerment) in the late 1800s and the early 1900s.[9] It was pointed out that Chinese scholars tended to emphasize the "power" aspect of *minquan* which was taken to mean "people's power in politics" (Svarverud, 2001, p. 140). Reformers and intellectuals such as Kang Youwei (1858–1927), Liang Qichao (1873–1929), and Sun Yat-Sen (1866–1925) were primarily concerned with China's power to recover its sovereign rights. Others, like Yan Fu (1854–1921), understood the importance of individual rights, but saw rights ultimately in terms of their contribution toward strengthening China (G. Wang, 1991, p. 167). These intellectuals were talking about people's power, not individual rights or civil liberties. In the use of *quan* in *minquan,* that generation of Chinese gave emphasis to the political power due to the people, their share in determining the destiny of China, their role in saving China (G. Wang, 1991, p. 180).

In the more recent past and present China, the association and meaning of power and authority in *quan* remains. First, *quan* 权in modern Chinese still means first and foremost power and authority. For instance, in the Chinese Constitution, it states, "All the power (*quanli* 权力) of the People's Republic of China belongs to the people" (Art. 2), and "The National People's Congress of the People's Republic of China is the highest organ of state power" (*quanli* 权力) (Art. 57). Apart from *quanli* (power), other phrasal combinations with *quan* include *quanwei* (authority, authoritative), *quanxian* (limit of power, competence or jurisdiction), *quanneng* (power and function), *quanshu* (power games), *dangquan* or *zhangquan* (in power), *yuequan* (to overstep or exceed one's authority), *shouquan* (to authorize), *baquan* (hegemony), *quanyu* (lust for power), *quanzha* (political trickery, craftiness or political expediency), *quanmou* (political tactics, trickery). Other phrases with *quan* are *zhengquan* (political power), *tequan* (special power and privilege), *jiquan* (absolute power, dictatorial or totalitarian rule), *zhengduo quanli* (fight for power and privilege), *xingzheng quan* (executive power), *sifa quan* (judicial power), *lifa quan* (legislative power), and *zhuquan* (sovereignty or sovereign power). All these phrases are in common use in modern Chinese political discourse, with *quan* a high-frequency word, widely used with strong connotations associated with political power and authority. All the phrases in Chinese beginning with *quan* carry the meaning of "power," with the only exception of *quanli* (rights).

As for the sense of "rights," *quanli* (权利) is the only Chinese word associated with such a meaning, with no synonyms, unlike in English where you have "rights," "entitlements," "just due," among others. It is the only word that begins with *quan* but does not mean "power." *Quan* in this "rights" sense is often used after other words to denote various rights, for instance, *gongmin quan* (citizen's rights), *xuanju quan* (the right to vote), *nannü pingdeng quan* (the right of gender equality), *shou jiaoyu quan* (the right to receive education). There are also *caichan quan* (property rights), *minquan* (civil rights), *fading quan* (legal rights), and others. In recent years, many more new words have appeared associated with rights, for instance, *maogou quan* (cat and dog rights), *dongwu quan* (animal rights), *xiaoxiang quan* (the right to one's image or portrait), *yinsi quan* (the right to privacy) and *chenmo quan* (the right to remain silent), and *shengcun quan* (right to survival or to life). Other recent terms include *weiquan* (to uphold or demand one's rights) and *weiquan lüshi* (rights lawyer). However, in the past few years, the Chinese government has been targeting and cracking down on rights lawyers in China, making *weiquan lüshi* a derogative term.

As for the use of *renquan* (human rights), not the focus of this chapter, *renquan* was used in the late 1800s in the famous *tianfu renquan* (natural rights or naturally endowed rights), and the phrase was first used in 1887 by Chinese writers in their writings in explaining the Western idea of "natural rights" (G. Wu, 2014).[10] In the 1950s to the 1980s, *renquan* was a taboo in China, not to be promoted or even mentioned. It became more visible in the past ten years or so in official Chinese media and political discourse. *Renquan* has now gained wider publicity and legitimacy in usage in China. The Chinese Constitution added the word *renquan* in the 2004 constitutional amendment, stating that "the state respects and protects human rights" (Art. 33).

In short, *quanli* (rights) is not indigenous to Chinese language and culture, and its evolution has been fraught with complications since its introduction into Chinese. Its linguistic and conceptual ambiguity and multiplicity may reveal the ambivalence toward the notion and practice of rights in modern Chinese society, and one thing for certain is that it is not at all identical to the original English word "rights" where it came from.

CULTURAL MEANINGS OF *QUANLI*

As elaborated above, the Chinese language in its classical form does not have a semantic equivalent to the concept of "rights." The significance of the linguistic absence in the long history of Chinese culture was not lost in many of the discussions concerning rights in China. It signifies more than just a semantic absence. There was a conceptual absence of rights in classical Chinese as well.

To begin with, ancient Chinese laws did not have provisions concerning various rights of individuals. Furthermore, there were no intellectual discussions and debates about natural rights in imperial China, unlike those during the Renaissance and Enlightenment periods in Europe. Instead, what traditional China had in terms of philosophical debates were predominantly moral teachings from Confucius among others. Rights and individual liberty were not mentioned in Confucius, not part of the Confucian thoughts and principles. The most important Confucian moral teachings included rites (instead of rights), duties, collectivism, and the so-called eight virtues of Confucius—benevolence, righteousness, courtesy, wisdom, fidelity, loyalty, filial piety, and service to elders. In the more recent history, in the late nineteenth century, the Chinese were keen to embrace Western ideas in their desperate attempt to save China. However, the response to the West took place within a framework of concepts and categories furnished by the Chinese intellectual tradition (Schwartz, 1964, pp. 5–6). Many of the new introduced ideas had been built on Confucianism and other Chinese indigenous ideas because Chinese traditional values, in particular, Confucianism, were the spiritual and intellectual world within which these literati lived and breathed within the Chinese world (Schwartz, 1964, pp. 5–6).

Directly related to our discussion of rights are the ideas of collectivism and duties, especially from classical Confucianism. In terms of collectivism and individuals, in traditional China, there were no discussions or mention of individuals being entitled to naturally endowed rights. One must earn privileges, interests, and benefits by achieving some minimal level of humanity with required demonstration of credentials as a participating member of society (Peerenboom, 1993, pp. 40–41). Instead of positing some intrinsically residing features, some self-same identical characteristic that qualifies all human beings as members of a natural humankind, in the Chinese mind, people were to be understood by exploring relevant associations that constitute their specific patterns of meaningful relations. Persons were not perceived as superordinated individuals, not as agents who stood independent of their actions, but rather were ongoing events defined functionally by constitutive roles and relations within the context of their specific families and communities, that is, through the observance of rites or ritual propriety (*li*) (Ames and Rosemont, 1998, p. 29). Due to the social nature of humans, a human becoming a human was a function of socialization (Peerenboom, 1993, p. 41). As social animals, people had social roles and obligations. One consequence of this thinking was that people could acquire different social, economic, and political standing in the process of becoming a human and a gentleman. People were differentiated according to status and they were regarded as unequal. Traditional Chinese law was known for legalizing inequality and unequal treatment of different classes of people, some being superior to others.

In addition, although Confucianism recognized the existence of private interests in society, they were viewed as belonging not to the individual but to the group—a family, lineage, or community (Nathan, 1986, p. 138). In such a view, people were born into society and could not prosper alone; the individual depended on the harmony and strength of the group (Nathan, 1986, p. 138). The individual must cultivate oneself, not for oneself but to contribute to the welfare of family and community. As pointed out, the basic unit of traditional Chinese society was not the individual but the collectivity: family, clan, village, gentry (Lubman, 1999, p. 17). While there is evidence to suggest that the role of the individual was once highly prized and later suppressed as a result of the political and ideological imperatives of the Chinese state, the collective tradition has remained a dominant feature of Chinese culture (Potter, 2001, p. 61).[11] As Turner notes,

> It is this ultimate focus on the decisions of rulers and officials to guide and to define the goals of the legal system that distinguishes the classical Chinese idea of the function of law from that produced in classical Greek and Rome, and from what the late classical Chinese theoretical texts, legal procedural manuals and histories demonstrate, the Chinese elites who formulated and implemented the law were servants of the state, charged with protecting its interests. The law was a component of an authoritarian state, and when it operated in such a way that the good of the state coincided with the good of the larger community, one might argue that law served "justice." But the idea that all humans possessed the means and the right to decide what is just and lawful did not take root in early China. (Turner 1992, p. 44)

The Confucian understanding of the empirical and ethical relationships between the individual and society continues to inform Chinese political thought in modern China (Nathan, 1986, p. 138; Munro, 1977). The superior importance accorded to collective interests ahead of individual rights forms part of a longer constitutional tradition that surfaced during the Chinese Republican period and continues today (Nathan, 1986). At the turn of the twentieth century, interestingly, reformers such as Liang Qichao and Sun Yat-Sen, influenced by Confucianism, believed that the Chinese traditionally were too individualistic, too centered on oneself and one's family and that the Chinese people lacked the sense of group loyalty and group participation necessary for asserting one's rights and fulfilling one's duties as citizens (de Bary, 1998, p. 116). Thus, Sun Yat-Sen came to advocate the idea of the need of the Chinese not so much for freedom of the individual as for the freedom of the nation (de Bary, 1998, p. 116). Similarly, Liang Qichao believed that the Chinese lacked group consciousness, the sense of rights, and responsibilities of citizens. Consequently, Liang strongly advocated the need for the empowerment of the people as rights-bearing citizens in an effective political infrastructure and civil society (de Bary, 1998, p.116; see also Zarrow, 1988).

In contemporary China, the introduced idea about rights was also influenced by Marxist ideology, seeing individual rights as a means to state ends to enhance state powers. Importantly, these are class rights or group rights, rather than individual rights. A manifestation of the collective view of rights is found in Chinese legal discourse and law. The priority given to the collective over the individual and individual rights as embodied in the Constitution has its concrete expressions in Chinese laws. For instance, Article 51 of the Constitution states that "The exercise of citizens of the PRC of their freedoms and rights may not infringe on the interests of the state, of society, and of the collective, or on the lawful freedoms and rights of other citizens." Other indications in the Constitution that highlight and give priority to collective interests over the individual include the expression "in the public interest" as in "the state may, in the public interest, requisition land" (Art. 10), and "the state may, in the public interest, requisition private properties" (Art. 13). In the past two decades with much influence from Western laws, an increasing emphasis has been given to individual rights in the Chinese society as a whole by both individuals and the state.

A related word and concept is "duty" or "obligation." When *quanli* (rights) was introduced to China, another strong competing notion within China was the indigenous idea of duty or obligation. In fact, the emphasis on duty may very well be responsible to the absence of the notion of rights in Chinese culture. It may have overwhelmed, suppressed, and killed any development of the conception of individual rights. Kang Youwei, one of the leading reformers in the late nineteenth century, believed that the failure of the Chinese people to conceive of their individual rights could be traced directly to the Confucian obsession with the performance of familial duties in the single-minded effort to maintain harmony of the Chinese social order (Weatherley, 1999, p. 81). People were understood in terms of the duties they owed to others. In Confucianism, the obligations between people were differentiated, but they were mutual and shared, involving reciprocity (de Bary, 1998, p. 18). Thus, in the late 1800s, the Confucian notion of duty was assumed or assimilated into the new notion of rights. The Confucian emphasis on duty has its modern manifestation in China in the belief that rights are seen as correlative to duties. This line of thought has its presence in the Constitution as well. For instance, chapter 2 of the Constitution is entitled "The Fundamental Rights (*quanli*) and Duties (*yiwu*) of Citizens." Here *yiwu* can be translated as either "duties" or "obligations." Article 33 states, "Every citizen is entitled to the rights and at the same time must perform the duties prescribed by the Constitution and the Law." Relevantly, another meaning of *yiwu* when used as an adjective is "voluntary" as in *yiwu gongzuo* (volunteer work). *Yiwu* was also a new word created in the late 1800s. In traditional China and classical Chinese, there were many specific words for specific duties such as filial piety, but not a general or generic term for duties or obligations as in English corresponding to rights.[12]

To sum up, *quanli* for rights and the introduced idea of rights met with the Chinese cultural tradition and thinking. In the process, *quanli* as a notion for rights has acquired Chinese contents. Although one can never be absolutely sure that there was a complete absence of an idea similar to or resembling rights in traditional China (see more later), so far evidence suggests that until mid-1800s, there was no such concept as rights in China, certainly not a correlative of rights and obligations, linguistically, conceptually, and pragmatically. Chinese sociologists and legal scholars have long warned against interpreting traditional Chinese society in terms of the Western and modern concept of rights or interpreting Chinese traditional laws in terms of modern concept of rights (see Z. Liang, 1989).

HOW UNIVERSAL ARE "RIGHTS" AND OTHER LINGUISTIC SIGNS?

In view of the account of the linguistic and conceptual absence of rights in classical Chinese and the linguistic creation and innovation relating to *quanli* (rights), a number of implications can be drawn.

First, as stated in the beginning, Jackendoff suggested the cultural universality of the concepts of rights and obligations. He further proposed that they are "largely if not entirely innate, a specialized way of thinking wired into the brain by the human genome," and these concepts "would form preestablished species-wide skeleton of social understanding over which each particular culture builds its own flesh" (Jackendoff, 2007a, p. 355). He also previously proposed that "rights and obligations are fundamental in the fabric of human social organization" (Jackendoff, 1999, p. 68). This was also explained as a principle: If person X has a right to do action Y, that person Z prevents X from doing Y, then X acquires a right to impose sanctions on Z (Jackendoff, 2007a, p. 414). The foregoing discussions show that the concept of "rights" may not be as universal or innate to all humans and all human societies as has been claimed. Otherwise, it would have to exclude a very large speech community of the human race and one of the longest continuous human civilization and culture, that is, Chinese. Relevantly, as has been long pointed out, in Western rights discussions, the idea that human beings have rights by virtue of being human is often said to be self-evident, but the non-obviousness of the idea may also be illustrated by the fact that there is no expression in any ancient or medieval language correctly translated by the word "a right" until near the close of the Middle Ages: the concept lacked the means of expression in Hebrew, Greek, Latin, Arabic, classical or medieval, before 1400, also in Old English and Japanese until mid-1800s (MacIntyre, 1981). In direct response to Jackendoff's claim in 2007 cited in the beginning of the paper, Wierzbicka stated that the words "rights" and "obligations" are English words without exact semantic equivalents in most other languages, and such English words contain a wealth of history, not a universal history but one that is specific to English culture (Wierzbicka, 2007a, pp. 402, 406). It involves much more than just translation.

Secondly, the history of *quanli* (rights) in Chinese also illustrates that the idea of rights is not indigenous to Chinese, but it does not mean that the idea is incompatible with Chinese culture. Rights, like other terms and institutional practices such as democracy, rule of law, constitutional government, and human rights, are all decidedly Western concepts and inventions. Indeed, the centrality of rights in our time is a product of Western liberalism, tracing back to Locke and other Western thinkers (Raz, 1989). This Western birth origin does not and did not prevent the ideas and practices from being exported, and successfully transplanted, applied in other lands and other minds (in China's case, it is yet to flourish). Instead of seeing rights as a universal innate concept, I regard "rights" as cultural objects or units, cultural traits, or memes in Dawkins's (1989) language, that can be culturally transmitted from person to person and culture to culture. In China's case, the introduction and acceptance of the idea of rights in Chinese culture is a long and difficult process of cultural evolution that is still ongoing. As discussed earlier, the word *quanli* for rights and the idea of rights represents an innovation. It is a mutation that involves the change of the meaning of old classical words and adding a new meaning. The story of *quanli* (rights) also tells us that a seemingly simple word can tell a great deal about a culture and society. Language changes much faster than culture does. Linguistic change, in particular, the creation of new words, is much more visible while culture evolves in a more subtle and complex fashion and much more slowly. Just as the Chinese language and many Chinese words such as *quanli* have complicated history and stories, English and many of its words such as rights also have certain cultural assumptions and values embedded in them (Wierzbicka, 2010, p. 5). Neither is totally neutral free from the baggage of its history and tradition. Every language carries with it a specific interpretation of the world and such interpretations are not the same.

Thirdly, there may be a need to distinguish universality and innateness of words and concepts.[13] Part of the Jackendoff's proposition about the universal applicability of the concept of rights may be true if we consider the words of rights and obligations in the present context in our time. Words such as rights and obligations are time-restricted. For instance, as shown in this chapter, the Chinese language and culture now have an equivalent to "rights," as do most if not all other languages now in contemporary societies, although not identical to English, and complete identity is not necessary. Similarly, the concept of human rights has also found its equivalence linguistically and legally in China today. Thus, such words and concepts can be considered universally applicable referring to the present time, but not universal in the sense of universally indigenous to all human societies. As for innateness, "innate" means as defined by Merriam-Webster dictionary (www.merriam-webster.com/dictionary/innate): (1). existing in, belonging to, or determined by factors present in an individual from birth: native, inborn; (2). belonging to the essential nature of something: inherent; and (3). Originating in or derived from the mind or the constitution of the intellect rather than from experience. Common sense and empirical studies tell me that "rights" cannot be described as possessing any of such meanings. It certainly cannot be described as being innate for the Chinese speech community, either of the past or now.

Fourthly, of course, when dealing with language and culture, one can never be absolutely certain that a certain language or culture does not have fragments or certain resemblance of a certain idea. One could even argue that there were some of the conditions and environment for the notion of rights to emerge in early human societies. Nevertheless, the linguistic evidence so far is that no Chinese word or cluster words or cluster concepts resembling "rights" existed until the creation of *quanli* in the 1800s. There was no equivalent intellectual discussion of natural rights in traditional China, unlike the eighteenth and nineteenth-century West. It is not a question either of the rights idea and word appearing in ancient China before it was suppressed and killed. It never emerged in the first place. Despite this, one could still contemplate that there may be some ideas in ancient China that could be interpreted as being associated with "rights." Feinberg (1980, p. 148) notes that the conceptual linkage between personal rights and claiming has long been noticed by legal writers and is reflected in the standard usage of claim-rights in English as distinguished from the liberties, immunities, and powers that are sometimes also called rights. As we have seen, although in traditional China, before the rights notion was introduced, no word for "rights" and no developed notion or law prescribing rights existed, the Chinese people had the sense of what was due between one another, and they did make claims against each other (Cao, 2004). This notwithstanding, as pointed out, the claims in premodern China might be considered claims that were grounded in relationships, familial, communal, or commercial (Lubman, 1999, p. 21). Such claims were not defined in objective rules promulgated by the state despite the existence of the fragmentary legislation, and they were not ordinarily vindicated by agencies of the state. In traditional China, the notion and activity of making claims never developed into a mainstream cultural trait or a concept of rights. Thus, I believe that the idea and practice of claim was present in traditional China, but not importantly present or contributing significantly to the shaping of the

Chinese cultural milieu to indigenously generate the concept of "rights" (Cao, 2004). Similarly, and alternatively, if we define rights as protected interests, the word "interests" certainly figured prominently in Chinese culture. There were interest holders, but with their interests deriving from social status and position, not rights.

Fifthly, a related issue is the claims about the existence of universal words and concepts. There is a need for empirical studies for proposing any such words and concepts, and importantly, empirical studies of different languages and cultures in addition to English (see Wierzbicka's (2007a, b) direct response to Jackendoff regarding empirical studies). In this regard, it seems that basic or culture-neutral words instead of value-loaded words are better candidates for plausible universals, for instance the theory and practice of Natural Semantic Metalanguage (NSM) as proposed and researched by Anna Wierzbicka and colleagues.[14]

Lastly, it is noted that given the divergent paths taken by Chinese and Western thought in their development, the problematics of the Anglo-European culture and that of China are quite distinct (Hall and Ames, 1995, p. 253). Therefore, the language used in the two traditions is distinct despite the fact that words when translated into the same language may sometimes sound similar. In particular, culturally loaded words such as law, justice, interests, duties and rights do not carry the same meanings in the two philosophical or semantic traditions. To put it another way, "Apart from mathematics, knowledge (including moral knowledge) is normally formulated in the words of a particular language, and the assumptions embedded in that language are likely to color all knowledge formulated in it" (Wierzbicka, 2014a, pp. 162–163). This is true for the Chinese language as well.

NOTES

1. http://plato.stanford.edu/entries/rights/
2. William Alexander Parsons Martin graduated from Indiana State University in 1846 and received his LL.D from the University of the City of New York in 1870. He once acted as an interpreter for William B. Reed, a U.S. government minister, in negotiating the treaty of 1858 with China. In 1857, Martin was made professor of International Law in Tongwenguan (Imperial College) in Beijing, and was its president from 1869 to 1895. He acted as an adviser for the imperial Chinese government on questions of international law for disputes with European countries, notably during the conflict with France around 1884. In 1885, Martin was made a mandarin of the third class by the Chinese imperial court. For Martin's life and work, see Covell (1978).
3. The characters *quan* and *li*, separately, are used extensively in *Xunzi*, to mean "power" and "to weigh" for *quan* and "profit" and "benefit" for *li*. *Quan* and *li* are also commonly found in other Chinese classics.

4. Liu (1999) argues that *quanli* (rights) like *zhuquan* (sovereignty) and many other nineteenth-century coinages no longer strike us as strange or un-Chinese, because they have been naturalized in the history of Chinese (and Japanese) political discourse and through "repeated usage" for the past 135 years. Liu calls such neologism "hypothetical equivalence" between English and Chinese. However, I believe that this is not entirely correct as much more than "repeated usage" is involved, and such equivalences are far from being mere "hypothetical."

5. The English translation is taken from Svarverud (2001, p. 134).

6. According to Pulleyblank (1991, pp. 188–189), the two characters for *li* were distinguishable in ancient Chinese pronunciation. They are pronounced exactly the same in modern Chinese.

7. http://ling.cuc.edu.cn/RawPub

8. For further discussions of the power and rights of the father (*fuquan*) in traditional China, see Ch'ü T'ung-tsu (1965, 1998).

9. For further discussion of the intellectual development related to rights thinking in late Qing China, see Zarrow (1998).

10. The two Chinese writers who were among the first to use *tianfu renquan* were He Qi (also known as Sir Kai Ho, 1859–1914) and Hu Liyuan (1847–1916); it is believed that the reasons for translating "natural rights" as *tianfu renquan* (Heaven given rights to humans) were that the classical Chinese word for nature or natural (*ziran*) is very different in its usage and philosophical meaning from the English word, while *tian* (Heaven) is closer to the meaning of natural rights (see G. Wu, 2014). See Cao (2015b, pp. 12–16) for discussion of the meaning of *ziran*/nature in classical Chinese philosophy. See also chapter 3 for discussion of the translation of *tian* between Heaven.

11. De Bary (1998, pp. 23–29) calls Confucian individualism "personalism," distinguished from Western individualism since Confucian personalism shares some common ground with forms of personalism in Western tradition, distinct from modern liberalist individualism. According to de Bary, Confucian personalism expresses the worth and dignity of the person not as a raw, "rugged" individuals, but as a self-shaped and formed in the context of a given cultural tradition, its own social community, and its natural environment to reach full personhood. In de Bary's view, the Confucian ideal was a balance of public and private, not an assertion of one over the other.

12. It is noted that when we use the word "duty" for the Chinese context, its meaning is not identical to the English word. According to Wierzbicka (2014a, p. 145), the rise of duty as a keyword in seventeenth-century English has its roots in the Puritan tradition, and the word was historically related to the concepts of conscience and of right and wrong.

13. See Mooney (2014, p. 170) who argues against the claim of the innate nature of primitive words including the primes in Natural Semantic Metalanguage.

14. Briefly, for NSM, researchers have conducted extensive cross-linguistic investigations across many different languages (in Europe, Asia, Africa, North America, and Oceania), and on the basis of these investigations have identified a set of 65 universal semantic primes (see Goddard, 2010, 2011; Wierzbicka, 1996; Goddard and Wierzbicka, 2014). This set includes elements such as i, you, someone, something, this happen, move, know, think, want, say, where, when not, maybe, like, the so-called

semantic primes, grounded in ordinary linguistic experience, not cultural specific words. They also proposed that in addition to the universal semantic primes, there are some universal semantic molecules–fairly complex meanings that can be defined in terms of primes but that function as integrated units and thus facilitate a kind of conceptual chunking in the building of more complex concepts, for instance, men, women, children, to be born and to kill (Goddard, 2010, 2011; Wierzbicka, 1996; Goddard and Wierzbicka, 2014).

Chapter 6

Legal Speech Acts and Chinese Legal Performatives

Law relies on language and particularly, it relies on the performative nature of language use. Legal effects and legal consequences are commonly obtained by merely uttering certain words, for instance "You are guilty" or "You are sentenced to ten years' imprisonment" as regularly pronounced in court. By uttering words, one accepts public and private legal responsibilities and assumes legal roles and qualities; one transfers one's legal rights and imposes legal obligations onto others (Jori, 1994, p.2092). Thus, legal performatives are said to be constitutive of their effects. However, despite the frequent reference to legal usage in the development of speech act theories by such authors as Austin and Searle, it seems that more and in-depth discussions and analysis are needed to explore the intricacies of speech acts in the legal context for the benefit of linguistics, pragmatics, and legal theory.

This chapter examines the performative utterances and speech acts in the legal context. It first discusses and reviews the general speech acts theories originally proposed by Austin and further developed by Searle. It then turns to discuss legal speech acts including legislative and judicial speech acts and attempts to characterize the general and basic features and the illocutionary forces of such speech acts with reference to Habermas's speech acts theory. This approach to legal speech acts differs from the traditional Austin and Searle's theories in that speech acts in this theory entail the notion of communication as social action. Such speech acts have an intersubjective rather than individual basis in communication and in establishing relationships between the various participants in the legal contexts. This is regarded particularly important in the study of legal speech acts. The second part of this chapter focuses on Chinese speech acts and the illocutionary forces in Chinese legislative language in China and Taiwan and points to a universalism in the illocutionary functions of legal language.

SPEECH ACTS

The notion of speech acts starts with the assumption that the minimal unit of human communication is the performance of utterances such as asserting a proposition, asking a question, making a command, or expressing a desire, among other things. Words are not only something we use to say things, and Austin (1962) calls this "constative." We also use them to do things, the "performative." Austin (1962) distinguishes two kinds of utterances: the constatives which are statements or assertions and which describe or report things and events; and utterances which perform actions merely by virtue of the utterances being made; and the second type of utterances is called "performatives" by Austin to recognize their actional nature of what they do as opposed to constative utterances of what they say. For performative utterances, we do something rather than merely say that something is or is not the case. Uttering a performative is to constitute the performing of a further act in addition to the linguistic act itself. To say "I promise that . . ." is performing the very act of promising that can only be accomplished by saying the right words. These words do not describe the fact that a person is promising; they are the act itself. Such types of acts are illocutionary acts. An illocutionary act is the minimal complete unit of human linguistic communication (Searle, 1969, 1979, 1998).

In the attempt to understand speech acts, in Searle's analysis (1969, 1979, 1998), we need to distinguish the content of the act and the type of act it is. According to Searle, utterances can be in general analyzed into a propositional content and an illocutionary force. Take for example, in the utterances: "I assert that *p*," "I promise *p*," "I command that *p*," the same propositional content *p*, appears with varying illocutionary forces as indicated by "assert," "promise," and "command," respectively. Thus, the structure of illocutionary acts can be represented as F(*p*), where F stands for illocutionary force and *p* for propositional content. The part of the speech act that constitutes its illocutionary type or illocutionary force and the part that constitutes its propositional content are the standard double structure of speech acts. According to Habermas (1998, p.63), these two components, the illocutionary and the propositional, can vary independently of one another, and we can hold a propositional content invariant vis-à-vis the different types of speech acts in which it occurs. The propositional content can be infinitely diverse as the same propositional content can occur in different types of illocutionary acts. The dominating sentence (the main clause: I …) establishes the illocutionary force of the utterance and the mode of communication between the speaker and hearer, thus the pragmatic situation of the dependent sentence (the predicative clause: that …). The dependent sentence, consisting in general of an identifying (referring) phrase and a predicate phrase, establishes the connection of the communication with the world of objects and events.

Then, what are the different types of speech acts? Various attempts at the taxonomy of illocutionary acts have been offered over the years. The most influential ones are Austin and Searle's. Austin distinguishes five basic types of performative verbs as exercitives, verdicative, commissives, behavitives, and expositives. But as Searle (1969, 1976) points out, there are no clear principles by which Austin collects them into his classes. Searle expands Austin's theory and classifies five categories of illocutionary forces as representatives, commissives, expressives, declaratives, and directives (Searle, 1969, 1976). Furthermore, for speech acts to be performed, there are certain conditions, felicity conditions for Austin, and conditions of satisfaction for Searle, (as opposed to Habermas conditions, see later) that must be accompanied. These conditions must be fulfilled for performative utterances to be successful or valid.

In this study, speech acts, apart from the presumptions in the traditional Austin and Searle's theories, also entail the notion of communication as social action from Habermas's speech act theory. In this thinking, speech act has an intersubjective rather than individual basis. This is regarded as particularly important to legal speech acts.

Habermas's speech act theory forms the core of his universal or formal pragmatics, the theoretical underpinning for his communicative action theory, which in turn is a crucial element in his theories of society and of law. According to Habermas (1998), communicative action is an action whose success depends on the hearer's responding to the validity claims raised by the speaker. In Habermas's (1998) theory, there are three basic types of validity claims that are raised by a speaker in his/her speech acts: (1) a claim to the truth of what is said or presupposed, (2) a claim to the normative rightness of the speech act in the given context of the underlying norm, and (3) a claim to the truthfulness of the speaker. In using linguistic expression communicatively, the speaker raises all three claims simultaneously.[1] But typically, just one of the claims is raised explicitly, and the other two remain implicit presuppositions of understanding the utterance. These three universal validity claims provide a basis for classifying speech acts. In Habermas's (1998) view, communicative utterances can be divided into three broad categories according to the explicit claims they raise: (1) *constative* speech acts are connected with truth claims; (2) *regulative* speech acts with claims to normative rightness; and (3) *expressive* speech acts with claims to truthfulness.

In contrast to Searle's classification cited earlier which is based on the illocutionary aims or intentions of the speaker, Habermas's (1998) system of validity of speech acts oriented toward reaching understanding underlies the differentiation of types of speech acts. He argues that, if we start from the fact that the illocutionary aims of speech acts are achieved through the intersubjective recognition of claims to power and validity, and if we introduce normative rightness and subjective truthfulness and truth as validity claims, and interpret them in terms of actor/world relations, then, speech acts of the constatives, regulatives, and expressives that are communicative use (as opposed to strategic use in imperatives) can be justified. Besides, there are also the communicatives as a subclass of regulatives, and operatives that designate the application of constructive rules. So, commissives and declaratives (as in Searle) as well as institutionally bound speech acts and satisfactives all subsume under the same class of regulatives (Habermas, 1998, pp.154–164).

According to Maeve Cooke (1998, p.2), Habermas's speech act theory has two important characteristics: first, speech acts are cooperative relationships of commitment and responsibility: participants in communicative interaction undertake to behave in certain ways, and the success of the interaction depends on the cooperation of both parties involved; and secondly, the relationships of mutual recognition characteristic for communicative action have an inherent rational dimension: the communicative actor undertakes an obligation to provide reasons for the validity of the claims he raises with his utterances while his counterpart in action may either accepts the proffered reasons or challenge them on the basis of better reasons. Habermas's theory stresses the connection between the meaning of utterances and social practices, drawing attention to the institutions and conventions of the forms of life in which communicative activity is always embedded (Cooke, 1998).

Habermas developed his speech act theory on the basis of Austin and Searle's, taking an emphasis on utterances rather than sentences as the central unit of analysis, going beyond the traditional focus of linguistics. But Habermas's conception of illocutionary force goes beyond Austin and Searle's (Cooke, 1998, pp.7–8). Habermas objects to Austin's distinction between *force* and *meaning* as this, Habermas believes, overlooks the fact that utterances have a meaning distinct from the meaning of the sentences they employ; and he also objects to Austin's classification of speech acts into constative and performative.[2] His theory of utterance meaning brings together meaning and force, and extends the notion of illocutionary force to all utterances that are used communicatively. His theory gives an account of the meaning of utterances as inseparable from the act of uttering them, and defines utterances as acts of raising validity claims Searle's (Cooke, 1998, pp.7–8).

When illocutionary acts succeed, they will result in bringing about an interpersonal relation. Then, what is illocutionary force (IF)? According to Habermas (1998, pp.81–88), IF has a rational foundation. The illocutionary force of an acceptable speech act consists in the fact that it can move a hearer to reply on the speech-act-typical obligations of the speaker, that is, it can motivate the hearer to base his action on the premise that the speaker seriously intends the commitment he or she indicates (Habermas, 1998, p.85). IF is bound up with the speaker's assumption of a warranty, if challenged, to provide reasons in support of the validity of the claims he or she raises.

IF is a rational force, for in performing a speech act, the speaker undertakes to support what he/she says with reasons, if necessary. According to Habermas, we understand the meaning of an utterance when we know what makes it acceptable. We know what makes a speech act acceptable when we know the kind of reasons that a speaker can offer, if challenged, in order to reach understanding with a hearer concerning the validity of the disputed claim (Cooke, 1998, pp.7–8). Habermas argues that, if the speaker and hearer are to reach an understanding, they must communicate simultaneously at two levels: (a) the level of intersubjectivity on which the speaker and hearer, through illocutionary acts, establish the relations that permit them to come to an understanding with one another; and (b) the level of propositional content about which they wish to reach understanding in the communicative function specified in (a) (Habermas, 1998, p.64). Thus, Habermas's theory of speech acts and his theory of communicative action are based on an intersubjective, rather than individual, paradigm of communication and mutual understanding.

Finally, in Habermas's view, to understand an utterance is always to understand it as an utterance in a given situation which in turn may be part of multiple, extended contexts (Habermas, 1998). He draws attention to different kinds of often implicit background knowledge. This background knowledge of the lifeworld forms the indispensable context of the communicative use of language. Thus, according to Habermas, various types of speech act are linked to specific social institutions. For example, norm-conformative action (i.e., regulative speech act) is founded on institutional norms of moral behavior with which social actors must comply. Each type of action has its own rationality—its own notion of truth. Habermas's (1998) ideal speech situation oriented to rationally motivated critique and understanding treats agreement as the telos of speech and as something that speaker and hearer arrive at through uncoerced consensus.

Thus, Habermas's speech act theory incorporates and extends the classical speech act theories of Austin and Searle, and takes it to another level in the understanding and description of human communication and social interaction through language. This is particularly crucial for the discussion of legal speech acts, in particular in terms of the intersubjective and non-intentionalist paradigm and communication oriented toward mutual understanding and consensus if it is applied to law and law making.

LEGAL SPEECH ACTS

As said earlier, law relies on speech acts. Then, what makes legal speech acts different from ordinary speech acts? How can we characterize the illocutionary forces in the legal context?

In relation to legal discourse, Danet (1980) classifies speech acts based on Searle's classification in the following way:

1. representatives which are utterances that commit the speaker to something being the case or assert the truth of a proposition, including testifying, swearing, asserting, claiming and stating;
2. commissives which commit the speaker to do something in the future, such as in contracts, marriage ceremonies and wills where both the relevant parties engage in commissive acts;
3. expressives which express the speakers' psychological state about or attitude to a proposition, including apologising, excusing, condemning, deploring, forgiving and blaming;
4. declaratives whose successful performance brings about a correspondence between their propositional content and reality, including marriage ceremonies, bills of sale, receipts, appointments, and nominations; and the legislative stipulation of rights and of definitions of concepts; lawyers' objections, sentences, and appellate opinions, indictments, confessions, pleas of guilty/not guilty, and verdicts; and there is a subcategory of representative declarations for certain institutional situations, e.g., an umpire or a judge making factual claims, requiring claims to be issued with the force of declaration, and also require the speaker to have certain authority, representative declarations share with representatives a sincerity condition. This would cover marriage ceremony, bills of sale appointment or nominations, legislative stipulation of rights and definitions of concepts, indictments, confessions, pleas of guilty/not guilty, verdicts etc.; and
5. directives which are future-oriented speech acts, seeking to change the world, to get someone to do something, most prominent in legislation that imposes obligations.

As we can see, Danet's classifications are based on the types of illocutionary forces of legal usage. However, within each category of speech acts as described by Danet, there are significant differences, for example, within the category of declaratives, the declarative of marriage ceremonies is very different from another type of declarative of legislation; or the declarative of lawyers' objections, confessions, or indictments are very different from the declarative of bills of sale, and so forth. Therefore, it is believed that it is necessary to distinguish, within the legal setting, different types of speech acts according to different types of language use and purpose of use. There are significant differences in legal speech acts in different legal contexts.

Thus, if we are guided by the type of legal settings in our analysis, we can divide legal speech acts into three broad categories of (1) legislative speech acts, consisting of statutes in the written language; (2) judiciary speech acts, including oral and written utterances during court proceedings such as oral and written evidence, oral and written judiciary pronouncements, oral arguments and other presentations from lawyers, plea, swearing, verdict, and other court room speech acts; and (3) other legal utterances in oral and written forms and this may include private legal documents such as contracts, wills, and other legally binding oral and written texts. These speech acts all involve the law and they share similarities as well as differences.

We can follow Habermas's classification and divide legal speech acts based on validity claims (instead of illocutionary forces as in Danet) into (1) *constative* speech acts are connected with truth claims; (2) *regulative* speech acts with claims to normative rightness; and (3) *expressive* speech acts with claims to truthfulness. Within each of these types of speech acts, the legal utterances or texts (both written and oral) can have different illocutionary forces, for example, legislation may contain both regulative and constative speech acts; or judicial speech acts such as lawyers' objections, sentences, and appellate opinions, indictments, confessions, pleas of guilty/not guilty, and verdicts, may be expressive, constative, and regulative speech acts.

For their similarities, legal speech acts, legislative, judiciary and others, are institutional speech acts as opposed to ordinary everyday speech acts between two private communicators. Institutional speech acts are different from ordinary speech activities for everyday communicative purposes. Legal speech act performance is closely tied to or presumes the existence and functioning of the relevant legal institutions and conventions, and the relevant legal system, whether it is in the court room or in parliament. They are institutionally bound speech acts.

Legal speech acts in different legal settings also manifest differences. First, in terms of addresser and addressee, for instance, one of the major differences is found in the status and relationships between the Speaker (addresser) and Hearer (addressee) in these three different settings and classes. For legislative speech acts, the speaker is the legislature and the hearer is the public, and they are both collective entities (see later). For private legal documents, for instance for a contract, there are normally two identifiable contracting individuals or parties, addressing each other. Another difference between legislative and judicial speech acts is that the medium of communication is different. Legislation is written in the written language as opposed to oral evidence in court. Furthermore, oral testimony in court may be between a legal counsel and the witness, between two individuals, and it may also involve the judge, and jury and court officers. For court room speech acts, all the utterances must follow certain procedures and conventions. For instance, the order of speaking by the various parties, the linguistic form that must be used, for example, "Guilty" or "Not guilty" as verdict must be uttered by the judge or the foreman of the jury at the appropriate stage of the court proceedings and words must be uttered in a certain linguistic form, for example, "We find the defendant guilty." Contracts, wills, and legislation in different jurisdiction must also follow certain styles and forms.

Within each of the three categories of legal speech acts, the illocutionary forces are also different (see later). For instance, for legislation, individual provisions in a statute may be declaratory acts and directives in Searle's terminology. For a contract, the illocutionary forces are mostly commissives from both parties. A judiciary speech act in the form of a verdict may entail a representative declarative. If we use Habermas's classification, some legislative speech acts may involve regulative speech acts while judicial speech acts may also involve imperatives and expressives.

In this regard, legal speech acts as institutional speech acts are different from other types of institutional speech acts such as speech related to religion or a referee in a football game. This is firstly found in the specific context, that is, the differences in the institutions involved. There are conventional procedures and conventions attached to different contexts. To understand the meaning of an utterance, we must refer to its social context, be it "The court is in now session," or "You are out" in a sport competition. Context is consequently a vital constituent of any attempt to apprehend an utterance's performative strength. Secondly, legal speech acts are norm-conformative action and they are founded on legal norms of behavior with which social actors must comply. Thirdly, just as we create institutional facts by performative utterance, legal speech acts create legal facts. In law, the constitutive rules, derived from either the constitution or convention, establish the legislature and its acts as institutional facts. Legal speech acts create or bring about institutional acts merely by declaring them through legal instrument. In these cases, performance does not depend on purely linguistic competence, but on socio-linguistic, political, and legal facts about the world.

CHARACTERIZING LEGISLATIVE SPEECH ACTS

Of the three types of legal speech acts, we now turn to legislative speech acts. To characterize statutes as speech acts, legislative speech acts are mostly regulatives, involving the domain of our world of society in social reality that the law tries to regulate. They display the basic attitude of norm-conformative on the part of the language users, that is, the legislature. The thematic validity claim is that of normative rightness and the general function of legislation is the establishment of legitimate interpersonal relations and regulation of society and behavior. The mode of communication is interactive between the lawmaker and the general public. The type of action is normatively regulated action and the action is oriented toward reaching understanding.

In terms of the linguistic form in legislative speech acts, it must follow the relevant legal institutional conventions. Statutes are written in a different structure from that of ordinary performatives. In ordinary speech acts, usually, the first person pronoun is used followed by the simple present form of the verb, for example, "I promise. . . ," or "I bet. . . ." However, the provisions are not written in the first person, but they may be paraphrased in such a form. For instance, "We hereby declare that. . . " or "We hereby enact that. . . ." The part of the statute that contains the explicit performative verb is known as the enacting formula, and it is usually found at the beginning of each statute. In Britain and the United States, the enacting formula usually has the form of "Be it enacted that. . . ." The explicit use of performative verb in legislative texts is found only in common law countries (Kurzon, 1986). In the legislation from China, similar to some jurisdictions in the continental system, there is no such formula. Kurzon (1986) calls such cases "implicit performatives" since it is only the occasion—the promulgation of a law—not the linguistic form, that allows for a performative interpretation. In Chinese statutes, normally, below the title of an act are the words in brackets that the law was passed at such and such a date by the legislature (or a government department with lawmaking powers) at such and such a session, reporting the fact that the legislature has passed the law. It uses similar wording for amended laws except using the word "amended" instead of "passed." For subordinate legislation, usually the words that "at such a date the regulation was announced by such and such a government body" are used. In the main text, in the first article of an act, it states that for such and such a purpose, this particular act is hereby enacted. Sometimes it also names the particular law that gives the authorization for making the law, for instance the Constitution or a basic law.

Within a statutory text, specific provisions do not normally follow particular formulas. However, statutory language in its special formal legal style, and register in the form of legal language is to be followed. In different countries and jurisdictions there are different linguistic conventions for legislative drafting.

Furthermore, for a legislative illocutionary act to be successful, apart from meeting the verbal requirements of what the convention requires, it must also be issued by the right person under the right circumstances, meeting the specifications of the relevant convention. Conditions for statutory validity include the capacity and authority of the persons making the law and the appropriateness of the occasion of enacting and promulgation. Besides, if we see communication as primary as Habermas does, and if we see legislation as communicative in nature, then, who are communicating with whom in the constitutional speech act? Who are its addressor and addressee?

Specifically, the lawmaker is the speaker, the author or addresser of legislation, that is, the legislature, the body which has the legislative authority to enact legislation. Furthermore, the hearer is the audience, the general public the law is directed at. The hearer is the receiver or addressee of the legislation, and this may also include the judiciary. Some commentators (see Bowers, 1989 and Kurzon, 1986, to some extent) seem to regard the addressee as consisting of only the judiciary for the purpose of statutory interpretation. This may not be an entirely accurate description. The judiciary can be regarded as one addressee of the collective addressees of legislation. But judges' interpretation of statutes as contained in decisions is a different type of speech acts. In judiciary pronouncements, the judge then is the addresser, talking to the litigating parties and the public at large, performing different illocutionary acts. So, the main addressee of legislation is the public that legislation is directed at, in guiding behavior. We may also include the executive government as another addressee. Although the executive's intention is usually embodied in legislation and in this sense the executive is the de facto author, the executive government is also a receiver or addressee in the sense that law is enforced by the executive and in the sense that the executive is to follow the legislative directives just as the general public. A different way to look at this is the one offered by Kurzon (1986). He describes the addresser and addressee of legislation in Western legal systems as consisting of the author, the implied author and the instantial author on the one hand, and the reader, the implied reader and the instantial reader on the other. He argues that they in fact are all lawyers. Such a description is true to some extent and true technically, as lawyers are usually employed to draft laws, and they are also the people who read and understand laws to convey the meanings to the public to advice clients. Undoubtedly, lawyers play a very important role in lawmaking in any society, but this seems simplistic or cynical and not a true depiction of a constitution when political and other factors are considered. Besides, in democratic discursive lawmaking, the addressee may also become an addresser.[3]

With regard to the legal competence of the addresser of legislation, an important component and a distinctive feature of legislative speech acts as part of the legal convention requirement is that the addresser, that is, the lawmaker, must have the *authority* in making legislative utterances in lawmaking. Normally, the legislative authority derives either from convention and long-standing custom as in the case of United Kingdom. or from a written Constitution as in the United States. In Australia, a country with a written Constitution, the authority for all the statutes derives from the Constitution which delegates to the legislature the ultimate legislative but limited powers to make law over its jurisdiction. Thus, a statute is a document with the highest constitutional authority with legal effect within its jurisdiction (see Bowers, 1989). However, if we take Habermas's view, legislative authority and the legitimacy of legislation emerges from communicative actions or deliberative democracy. The law employed by the state must be legitimated through a broader discourse of citizens and their representatives, and this process of legitimation must be included in the legal system (Habermas, 1996, p.38).

Finally, an act of making law must also be performed on the appropriate occasion recognized by convention or law to be the occasion on which such acts take place. A statute has to be enacted in a prescribed manner. For instance, in Australia as in the United Kingdom, this entails, *inter alia*, the passing of the statute through both Houses of Parliament and its receiving the royal assent in the required manner.[4] Analogous to this situation is the example of naming a ship. The prime minister or a certain person who is authorized to name a ship, that is having the appropriate authority, on the occasion says: "I name the ship Elizabeth." This very utterance is an act that confers that name to the ship. If another person unauthorized, at the same ceremony, or a person sitting at home watching the launching ceremony on television, utters the same words, the ship is not so named.

As said earlier, an important feature of legislative speech act is that they are institutional speech acts that involve institutional behaviors and institutional facts. The performance of legislative acts depends on institutional facts as in government and legislature, and such performative acts hereby create further institutional facts. For instance, when a parliament promulgates laws, the very act of promulgation presumes and depends on the existence of a parliament or a lawmaking institution and the relevant institutional rules and conventions. Furthermore, as conventional illocutionary acts, they effect changes in institutional states of affairs. In some cases, they affect the institutional position or social status of persons or things. In other cases, they create institutional rights and obligations, and prescribe behaviors and prohibitions. In still others, they are part of some institutional practice, process or procedure. When a parliament passes a law introducing a new tax, a new tax regime as reality and fact is thus created by the very declaration of the law, and obligations thus follow. In short, a law creates legal or institutional facts.

INTERSUBJECTIVE UNDERSTANDING IN LEGISLATIVE SPEECH ACTS

Apart from clarifying the addresser and addressee of legislation, we also need to consider, more importantly, whether legislative speech acts are communicated successfully in reaching understanding and establishing relationships between the two communicating parties, that is, before the lawmaker and the public, and how legislative speech acts perform the functions between the addresser and addressee linguistically and non-linguistically reaching understanding and establishing relations.

In the traditional theory of speech acts as in Searle, the hearer's recognition of the intention of the speaker and conditions of satisfaction must be satisfied for happy or successful execution of illocutionary forces in speech act (see also Bach and Harnish, 1979). However, Habermas argues that this is not the case. According to Habermas (1998, p.269), with a speech act, the speaker or addresser not only provides the hearer, the addressee, with the opportunity to become aware of his/her own intention. The speaker cannot achieve his/her illocutionary aim of conveying a fact, giving an order, making a request or a promise or revealing a subjective experience if he/she does not at the same time make known the conditions under which his/her utterance could be accepted as valid, and he/she must do so in such a way that in claiming that these conditions are satisfied, he/she implicitly also offers to provide reasons in support of his/her claim, if necessary (Habermas, 1998, p.269). A speaker can rationally motivate a hearer to accept his/her speech act offer because, on the basis of an internal connection between validity, validity claim, and the redemption of a validity claim, he/she can assume the warranty for providing if necessary convincing reasons that would stand up to a hearer's criticism of the validity claim (Habermas, 1989, p.269). Habermas (1998, pp.83–84) states:

> The essential presupposition for the success of an illocutionary act consists in the speaker's taking on a specific commitment, so that the hearer can rely on him. An utterance can count as a promise, assertion, request, question, or avowal if and only if the speaker makes an offer that he is ready to make good insofar as it is accepted by the hearer. The speaker must commit himself, that is, indicate that in certain situations he will draw certain consequences for action. The type of obligation determines the content of the commitment, from which the sincerity of the commitment is to be distinguished.

Thus, according to Habermas, the communicative use of language oriented to mutual understanding functions in such a way that the participants either agree on the validity claimed for their speech acts or identify points of disagreement which they conjointly taken into consideration in the course of further interaction of practical discourse. Every speech act involves the raising of criticizable validity claims aimed at intersubjective recognition. The content of the speaker's commitment is determined by both the specific meaning of the interpersonal relation that is to be established and a thematically stressed universal validity claim (Habermas, 1998, p.86). In Habermas's words:

> In the final analysis, the speaker can illocutionarily influence the hearer and vice versa, because speech-act-typical obligations are connected with cognitively testable validity claims—that is, because the reciprocal binding and bonding relationship has a rational basis. The speaker who commits herself normally

> connects the specific sense in which she would like to take up an interpersonal relationship with a thematically stressed validity claim and hereby chooses a specific mode of communication. (Habermas, 1998, pp.85–86)

If we examine this in terms of legislative speech acts, in regulative speech acts as in legislation, the thematic validity claim is that of rightness and appropriateness and the theme is interpersonal relation. In regulative speech acts, the obligation to justify refers directly to the claim that the speech act performed fits an existing normative background. The claims to the rightness or appropriateness for norms or values that in a given context justify an interpersonal relation that is to be established performatively. But in every instance of communicative action, the system of four validity claims (comprehensibility, rightness, truth, and truthfulness) are raised simultaneously, and come into play, and they must be recognized as justified for the speech act to be acceptable and thus results in successful communication (Habermas, 1998).

Furthermore, according to Habermas (1998), the illocutionary force of the legislative speech act consists in its capacity to move the public to act under the premise that the commitment signaled by the lawmaker is seriously meant. The lawmaker and the public can reciprocally move one another to recognize validity claims because the content of the lawmaker's commitment is determined by a specific reference to a thematically stressed validity claim, whereby the lawmaker, in a cognitively testable way, assumes with a rightness claim obligations to justify for regulatives, and implicitly and secondarily, with a truth claim obligations to provide grounds and with a truthfulness claim obligations to confirm.

In addition, according to Habermas (1998, p.267), to understand the directives or regulatives as embodies in statutes, the hearer must know not only the satisfaction conditions for the state of affairs represented in it, but also the conditions under which it can be regarded as legitimate or as binding. Illocutionary acts owe their motivating force to the validity claims they carry, since these claims are capable of being intersubjectively recognized to the extent that they are based on reasons that counts as reasons for all parties involved.

The legislative speech acts tell us that the lawmaker (speaker) by raising a validity claim concomitantly takes on a sufficiently credible guarantee to vindicate the claim with the right kind of reasons, should this be necessary (Habermas, 1996, p.18). They rely on reasons or potential reasons. Any speech act therewith refers to the ideally expanded audience of the unlimited interpretation community that would have to be convinced for the speech act to be justified and hence rationally acceptable (Habermas, 1996, p.19). Often, we are told, enough law provides illegitimate power with the mere semblance of legitimacy (Habermas, 1996, p.40).

Now let us use the Chinese Constitution as a speech act to illustrate the way the addresser and the addressee of the law in the success or failure of intersubjective communication and in contesting the truthfulness and truth claims in the constitutional speech acts. Regarding truth claims, if we take a Peircean perspective, truth claims or meanings arise through language only when an idea or concept can be related to by something else already existing in the mind of an interpreter. In our present situation, for instance, the Chinese legislature says as it did: We declare in the Constitution that Chinese citizens enjoy freedom of speech, of the press, of assembly, of association, of procession and of demonstration. To such a statement, what kind of response could be generated from a Chinese hearer living with the everyday realities of China? Possibly:

1. You (lawmaker) are not serious in saying that.
2. You must be lying and cannot be trusted.
3. You have never meant or guaranteed that.

To be fair, people do enjoy a certain degree of freedom in today's China, much more than in the past, but only to some degree, a degree that the government deems permissible measured against its own interest. It is common knowledge that the Chinese press is not free, in particular with regard to political freedom of expression. They are not freedoms guaranteed but permitted subject to heavy political qualifications. Hence, there are not many reasons that the Chinese lawmaker and the government can actually or potentially provide to move or convince the public of the claims in the Constitution that they are true, even if they are truthfully uttered and even if they satisfy the normative rightness claim. As Habermas (1996) points out, understanding and reaching understanding are not the same, and a valid utterance and one that is merely held to be valid are not the same. Law, as Habermas (1996) conceives it, and its legitimacy, stems from its being at once self-imposed and binding. Moreover, all persons subjected to law must be treated as free and equal actors, and laws that are self-imposed and binding must successfully reconcile legal and factual equality (Habermas, 1996).

To sum up, in the foregoing, we have considered different types of legal speech acts and in particular legislative speech acts with reference to Habermas's theory of speech act and his general theory on discourse theory of law. When we consider legislative speech acts, positive laws (legislation) which are not just command backed by the threat of sanction as is now commonly accepted, especially laws in a democratic country, should appeal to reason that citizens who are affected by the law should find acceptable, and should be the equal participants in lawmaking in reaching understanding and establishing interpersonal, legal, and social relations.

ILLOCUTIONARY FORCES IN LEGISLATIVE TEXTS

The legal rules conveyed in legislation may and do vary considerably from country to country and from jurisdiction to jurisdiction in terms of content, legal force, and linguistic expression. However, they are all linked to the basic function of law in regulating human behavior and relations by setting out obligations, permissions, and prohibitions in society. The law expresses its functions through the use of language. In this regard, one prominent feature of legislative texts is that of the illocutionary force of statutory utterances, through the deployment of performative indicators to express illocutionary forces of legislative provisions. In particular, the use of directives and declarations is most significant in setting out obligations, permissions, and prohibitions. The illocutionary forces of language are of paramount importance in law.

The illocutionary forces of legislative provisions have been divided into three categories that are generally adopted for interpreting statutes in common law jurisdictions. They are: (1) imperative language that imposes an obligation to do an act, (2) facultative language that confers a right, privilege or power, and (3) prohibitive language that imposes an obligation to abstain from doing an act. To convey these illocutionary forces in English statutes, the words "may," "shall," and "shall not"/"may not" are generally used respectively. In other words, in legislative texts, sentences containing such performative auxiliary verbs function as speech acts with the illocutionary forces of permission or conferring a right (may), ordering or imposing an obligation (shall) or prohibition (shall not) (Bowers, 1989, pp.30–31; see also Kurzon, 1986). Thus, "shall," "may," and "shall not"/"may not" are the main legal performative indicators in English. Specifically, according to Sullivan (2002, pp.56–57), "may" can be used to confer an authority or a power, confer a right, impose conditions on a grant of authority or a right, "shall" can be used to impose a duty—create formal or substantive conditions precedent, declare legal effects or state definitions of words. To prohibit conduct, "shall not/may not" is used. In some jurisdictions, in recent years, due to the plain English movement, "must" is sometimes used in addition to or in place of "shall." [5] These are the indicative performative words used in English. The equivalent Chinese words are analyzed in the following sections.

In sum, statutes as legislative speech acts carry various illocutionary forces, communicating a range of propositions—conferring rights, imposing obligations, establishing institutional facts, and imposing prohibitions. "Shall" is used to indicate obligations. Such obligations are mandatory or directory. "May" signifies permission or discretion. "Shall not/may not" is a prohibition where legal consequence or penalty will arise for violation. The importance of legal texts as speech acts goes to the very heart of the nature of law and legal language, irrespective what language it is.

CHINESE LEGISLATIVE SPEECH ACTS IN ACTION

Now we turn to the linguistic representation of legislative speech acts in Chinese. We focus on Chinese legal language and examine statutory laws of China and Taiwan to document and compare the similarities and differences of a pragmatic feature of Chinese legal language by analyzing the illocutionary forces in legislative texts in China and Taiwan.

First, what it is meant by "Chinese legal language"? Many years ago, a prominent Chinese law expert and lawyer, Lubman (1970), said that there was no such a thing as legal language in China. This is not true, in either imperial China or modern China, although legal language in Chinese was and is very different from legal language in English. In this book, legal language refers to the language of and related to law and legal process. This includes language of the law, language about law, and language used in other legal communicative situations (cf. Kurzon, 1989 and 1997, who distinguishes language of the law and legal language which is language about law). Legal language is a type of register, that is, a variety of language appropriate to specific occasions and situations of use, and in this case, a variety of language appropriate to legal situations of use, language for legal purposes (LLP). Thus, "Chinese legal language" refers to the language of and related to laws and legal processes of the People's Republic of China (PRC) and of the Republic of China (ROC, i.e., Taiwan). This does not imply that the Chinese legal language used in the PRC and Taiwan is identical. Here "Chinese legal language in China" and "Chinese legal language in Taiwan" are used to distinguish them, but the phrase "Chinese legal language" is used to refer to legal language used in both China and Taiwan. The Chinese language is one language but China and Taiwan as two separate speech communities. It is also noted that Taiwan law in this chapter refers to the law of the ROC, that is, Taiwan under the administration of the ROC, and does not include the laws of Taiwan under Japanese or Dutch rule. In other words, it refers to the ROC law.

Furthermore, we may also distinguish four major variants or subvarieties of Chinese legal language in the written form: (1) legislative language, for example, domestic statutes and subordinate laws, international treaties and multilingual laws, and other laws produced by lawmaking authorities; (2) judicial language produced in the judicial process by judicial officers and other legal authorities; (3) legal scholarly texts produced by academic lawyers or legal scholars in scholarly works and commentaries; and (4) legal language used in private legal documents, for example, contracts, leases, wills, and litigation documents (see Cao, 2007a).[6] These subtext types have their own peculiarities as well as sharing similarities unique to all legal texts. As noted, legal language is not homogeneous, not just one legal discourse, but "a set of related legal discourses" (Maley, 1994, p.13). Legal language does not just cover the language of law alone, but all communications in legal settings.

In this connection, it is necessary to clarify and distinguish classical Chinese legal language and modern Chinese legal language. Classical Chinese legal language refers to the language of and about law and legal process in imperial China which ended in 1911. Modern Chinese legal language began taking shape around the late 1800s and early 1900 when Western laws were translated and introduced to China and formally came into use in 1911 when the ROC was founded. Although some of the legal texts translated into Chinese from Europe in the late 1800s and early 1900s were written in classical Chinese, new legal concepts and vocabulary of modern legal systems and law, completely different from imperial Chinese law, were introduced and created in modern Chinese (see Cao, 2004). They helped to lay the foundations of modern Chinese legal system and of modern Chinese legal language. The laws enacted by the ROC from 1911 onwards signal the formal start of modern Chinese law, hence the start of modern Chinese legal language. Due to the historical and linguistic continuity of the Chinese written language, all the important law-related words used in classical Chinese are an integral part of the modern Chinese legal language. Modern Chinese legal language was greatly enriched in the late 1800s and early 1900s when many new words were coined to introduce Western legal concepts and practices, often via borrowing from the Japanese (see Lackner et al., 2001; Cao, 2004).

CHINESE LEGAL PERFORMATIVES

By applying the general theory of legal speech act to legislation from the PRC and ROC, certain characteristics in the use of performative expressions have been identified. Although there does not seem to exist any explicit statutory or other written rule governing the uses of legal performative expressions in either China or Taiwan, it is observed that the general usages are followed in practice with few exceptions, and can be generalized. For the purpose of this study, a large number of major statutes in China and Taiwan were examined, but in the following analysis, only a small number of statutes of China and Taiwan are referred to for the sake of clarity and convenience.

Generally speaking, there are five types of legal performative patterns common to both China and Taiwan. For China, the Chinese performative verb uses are:

a. verb preceded by *bixu/xu* (必须/须 must/shall);
b. verb preceded by *yingdang/ying* (应当/应 shall);
c. verb in the present tense without any modal verbs—zero performative;

d. verb preceded by *keyi* (可以 may); and
e. verb preceded by *bude* (不得 may not/shall not).

For Taiwan, the legal performative modal verb patterns are largely similar to those in China but not identical. They can be summarized as:

a. verb preceded by *xu* (须 must/shall);
b. verb preceded by *ying* (应 shall);
c. verb in the present tense without any modal verbs—zero performative;
d. verb preceded by *de* (得 may); and
e. verb preceded by *bude* (不得 may not/shall not).

In China, there are also other words used, for instance, *yinggai* for "should" which is similar to *yingdang/ying* in meaning; *bubi* ("not need to," an informal and colloquial expression), *xu* ("need to," a different character from the one used in *bixu*), and *yao* (should) among others are occasionally used but they are not common.[7] In Taiwan, the use of the performative indicators seems to be uniform and consistent. In the following section actual uses of these words are cited and discussed.

ILLOCUTIONARY FORCE OF ORDERING OR IMPOSING AN OBLIGATION

The first category of performative indicators in Chinese is the various words used for indicating orders and obligations. For this illocutionary force, there are two sets of words: *bixu* or its short form *xu*, and *yingdang* and its short form *ying*.

Firstly, *bixu* 必须 and its short form *xu* 须is an imperative modal verb equivalent to the English "must" or "shall" to order someone to perform certain acts or to fulfill certain obligations, denoting the mandatory and compulsory weight of the relevant provision. For instance, the PRC Constitution (1982, as amended) states:

(1) 第五条 …… 一切国家机关和武装力量、各政党和各社会团体、各企业事业组织都必须遵守宪法和法律。一切违反宪法和法律的行为□必须予以追究。

Article 5 … all state organs, the armed forces, all political parties and public organizations and all enterprises and institutions *must* [*bixu*] abide by the Constitution and the law. All acts in violation of the Constitution and the law *must* [*bixu*] be investigated (emphasis is added for all the quotations):

(2) 第一百零一条 …… 选出或者罢免人民检察院检察长□须报上级人民检察院检察长提请该级人民代表大会常务委员会批准。

Article 101 … The election or dismissal of chief procurators of people's procuratorates *must* [*xu*] be reported to the chief procurators of the people's procuratorates at the next higher level for submission to the standing committees of the people's congresses at the corresponding level for approval.

For Taiwan, *xu* is always used instead of *bixu* with the same usage and meaning as in China. But it is also noted that *xu* is much less frequently used than *ying* in Taiwan laws (see below). For instance, an article in the ROC Constitution states:

(3) 第三十九條 總統依法宣佈戒嚴。但須經立法院之通過或追認 …… 。

Article 39 The President [may], in accordance with law, declare martial law but this *must* [*xu*] be done with the approval of, or subject to confirmation by, the Legislative Yuan.

In contrast to English which only uses "shall" or "must" for ordering or imposing obligations, apart from *bixu/xu*, there is in Chinese of both the PRC and Taiwan an additional word *yingdang/ying* (should/ought to) that functions in more or less same manner as *bixu/xu*. For the PRC, *yingdang* is more often used than *ying*, but in Taiwan, *ying* is always used. As the next examples show, *yingdang/ying* denotes the sense of command and compulsory obligation, in the same sense as *bixu/xu*. For instance, in the PRC Constitution:

(4) 第一百三十四条 各民族公民都有用本民族语言文字进行诉讼的权利。人民法院和人民检察院对于不通晓当地通用的语言文字的诉讼参与人，应当为他们翻译。

在少数民族聚居或者多民族共同居住的地区，应当用当地通用的语言进行审理；起诉书、判决书、布告和其他文书应当根据实际需要使用当地通用的一种或者几种文字。

Article 134 [Chinese] citizens of all ethnic groups have the right to use the spoken and written languages of their own ethnic groups in court proceedings. The people's courts and people's procuratorates *shall* [*yingdang*] provide interpreting [translation] for any party to the court proceedings who is not familiar with the spoken or written languages commonly used in the locality.

In an area where people of an ethnic minority live in a concentrated community or where a number of ethnic groups live together, court hearings *shall (yingdang)* be conducted in the language or languages commonly used in the locality; indictments, judgments, notices, and other documents *shall (yingdang)* be written, according to actual needs, in the language or language commonly used in the locality.

In this provision, the obligation on the part of the judicial authorities is mandatory, not optional. Conversely, this provision confers on the citizens of ethnic origin in China a legal right to an interpreter in judicial proceedings, not just a discretionary option or choice.

From the Taiwan Constitution, similarly, the use of *ying* means "shall" or "must":

(5) 第八條 人民身體之自由應予保障。

Article 8 Personal freedom of the people *shall* [*ying*] be guaranteed.

Again here, the Constitution confers a legal constitutional right on Taiwan citizens and imposes a mandatory obligation on the authorities, without any discretionary leeway. It is noted that in Taiwan's statutes, *xu* is used in the same sense as *ying* to indicate orders or obligations, but there may be some subtle differences, for instance, *ying* is used to indicate orders or obligations while *xu* is also used to indicate conditions precedent or incidental requirements.

Another relevant feature of the linguistic use is that a comparison of the statutes in China and Taiwan shows that in China, *bixu* and *yingdang* are more often used than the short form *xu* and *ying* while in Taiwan *xu* and *ying* are always used instead of *bixu* and *yingdang*. This trend and usage is more evident in the laws enacted in more recent decades in China than in the more distant past. In China in the 1950s, *xu* and *ying* were more often used than the long form *bixu* and *yingdang*. For instance, the Marriage Law (1950) of the PRC states:

(6) 结婚须男女双方本人完全自愿, ……

Article 3 The male and female parties to the marriage *must* [*xu*] each be completely voluntary….

(7) 第六条 结婚应男女双方亲到所在地 (区、乡) 人民政府登记。

Article 6 To marry, both the male and female parties *shall (ying)* go to the local (or district or county) people's government in person to register.

In contrast, in a later statute, the Marriage Law (1980), which replaced the 1950 Marriage Law, the word *bixu* replaced some of the *xu*. It states:

(8) 第四条 结婚必须男女双方完全自愿, ……

Article 4 The male and female parties to the marriage *must* [*bixu*] be completely voluntary….

Similarly,

> (9) 第六条 要求结婚的男女双方必须亲自到婚姻登记机关进行结婚登记。
>
> Article 6 Both the male and female parties who request to be married *must* [*bixu*] go to the marriage registration authorities in person to register.

However, *bixu* has not completely replaced *xu*. Both are used with the same meaning but with *bixu* and *yingdang* used more frequently. For instance, in the same Marriage Law (1980), *xu* and *ying* are also used:

> (10) 第二十四条 男女双方自愿离婚的，准予离婚。双方须到婚姻登记机关申请离婚。
>
> Article 24 The male and female parties to a marriage who voluntarily want a divorce [shall] be granted divorce. The two parties *must [xu]* go to the marriage registration authorities to apply for divorce.

> (11) 第二十五条 …… 人民法院审理离婚案件，应当进行调解；如感情已破裂, 调解无效, 应准予离婚。
>
> Article 25 … The People's Court that handles divorce cases *shall* [*yingdang*] mediate; for those couples whose emotional relationships have broken down, the Court *shall* [*ying*] grant divorce.

The statutes enacted in the 1990s in China show that now *bixu* and *yingdang* are more commonly used than the short forms and this seems to have stabilized. In contrast, in Taiwan, relatively little change has occurred in the use of performative modal verbs during the years since the enactment of the early ROC statutes of the 1930s and 1940s up to the present day.

A number of comments can be made regarding the foregoing examples. The survey of both the PRC and ROC statutes shows that *yingdang/ying* is much more frequently used than *bixu/xu*. *Yingdang/ying* is the dominant performative modal verb for Chinese statutes for the sense of ordering and imposing obligations while *bixu/xu* is a subordinate indicator used only occasionally. It is apparent that both have the same function with the same illocutionary force to impose obligations or to order as demonstrated in the abovequoted legislation. They are imperative words equivalent to the English "shall," to order people to perform certain acts or to fulfill certain obligations, denoting mandatory and compulsory weight of the relevant provisions. However, it is not possible to find any regularity or any written explanations or rules from either the PRC or Taiwan for the selective use of either word. In ordinary non-technical Chinese, *yingdang/ying* and *bixu/xu* do not have the same meaning. As used in law, they are ambiguous (see Cao, 2007b for a discussion of ambiguity of legal language). However, it is argued that in legal language *yingdang/ying* as found in Chinese statutes is a special legal usage (see Cao, 1999, 2004), and both academic and judicial opinions seem to favor the view. For instance, Wu et al. support the view that *yingdang* is identical to *bixu* in legislative usage (1992, p.721). They further state that if *yingdang* used in legislation can be substituted by *bixu*, *yingdang* is used correctly, meaning that *yingdang* and *bixu* can be used interchangeably (Wu et al., 1992, p.721). In all the above examples, *yingdang/ying* can be substituted by *bixu/xu* and vice versa. In a case decided some years ago in China, a statutory provision containing the word *yingdang* was interpreted as a compulsory obligation, not a matter of "should" or "should not" at the discretion of the parties.[8]

In semantic terms, *bixu/xu* is, in general usage, stronger and more forceful than *yingdang/ying* (see also Liu, 2003). *Yingdang/ying* carries a sense of being compelled to do something and a sense of moral judgment, a sense of what is right or wrong. In addition, the negative form of *yingdang/ying* in ordinary Chinese is *bu yingdang/bu ying* (should not). But in legal Chinese, its negative form is *bude* (may not/shall not), which is also the negative form of *bixu*.[9] This also lends support to the view that *yingdang* has a legal usage, not entirely identical to its general use. Nevertheless, when used in legislation, these two terms have legislative connotations, but the original meanings of the words as used in ordinary Chinese are not entirely lost, that is, both *bixu/xu* and *yingdang/ying* carry the sense of compulsion but *yingdang/ying* also implies a moral obligation. So, *yingdang/ying* denotes both a sense of ordering and a sense associated with morality. The translation of *yingdang* into "shall," however, is a preferable option for its effect of reducing ambiguity, although it loses the moral connotation.

In this regard, I argued previously (Cao, 2004) that the use of *yingdang/ying* in Chinese legislation may be attributable to the classical or traditional Chinese view of law and morality. Essentially, it is proposed that *bixu/xu* and *yingdang/ying* are manifestations of the traditional Chinese thinking associated with law and morality symptomatic of its hidden but enduring influence. I continue to advocate this position. For the purpose of this chapter, I have also examined imperial Chinese statutes and found *ying* together with *de* and *bude* used in the Tang and Ming Codes (see Xue, 1998 and the Tang and Ming Codes). It is believed that the use of *ying*, not only in legal philosophical terms, but also in actual linguistic usage, is a residual word inherited from the imperial Chinese legal language of the distant past.

ZERO PERFORMATIVE

Another category is legislative clauses that impose obligations without the use of any imperatives. It is referred to as zero performative. The term "zero performative" is used here in the sense that no actual performative lexical indicator is used. It does not mean that an utterance without a performative indicator is not a performative. For example, from the PRC Constitution:

(12) 第三十三条 ...... 中华人民共和国公民在法律面前一律平等。

Article 33 ... All the citizens of the People's Republic of China [are] equal before the law.

(13) 第三十五条 中华人民共和国公民有言论、出版、集会、结社、游行、示威的自由。

Article 35 Citizens of the People's Republic of China have freedom of speech, the press, assembly, association, procession and demonstration.

From the ROC Constitution:

(14) 第七條 中華民國人民, 無分男女、宗教、種族、階級、黨派, 在法律上一律平等。

Article 7 All the citizens of the Republic of China, irrespective of sex, religion, ethnic origin, class, or party affiliation, [are] equal before the law.

(15) 第十一條 人民有言論、講學、著作及出版之自由。

Article 11 The people have freedom of speech, teaching, writing and publication.

In the above examples, no performative modal verbs are used. As it is apparent, these provisions are statements of rights. In the above examples, the legislative clauses are speech acts, and their legal status endows the entire text with the legal authority, which Kurzon (1986, p.20) refers to as the master speech act. The speech act of enactment determines the occurrence of certain other speech acts within the text (Kurzon, 1986, p.20). In other words, the entire statute may be seen as a speech act with the illocutionary force of enactment, and many of the sentences in the statute may also have a status as individual speech acts. Therefore, even if some sentences in a statute do not contain a performative verb (e.g., "shall"), they may still be considered as speech acts and each provision is a speech act that has the illocutionary force of enacting and also of ordering.

In terms of the above examples in Chinese legislation, due to the master and individual speech act of enactment of the entire statute, even if *bixu/xu* or *yingdang/ying* (shall) are not present in these particular provisions, statutory utterances should be interpreted as compulsory obligations and their violation will be a breach of rights and obligations with legal consequences. When Chinese laws are translated into English, the use of "shall" for such cases would be deemed optional. However, "shall" is preferable, in particular when *bixu/xu* (in the PRC) or *yingdang/ying* (in the PRC or Taiwan) are clearly implied in the context of unmistakably mandatory rules, to avoid any misinterpretation.

ILLOCUTIONARY FORCE OF PERMISSION OR CONFERRING A RIGHT

The next category of performative verbs in Chinese is verbs preceded by *keyi* (可以may) or its short form *ke* (may), a use of facultative language, that is, language conferring a right, privilege or power. For example, from the PRC Constitution:

(16) 第十条 …… 国家为了公共利益的需要，可以依照法律规定对土地实行征用。

Article 10 … The state *may* [*keyi*], in the public interest, requisition land for its use in accordance with the law.

From the PRC Marriage Law (1980):

(17) 第十六条 子女可以随父姓，也可以随母姓。

Article 16 The children [of the marriage] *may* [*keyi*] use the surname of the father and *may* [*keyi*] also use the surname of the mother.

(18) 第二十五条 男女一方要求离婚的，可由有关部门进行调解或直接向人民法院提出离婚诉讼。

Article 25 If one party to a marriage requests a divorce, the case *may* [*ke*] be mediated by the relevant departments or divorce may be filed for in the people's court directly.

Occasionally, *de* (may) is used in PRC legislation but only very rarely in laws in the 1980s onwards. For instance, the PRC Constitution (1980) states:

(19) 第三十一条 ……国家在必要时得设立特别行政区。

Article 31 … The state *may* [*de*] establish special administrative regions when necessary.

But in older statutes enacted in the 1950s, *de* (may) is often used. For instance, in the Marriage Law (1950):

(20) 第十七条 …… 男女一方坚决要求离婚的，得由区人民政府进行调解；……

Article 17 If one party to a marriage requests divorce, the case may [*de*] be mediated by the district people's government.

In Taiwan, however, instead of *keyi/ke,* the word *de* is used consistently without variation in facultative provisions conferring a right, privilege, or power. For instance, from the Taiwan Constitution:

(21) 第八條 …… 人民遭受任何機關非法逮捕拘禁時,其本人或者他人得向法院聲請追究, ……

Article 8 … When a person is unlawfully arrested or detained by any authority, the person or another *may* [*de*] petition the court to investigate. …

(22) 第三十九條 總統依法宣佈戒嚴 … 立法院認爲必要時, 得決議移請總統解嚴。

Article 39 The President [may], in accordance with law, declare martial law….. When the Legislative Yuan deems it necessary, it *may* [*de*], by a formal resolution, request the President to lift the martial law.

In Taiwan, the use of *de* (may) has not changed. It is used in the Constitution originally adopted in 1947 and it is also used in the latest constitutional amendments in the 1990s and other recent laws. As mentioned earlier, it is believed that *de*, together with *ying* and *bude,* originated in the Chinese imperial codes of almost one thousand years ago.

In statutory provisions that contain the word *keyi/ke* and occasionally *de* (may) in China and *de* (may) in Taiwan, there is no complication or ambiguity. It signifies a permissive sense, similar to "may."

ILLOCUTIONARY FORCE OF PROHIBITION

The last category is the use of *bude* (不得may not/shall not), a prohibitive indicator which denies permission to do something or imposes an obligation to refrain from doing something. For example, in the PRC Constitution,

(23)第五条……一切法律、行政法规和地方性法规都不得同宪法相抵触。

Article 5 … *No* law or administrative or local rule or regulation *may* [*bude*] contravene the Constitution.

Similarly, *bude* is also used in Taiwan laws for "shall not/may not," and it is used in exactly the same way as in PRC. For instance, in the Taiwan Constitution:

(24) 第八條 人民身體之自由應予保障。除現行犯之逮捕由法律另定外,非經司法或警察機關依法定程序, 不得逮捕拘禁。

Article 8 Personal freedom of the people shall be guaranteed. In *no* case except that of the arrest of convicted criminals, which shall be separately prescribed by law, *may* [*bude*] any person be arrested or detained other than by a judicial or police department in accordance with the procedure prescribed by law.

In the above case, *bude* is used as the negative form of *yingdang*, denoting a sense of prohibition. It can be translated into either "may not" as in the above translation or "shall not." Conversely, *bude* is used in Chinese to express both "shall not" and "may not," and this usage is identical and consistent in both China and Taiwan.

THE UNIVERSAL AND IDIOSYNCRATIC FEATURES OF CHINESE SPEECH ACTS

A number of implications can be drawn from the foregoing discussion with a broader reference to the Chinese legal language and speech act theory in general.

First, the use of performative indicators in Chinese legislative language can be summed up this way. There are four sets of usage for illocutionary force in Chinese legislation: (1) statutory provisions can have no explicit performative indicators but nevertheless carry legal force. (2) *Bixu/xu* and *yingdang/ying* are used in the same manner to impose order or mandatory obligation with the more persuasive *yingdang/ying* being the dominant indicator and the more direct and forceful *bixu/xu* used less frequently used. Both sets of words convey the same legal meaning and the same or similar illocutionary force. (3) The terms *keyi/ke* are used in China and *de* in Taiwan to confer discretionary power. (4) *Bude* is used for strict prohibition. For (1), (3), and (4), the Chinese and English legal languages do not display significant differences. The study points to a universalism in the illocutionary functions of legal language and the tendency to use performatives in legal texts and to use fossilized phrases across different languages.

Secondly, the study has shown that speech act theory developed in the Western linguistic system is generally applicable to the Chinese legal language in terms of Chinese statutes being speech acts with illocutionary forces of enactment and of ordering, conferring rights and duties, and imposing prohibitions. The Chinese legal language uses corresponding words for these three categories. The exception to the English usage is the use of *yingdang/ying* (should/ought to) which is linked to the Chinese cultural and legal tradition and classical Chinese legal language. This exception, if viewed in a wider semiotic context, and in particular, if considered interlingually and interculturally, could well be regarded as a norm rather than an exception if language is to be construed in its culturally coded textual medium. Potentially, all meanings of legal and nonlegal texts can be interpreted differently by people with different cultural backgrounds and social knowledge.[10] Therefore, speech act theory needs to take into account these cross-cultural variables in the interpretation of meaning.

In terms of speech act theory, one interpretation is that provisions with *yingdang/ying* could be viewed as a type of indirect speech act.[11] The significance lies in the kind of relationships implied between the Chinese legislature and Chinese citizens. There are two dimensions here. Sentences with *yingdang/ying* could be rephrased as "we suggest that an act be done" with the same or similar effect as a direct speech act, but as Tannen (1984, cited in Jackson, 1995, p.20) argues, that would change the metamessage, a message about the form of relationships between the two sides. Furthermore, we can consider the kind of relationships the Chinese legislature may want to establish with its people. If we believe that law is more than just command and law-as-command is not an accurate representation of the nature of law in general or of legislation in particular, *bixu/xu* can be viewed as direct legal command while *yingdang/ying* may signify a kind of indirect command latent with moral connotation. *Yingdang/ying* is a less forceful and confronting imperative to the ordinary Chinese although its actual legal force is by no means weakened. A predominant use of *yingdang/ying* with the occasional deployment of *bixu/xu* creates a configuration of legal command in the form of moral advice. Such an interpretation is in conformity with the moral teaching and reshaping motives of the higher authority of government or legislature in guiding, as well as ordering, the ordinary people in proper conduct in the Confucian tradition.

Lastly, if we compare the usage in China and Taiwan, there is the difference in the preferred use of *keyi/ke* for China and *de* for Taiwan. Similarly, in the use of *yingdang* vs *ying* and *bixu* vs *xu* where China prefers the two-character term and Taiwan prefers the single-character term, it is proposed that the use of these words provides us with an interesting glimpse of the evolution of the Chinese legal language from the two sides of the Taiwan Strait.

If we compare the language in general and the use of performative words in China and Taiwan, China's statutes are less formal and more modern and colloquial while Taiwan's statutes are much more formal and have retained the classical style and usage. This is also helped in Taiwan's case by the fact that many of the major foundational laws of the ROC were drafted and enacted in the 1930s and 1940s, for instance, the Constitution. They have been amended since but main provisions and the language of most of these laws remain, preserving the more traditional and classical style of writing and usage. Generally speaking, China's laws predominantly use ordinary language. It is still a formal and written language, but it is much closer to ordinary spoken Chinese (Mandarin) than to classical written Chinese. In contrast, the legal language in Taiwan is much more formal and classical in usage and style. The Chinese legal discourse in China in general utilizes ordinary language to a great extent, greater than its Taiwan or even English counterpart. For the present purpose, *yingdang* and *bixu* are used more often in spoken Chinese while *ying* and *xu* are more formal and more often used in writing. The use of *de* in Taiwan as opposed to *keyi/ke* is another very good example. Today, in modern colloquial Chinese in China and Taiwan, *de* is very seldom used if at all for the meaning of "may." It is now an exclusively legal usage.[12]

If we view this in terms of language evolution and change and of historical linguistics, it is proposed that social factors play a major role in the evolution of the Chinese legal language specifically in the use of performative indicators. "Language changes inexorably" (Hock and Joseph, 1996, p.7), and Chinese, as used in both mainland China and Taiwan, is no exception. Furthermore, if we compare the Chinese language used in China and Taiwan as shown in the foregoing, we can see that Chinese in China seems to have changed more than in Taiwan. In China, the legal language is much more informal and colloquial and uses very much ordinary and plain language. In contrast, Taiwan law has maintained much of the classical style and terminology from the previous age. This partly relates to the time of the making of the respective laws. The major Taiwan statutes were originally enacted in the 1930s and 1940s (although they have been amended extensively since) while most of China's laws were enacted in the 1980s and onward. Both societies and speech communities have changed and evolved over the period. We have seen as from the foregoing examples that small changes took place in China's legislative language with progressively greater preference shown for the more colloquial terms of *yingdang, bixu,* and *keyi* over the older and more formal but otherwise synonymous terms *ying*, *xu*, and *ke*, and now these legal usages have become more or less stabilized. Taiwan, on the other hand, has generally retained the linguistic usage of performative modal verbs from the early age. China's performative usage has not been entirely consistent or uniform while Taiwan's has been. The changes in China are largely motivated by the external social factors rather than internal linguistic perimeters. Both the PRC and Taiwan societies have changed dramatically over the last fifty years, but linguistic usages in written language and written law have changed a great deal more in China than they have in Taiwan over this period.[13] It is beyond the scope of this chapter to explore these issues in depth. Suffice to say that language, and legal language use as social behavior, including the Chinese language and Chinese legal language on both sides of the Taiwan Strait adapts to the extra-linguistic and social forces in the environment and society in which it is used to function. Fundamentally, mainland China and Taiwan as political and social entities, in the past half a century or so, have taken different paths in social transformation. A Chinese reader educated in modern times from either side of the Taiwan Strait can read the laws enacted by either side but only to a certain extent, the extent marked off by both legal and linguistic barriers. The language of the laws used in the two societies brings both familiarity and strangeness, both closeness and distance, to the Chinese eyes and minds, perhaps a situation of two societies separated and linked by one language and the passage of time.

NOTES

1. Habermas (1998) distinguishes between communicative and noncommunicative (strategic) use of language. Communicative actions aimed at reaching understanding are primary and fundamental while strategic form of communication such as lying, misleading, deceiving, manipulating, etc. is derivative and parasitic on speech oriented toward reaching understanding.

2. For Habermas's analysis of Austin and his objections, see Habermas (1998).

3. For discussions of legislative addresser and addressee, see Cao (2004).

4. As Jori (1994, p.2094) comments, when doing legal things with words not only a specific verbal formula is required which one is not allowed to substitute with different expressions of equivalent meanings. One may also even be required to accompany the uttering of words with a complex ritual, to wear special costume and to make use of symbolic objects. This is the case in the United Kingdom. (for both the judicial and legislative processes) and Australia (for the judiciary only). Legal realists insisted that this is somehow attributable to the outdated and primitive belief in modern legal thinking in the magical force of words.

5. See Bowers (1989, p.37) who argues that the negative form of "shall" is "may not," used for abridging a right, privilege, or power, or imposing an obligation to abstain. As for the difference between "shall" and "must," Bowers (1989, p.33) writes:The use of *must* as an alternative to *shall* is unhelpful in all respects. First, if as Driedger says, it does not directly create a duty, it is no more expressive than *shall*; second, it muddies the water to the extent of introducing uncertainties about the meaning of *shall*, in that where both words appear in a [*sic*] Act they must be viewed within the maxim *ut res magis valeat quam pereat* and the presumption that different words have different meanings; third, *must* is ambiguous as to the sense of logical necessity and obligation. "you must be kidding" and "you must be going" being minimal pair examples.....with a consequent effect on illocution such that "you must be kidding" is representative while "you must be going" may be an indirect directive. These considerations convince me that *must* is even less determinate than *shall*, which when preceded by an agent such as person is more directly imperative-looking. Coode's exclusion of *must* implicitly recognizes the greater clarity of *shall* and preserves a uniform expression of obligation. It is also noted that in contrast to the stance of plain legal English advocates, some legal stylists advocate making a consistent distinction between the English "shall" and "must" by reserving "shall" exclusively to impose duties and reserving "must" to create conditions precedent and subsequent, for example see Child (1992).

6. Cf. Jean–Claude Gémar (1995, cited in Sarcevic, 1997, p.11) identifies six subdivisions of legal language: there are the language of the legislator, judges, the administration, commerce, private law, and scholarly writings.

7. Another word *yinggai*, related to *yingdang*, is often used in ordinary Chinese as a synonym of *yingdang*, but it has seldom appeared in legislation. Other words with some degree of illocutionary force that are only infrequently and irregularly used in legislation include *bubi* ("not need to," an informal and colloquial expression), *yao* ("need to," a colloquial word), *buzhun* ("not permitted," an informal word as opposed

to *bude* cited above), and *buneng* (cannot). Because these words are rarely used in law, they are not classified among the legal performative modal verbs for discussion here.

8. *Jilin sheng tuchan xuchan jinchukou gongsi shu Changchun shi Chaoyang qu nongfu chanpin jingxiaochu gouxiao hetong jiufen an* [Native Produce and Animal By-products Import and Export Corporation of Jilin Province v. Chaoyang District Agricultural Produce Distribution Corporation of Changchun] 1994.

9. When statutes and other legislative instruments written in English are translated into Chinese, "shall" is often translated into *yingdang/ying* and "shall not/may not" are translated into *bude*. However, in the Chinese texts of some U.N. instruments, for example, the Law of the Sea Convention, errors were found in the use of *buying* (should not/shall not) for "shall not." *Buying* is not a legal usage and it was used wrongly in the Convention.

10. A reference could be made to the Sapir-Whorfian hypothesis here, although the author would hesitate to jump to any conclusion. For discussions of the Sapir-Whorfian hypothesis in relation to Chinese legal language, see Cao (2004).

11. For a discussion of indirect speech acts in law, see Jackson (1995, p.50).

12. To make things slightly more confusing, in Chinese, there is another word, 得 *de*, written in exactly the same way as *de* (may) used in law but pronounced *dei*, and this 得 *dei* is a colloquial word for "have to" or "need to."

13. In China, there were several language reform campaigns in the past few decades, including the simplification of the Chinese characters and literacy campaigns to educate the vast uneducated Chinese and make the written language more accessible to them. Somewhat differently, in Taiwan, there have also been government-initiated campaigns in the 1950s and onwards to the last decade or so and the compulsory national language policy to popularize Chinese in Taiwan among the population including the indigenous population whose first language is not Chinese. For Taiwan's Mandarin Chinese language use and language policy, see Tsao (1999), Yeh et al. (2004), and Sandel (2003).

Chapter 7

Is the Chinese Legal Language More Ambiguous and Vague?

"To read the recent news, one might think China is experiencing a mysterious bout of felonious squabbling. 'Picking quarrels and provoking troubles' [*xunxin zishi* 寻衅滋事] is the charge now facing a host of political activists, lawyers, and worker rights advocates. And this crime can earn one up to five years in prison, or ten years for multiple offenses, under Article 293 of China's amended Criminal Law."[1] This is how Bloomberg media reported in 2014. The situation in China is getting worse, not better, as more people have been charged with this crime. Article 293 has been labeled as a "pocket crime" (*koudai zui*) by Chinese legal professionals—meaning that because of its vague definition, literally "anything can be stuffed into it," referring to a situation where it is uncertain and unclear whether a particular act is illegal or not under the law, but the act may bear some resemblance to a crime.[2] Thus a catch-all charge such as *xunxin zishi* may be applied to a broad and unspecified range of offenses.[3] *Xunxin zishi* charge, along with several similar ones (Articles 290–293 of the Criminal Law (1997), are sometimes referred to more generally as "disturbing social order."[4] Similarly, the social order charges were also vague and broad, as the earlier crime of "hooliganism" that they replaced in 1997. The crime of hooliganism was used to jail people for everything from dancing provocatively and being gay to political dissent. For the new *xunxin zishi*, previously, the "picking quarrels and provoking trouble" charge was applied more narrowly to actions disrupting public order, involving actual assault or property damage.[5] However, Chinese legal authorities have announced clarification of the circumstances under which "picking quarrels and provoking troubles" can be punished. The Supreme People's Court and Supreme People's Procuratorate issued a joint legal interpretation in 2013 without actually providing a precise definition.[6] In 2013, the application of this charge was extended to the internet, meaning that it can be used to prosecute online commenters whose posts are false or deemed to be rumors and are widely circulated.[7] The charge carries under five years up to ten years' imprisonment depending on the seriousness of the acts. Despite the clarification, the definition of *xunxin zishi* remains fluid and uncertain. It has been used to detain, charge, and convict people with a wide range of acts from ordinary assaults and public brawls, to public drunken and disorderly conduct,[8] petition,[9] assaulting medical staff in hospitals,[10] destroying a roadside clothes donation bin,[11] to journalists[12] and rights lawyers.[13]

Vague, undefined and broadly worded language is common in Chinese law as in the case of Criminal Law (1997) and other Chinese legal provisions. Language is inherently indeterminate. Linguistic uncertainties sometimes lead to legal disputes[14] and become matters of contention in court (e.g., see Schane, 2002; Stratman, 2004). The Chinese language, like any other language, is inherently indeterminate, but one may ask: Are all languages equally indeterminate or are some languages more indeterminate than others? In our case, one may wonder: is the Chinese language, and for the purpose of this analysis, the Chinese legal language, more ambiguous and vague than English and the English legal language? In this chapter, some of these issues are addressed using examples from Chinese statutes. First certain inherent linguistic features of the Chinese language are identified that may render the Chinese legal language prone to uncertainty. Then the chapter discusses drafting issues in Chinese law that may have contributed to ambiguity and vagueness. Lastly, it considers the pragmatic legal implications of the contention that the Chinese legal language is more ambiguous and vague than English. In this chapter, "uncertainty" is used interchangeably with "indeterminacy."[15] "Chinese linguistic uncertainty" is used as a general term to cover the uncertain and indeterminate property of the Chinese language, including linguistic vagueness, generality, and ambiguity. Vagueness, generality, and ambiguity are distinguishable (see Williamson, 2001), but they are also relative, and sometimes may overlap (see Schane, 2004).

UNCERTAINTY IN CHINESE LAW

It is commonly acknowledged that contemporary Chinese law suffers from excessive generality and vagueness. This is the case despite the fact that over 2,000 years ago Han Feizi, the leading Legalist (see chapter 2), advocated the notion that in order to earn the respect of the people, written law must be plain, clear, and specific as important characteristics of law (see Chang, 2016, pp.290–391, 517). Correspondingly, a highly flexible and contextualist approach to law seems to prevail among Chinese lawmakers and lawyers.

Peerenboom (2002, p.247, 251) argues that Chinese legislation is characterized by excessive generality and vagueness, omissions, undefined terms, and inconsistencies. He cites examples of Chinese equity joint venture law, criminal law, and civil law. Keller (1994) in his study of Chinese law concludes that generality and flexibility are the guiding principles in Chinese legislative drafting; colloquially referred to by legislative officials as the policy of "preferring the coarse to the fine" (Keller, 1994, p.749). He further argues that generality and flexibility captures the essential guide in Chinese law making that legislation must reflect the unitary nature of the state while satisfying the needs of regional diversity. This also accords with the principle of legislative stability as it permits the effective amendment of the law through changes in interpretation rather than through alterations to the actual statutes (Keller, 1994, p.750). The justification offered for this central doctrine is that national legislation must be general and flexible so that it can be implemented throughout the country and adapted to local conditions (Keller, 1994, p.749). As Keller (1994, p.752) notes, Chinese lawmakers have not, in general, attempted to use legislative language supported by rules of construction to strengthen the internal structure and order of positive law. They prefer instead, particularly in relation to primary legislation, that the specific meanings attached to legislative language shift with their contexts. Similarly, Chinese administrative bodies also have a preference for broadly drafted laws that leave them free to act as they see fit in specific circumstances (Keller, 1994, p.752).[16] In this regard, Potter (2001, p.11) agrees that Chinese laws are intentionally ambiguous and are replete with vague passages that do not lend predicability or transparency to the regulatory process; but he believes that this is a consequence of legal instrumentalism prevailing in China that gives policy makers and officials significant flexibility in legislative interpretation and implementation. In contrast, Peerenboom (2002, p.251) submits that there may be many reasons for generality and vagueness in Chinese law, pointing specifically to the following reasons: many of China's laws are modeled after the laws of civil law countries, which are typically more general and broadly drafted than statutes in common law countries; China is a vast country undergoing profound changes, so broadly drafted laws and regulations allow sufficient flexibility in implementation to meet local conditions. He also suggests that the traditional emphasis on particularized justice characteristic of the Confucian tradition and the socialist emphasis on uniting practice and theory combined with the pragmatic orientation of current leaders all favor laws that are statements of general principles that must then be interpreted and applied to particular situations by local officials and administrators (Keller, 2002, p.251). Regardless of the reasons, such excessive generality and vagueness often undermine the predicability and certainty of Chinese law.

CHINESE LINGUISTIC FEATURES OF UNCERTAINTY

In this section, the linguistic issues that may have contributed to the uncertainty in Chinese law identified by the aforementioned legal scholars are discussed, examining specifically the linguistic nature of the Chinese language, legal language, and legislative drafting practice. Chinese is different from English in its linguistic form in that the Chinese language uses character as its linguistic representation (as opposed to an alphabet), and in how the Chinese characters are structured to express meaning, for example, grammar. Two linguistic features stand out in Chinese when compared with European languages: firstly, the absence of inflection that is words can assume a variety of grammatical functions without morphological change; and secondly, omission that is grammatically significant indicators can be omitted. These are the inherent linguistic features of the Chinese language.

Chinese characters are not words in the strict English sense and as such they can vary in meaning as their context changes. Even in the same general context, a character may have several different meanings. Chinese characters are more like word roots than words. There are no changes in the character in relation to tense, number, gender, person, or case; and there are no articles such as the English "the" and "a"/"an." Since the Chinese language does not have definite and indefinite articles as in English or other European languages, this aspect becomes more obvious when translating between Chinese and European languages, for example English. When translating into Chinese, the articles in English are often omitted. This can sometimes give rise to problems, as considerable meaning variation may result with or without the use of articles.

When Chinese texts are translated into English, there is the additional problem of the rare use of linguistic markers for plural nouns with no markers for plural verbs. As a result, ambiguity often arises as linguistically it is uncertain whether singular or plural meanings are intended. In many instances, the translator has to make the arbitrary decision of using or not using articles or choosing between the singular and plural in English, thus arbitrarily eliminating the uncertainties contained in the original Chinese text. This also arises when English is translated into Chinese: the definite article and plural form in English are omitted and their meanings lost in the translation; often introducing uncertainty when it was not there in the original text (for interlingual uncertainty in law, see Cao, 2007b).

One source of uncertainty is that Chinese does not have grammatical categories of tense or aspect (see Yang and Huang, 2004). There are particles that function as tense markers, but they are rarely used. As a result, the Chinese language is not a tense-prominent language like English and while the equivalence of tenses can be indicated by temporal adverbs or particles, more often than not, they are implied from context. There are two kinds of uncertainty related to the lack of tense: (1) the rare use of particles or tense markers and (2) certain tenses in English cannot be expressed in Chinese.

Another source of uncertainty in Chinese comes from omission. The language offers the option to omit grammatically significant and other parts in language use. The resulting elliptical sentence is a major source of structural ambiguity. Ambiguities of this kind may disappear and the meaning may become clearer if the omitted parts are supplied.

Apart from these inherent linguistic features that contribute to uncertainty, Chinese language users also have a linguistic habit of using words with uncertain meanings. Such vague and general expressions are commonly used in ordinary speech and ordinary written texts. They are also used in law. For instance, a common word in Chinese is the use of *deng* (meaning "etc.," "such as," "including") in Chinese legal texts. The habitual and sometimes over-frequent use of *deng* which allows for open-ended interpretations can cause a great deal of uncertainty and ambiguity. A further problem is that *deng* can indicate open-endedness both when listing things and when used to end a listing, a closure, to be all inclusive, depending on actual use and context.

Another linguistic feature that can cause uncertainly is the extensive use of adjectives, for instance, in Article 293 concerning "picking quarrels and provoking troubles" mentioned in the beginning of the chapter, the definition of the crime contains many such descriptive words:

> 第二百九十三条 有下列寻衅滋事行为之一, 破坏社会秩序的, 处五年以下有期徒刑、拘役或者管制:
>
> (一)随意殴打他人, 情节恶劣的;
>
> (二)追逐、拦截、辱骂、恐吓他人, 情节恶劣的;
>
> (三)强拿硬要或者任意损毁、占用公私财物, 情节严重的;
>
> (四)在公共场所起哄闹事, 造成公共场所秩序严重混乱的。纠集他人多次实施前款行为,严重破坏社会秩序的,处五年以上十年以下有期徒刑,可以并处罚金。

> Article 293. Whoever undermines public order with anyone of the following provocative and disturbing behaviors (*xunxin zishi*) is to be sentenced to not more than five years of fixed-term imprisonment, criminal detention or control:

1. *willfully* assaulting another person and the circumstances are *heinous*;
2. chasing, intercepting, or reviling and intimidating another person, and the circumstances are *heinous*;

3. forcibly taking away, demanding, or *willfully* damaging or seizing public or private property; and the circumstances are *serious*;
4. creating a disturbance in a public place, causing *serious* disorder in the public place.

   Whoever assembles other people to commit the acts as mentioned in the preceding paragraph many times, which *seriously* disrupt the social order, shall be sentenced to imprisonment of not less than five years but not more than ten years and may be fined in addition.

Words such as "heinous," "serious," and "willfully" are not further described or defined. Common sense tells us that such words can be understood differently by different people and in different situations. When such words are used in law, they may leave wide discretion to the judges, causing uncertainty. In common law countries, when such words are used in statutes, their imprecise and uncertain meanings are often made certain by common law judges over years of case law. Such practice of judicial interpretation or lawmaking does not exist in Chinese law.

LINGUISTIC UNCERTAINTY IN CHINESE LAW

The following section examines a major Chinese statute, the Criminal Law (1997 as amended), to demonstrate how the various linguistic features discussed above and other factors render the Chinese legal language vague, general, and imprecise.

The Criminal Law (1997) is one of the most important basic laws in the Chinese legal system. It was originally promulgated in 1979 and has been amended many times since and most recently 2015. The 1997 amendment was virtually a rewrite of the original law, substantively and substantially changing many of the provisions; increasing the total number of articles from 192 in eight chapters to 452 articles in ten chapters. A close reading of the Criminal Law (1997) reveals that there are many instances of linguistic uncertainty at the lexical and syntactical levels. These uncertainties caused by the inherent and other features of the Chinese language include lexical, grammatical and syntactical ambiguity, vagueness, and generality.

Two provisions are worthy of closer examination, namely Articles 338 and 339 relating to environmental crimes:

> 第三百三十八条 违反国家规定，向土地、水体、大气排放、倾倒或者处置有放射性的废物、含传染病病原体的废物、有毒物质或者其他危险废物，造成重大环境污染事故，致使公私财产遭受重大损失或者人身

伤亡的严重后果的，处三年以下有期徒刑或者拘役，并处或者单处罚金；后果特别严重的，处三年以上七年以下有期徒刑，并处罚金。

Article 338 Anyone who, in violation of the state regulation, release[s], dump[s] or dispose[s] radioactive waste[s], waste[s] containing pathogen of contagious disease[s], toxic material[s] or other hazardous waste[s] to land, water [and/or] atmosphere, [and/or] cause[s] [a] serious environmental pollution accident, [and/or] result[s] in serious consequence[s] causing serious loss to public [and/or] private property or personal injury [and/or] death is punished by no more than three years' imprisonment or detention, and is also punished with a fine, or is only punished with [a] fine; for [those accidents resulting in] particularly serious consequence[s], no less than three years' and no more than seven years' imprisonment is imposed together with [a] fine.

Similarly,

第三百三十九条 违反国家规定，将境外的固体废物进境倾倒、堆放、处置的，处五年以下有期徒刑或者拘役，并处罚金；造成重大环境污染事故，致使公私财产遭受重大损失或者严重危害人体健康的，处五年以上十年以下有期徒刑，并处罚金；后果特别严重的，处十年以上有期徒刑，并处罚金。

未经国务院有关主管部门许可，擅自进口固体废物用作原料，造成重大环境污染事故，致使公私财产遭受重大损失或者严重危害人体健康的，处五年以下有期徒刑或者拘役，并处罚金；后果特别严重的，处五年以上十年以下有期徒刑，并处罚金。

以原料利用为名，进口不能用作原料的固体废物、液态废物和气态废物的，依照本法第一百五十二条第二款、第三款的规定定罪处罚。

Article 339 Anyone who, in violation of the state regulation, dump[s], stockpile[s] or dispose[s] solid waste[s] from outside the border to inside the border is punished by no more than five years' imprisonment or detention and a fine. Anyone causing serious environmental pollution incident[s], resulting in serious loss t`o public [and/or] private property or serious harm to human health, is punished by no more than five years' and no less than ten years' imprisonment and by imposing [a] fine. For [those resulting in] particularly serious consequences, [they are punished] by more than ten years' imprisonment and [a] fine.

Anyone [who does] not have the approval of the relevant department[s] in charge under the State Council import[s] without authorization solid waste[s] as raw material[s], [and/or] cause[s] serious environmental pollution accident[s], result[s] in serious loss to public [and/or] private property or serious harm to human health, is punished by no more than five years' imprisonment or detention, and is also punished with [a] fine. For [those accidents resulting in] particularly serious consequences, no more than five years and no less than ten years' imprisonment is imposed together with [a] fine.

> Anyone who import[s] solid waste[s], liquid waste[s] and waste gas in the name of raw material[s] which cannot be used as such is punished under sections 2 and 3 of Article 152 of this Act.

There are a number of linguistic uncertainties in the above two provisions. First, all the articles "the" and "a" are added in the English translation.[17] Secondly, since Chinese does not distinguish in most cases between singular and plural forms as stated earlier, when translating Chinese into English, we may have to decide whether certain nouns should be translated and understood as singular or plural forms. In this particular case, there are ambiguities due to the lack of number markers in Chinese, but common sense tells us that words such as "waste" and "disease" in this context would not result in any substantive deviation or change in the meaning of the Act. Also, in Chinese, words such as "waste" are collective nouns, and do not present the problem of singular versus plural forms. Besides, even in common law, it is often stated and it has become an established rule of statutory interpretation that the singular form may represent the plural and vice versa (see, for example, the U.K. Interpretation Act 1978 s. 6[c]).[18]

However, this is not always the case. Another phrase the equivalent of "cause serious environmental pollution accident" in Chinese can be understood as "an accident" or "accidents." Would it mean that a person has to cause more than one such accident to be criminally liable or just one accident is sufficient? Such an issue would arise in both Chinese and English. Common sense may also tell us that it is likely that it means one accident if such an accident satisfies the qualification stated in the provision. Similarly, "fine" is imposed, and it could be one fine or many fines, although common sense and a reasonable understanding may dictate that one fine was intended. For another noun in Article 339, the equivalent of "anyone who does not have the approval of the relevant departments in charge under the State Council," "departments" here can be either "a department" or "departments." This ambiguity is more serious in practical terms than the examples discussed above. Since the Chinese version does not specify whether it is singular or plural, and the word "department" is qualified by "relevant" without specifying which department, and given the Chinese bureaucracy and lack of transparency in general, this could potentially mean numerous and countless numbers of departments that are either closely related or remotely related from which one has to obtain approval. This could potentially be a source of uncertainty.

In summary, the use or nonuse of singular and plural markers and lack of definite and indefinite articles are very much present in the Criminal Law (1997), giving rise to some ambiguities, although in many cases, not all cases, such ambiguities can be clarified or made clear from context or by a common-sense approach. This situation is similar in most Chinese statutes in general.

Thirdly, apart from grammatical ambiguity, there is also a syntactical or structural ambiguity in Article 338 as in:

> Anyone who, in violation of the state regulation, releases, dumps or disposes radioactive wastes, wastes containing pathogen of contagious diseases, toxic materials or other hazardous wastes to land, water [and/or] atmosphere, [and/or] causes a serious environmental pollution accident, [and/or] results in serious consequences causing serious loss to public [and/or] private property or personal injury [and/or] death is punished.

Here the main verbal phrases "releases, dumps, or disposes" and "causes a serious environmental pollution accident" have parallel structures in Chinese. It could well and reasonably be understood as to mean that anyone who releases, dumps, or disposes the prohibited materials commits an offense under the Act. Equally, it could also mean that anyone who causes a serious environmental pollution accident is also liable under the Act. Linguistically speaking, such interpretations would be correct. However, according to Wang (2004), a legal scholar from China, in terms of the law, under Article 338, the criminal liability arises only when one causes a serious environmental pollution accident which leads to the grave consequences of heavy losses of public or private property or human casualties. This means that a person can release, dump, or dispose any of the prohibited materials without committing any offense. Furthermore, a person can also release, dump, or dispose the prohibited materials causing an environmental pollution accident and still not commit any offense under the Act, so long as the serious environmental pollution accident does not result in the grave consequences of heavy losses of public or private property or human casualties. The act is only an offense when serious consequences as described in the Act result thereof. One may say that this interpretation is possible or acceptable in the Chinese provision. One may also say that this is a stretched and very restricted interpretation. In any event, the Chinese sentence is very loosely structured linguistically so that we can say that either interpretation is possible. Thus, the provision is ambiguous and uncertain linguistically.

We can also detect a structural ambiguity in Article 338 in some of the noun phrases used. These words are stringed together without the equivalent of the English "and" or "or" as in the case of *gongsi caichan* in Article 338, "resulting in serious loss to public [and/or] private property." Here in Chinese, the commonly used phrase *gongsi caichan* is literally "public private property" which can mean either "public and private property" or "public or private property." The Chinese can say without the omissions *gonggong caichan he siyou caichan* (public property and private property) or *gonggong caichan huo siyou caichan* (public property or private property), but in most cases, a short hand form is used *gongsi caichan*. One possible interpretation is that "or" is intended in the Criminal Law (1997).

Another example in Article 338 is *renshen shangwang* (literally "personal injury death"), so it could mean "personal injury and death" or "personal injury or death." It is ambiguous as to whether death must be involved for the offense to be committed. This is important as the offense under Chinese law, as mentioned earlier, very much depends on the seriousness of the conduct. However, in this case, we have no definitive way of knowing it. A reasonable understanding is that it could mean either injury or death but it must have produced serious consequences.

Hence, a clearer (or as clear as one can or should be) translation of Articles 338 and 339 could be (in any event English is not the language of the court in China):

> Article 338 Anyone who, in violation of the state regulation, releases, dumps or disposes radioactive wastes, wastes containing pathogen of contagious diseases, toxic materials or other hazardous wastes to land, water *or* atmosphere, *causing a* serious environmental pollution accident *that results in* serious consequences causing serious loss to public *or* private property or personal injury *or* death is punishable by no more than three years' imprisonment or detention, and is also punished with a fine, or is only punished with a fine; for those accidents resulting in particularly serious consequences, no less than three years' and no more than seven years' imprisonment is imposed together with a fine.
>
> Article 339 Anyone who, in violation of the state regulation, dumps, stockpiles or disposes solid wastes from overseas to China is punished by no more than five years' imprisonment or detention and a fine. Anyone causing serious environmental pollution incidents, resulting in serious loss to public or private property or serious harm to human health, is punished by no more than five years' and no less than ten years' imprisonment and by imposing a fine. For those resulting in particularly serious consequences, more than ten years' imprisonment and a fine are imposed.
>
> Anyone who does not have the approval of the relevant departments in charge under the State Council imports without authorisation solid wastes as raw materials, causing a serious environmental pollution accident that results in serious loss to public or private property or serious harm to human health, is punished by no more than five years' imprisonment or detention, and is also punished with a fine. For those accidents resulting in particularly serious consequences, no more than five years and no less than ten years' imprisonment is imposed together with a fine.
>
> Anyone who imports solid wastes, liquid wastes and waste gas in the name of raw materials which cannot be used as such is punished under sections 2 and 3 of Article 152 of this Act.

Fourthly, we can also see that in both Articles 338 and 339, the words *yanzhong* (serious), *zhongda* (serious, major or heavy) and *tebie yanzhong* (particularly serious) are used a number of times. These words are general or vague in Chinese and English. In fact, such words are typical expressions of vagueness or imprecision as they indicate borderline cases and there can be no clear determination as to whether or not such words apply to a particular situation. So, one may wonder how "serious" would be considered "serious" or "particularly serious." We have no way of knowing as nowhere in the law are these words further qualified or described. However, they touch on an extremely important aspect in Chinese criminal law.

As pointed out, in Chinese criminal legislation, determining what constitutes a criminal and capital offense can turn on interpretations of phrases such as "serious," "large amount," or "special circumstances" (Belkin, 2000). These are the most obvious and most frequently used words of vagueness in the Criminal Law (1997). These words are frequently employed to describe the degree of the seriousness of crimes, extent of harms or damage done by criminal acts, and amount of money involved in crimes for the purpose of prescribing penalties and punishment. In this regard, the legal definition of crime in the Chinese criminal law is relevant. Article 13 of the Criminal Law (1997) stipulates:

> A crime refers to an act that endangers the sovereignty, territorial integrity and security of the States, splits the State, subverts the State power of the people's democratic dictatorship and overthrows the socialist system, undermines public and economic order, violates State-owned property, property collectively owned by the working people, or property privately owned by citizens, infringes on the citizens' rights of the person, their democratic or other rights, and any other act that endangers society and is subject to punishment according to law. However, if the circumstances are obviously minor and the harm done is not serious, the act shall not be deemed a crime.

According to Wang (2004, p.153), in this legal definition of crime, what we should notice is not only the material characteristic of a crime in China, but also the requirement as to what constitutes a crime. According to Chinese criminal law and, principally, for the general definition of a crime, any harmful conduct will not be treated as a crime "if the circumstances are obviously minor and the harm done is not serious" (Wang, 2004, p.153). In the theory of Chinese criminal law, "the circumstances" are closely linked with the degree of the social harmfulness caused by the conduct. In the Specific Part of the Criminal Law (1997), the circumstances or the degree of the social harmfulness shall be clearly defined (Wang, 2004). This is reflected in the form of actual harmful consequences and the sum of the illegal money involved. In some cases, it might be also reflected in the criminal method or criminal mind, but in these cases, the final decisive factor in what constitutes a crime is still the actual harmful consequences (Wang, 2004, p.153). As Wang points out, because of this requirement of "the circumstances," the Chinese criminal law builds up its unique "guilty line" for differentiating guilty and innocent. Accordingly, most conducts which are treated as innocent in Chinese criminal law because they are below "the guilty line" would constitute crimes in other legal systems (Wang, 2004).

Thus, the seriousness of an act and the seriousness of its social consequence determines whether the act constitutes a crime or not and the punishment accordingly, but the vague words "serious" and "particularly serious" in the Criminal Law (1997) would pose considerable problems in the application of the law and in people's understanding of the law.[19]

Therefore, it is not surprising that the Supreme People's Court issued an explanation for these words in these sections of the Criminal Law (1997), The Interpretation of the Supreme People's Court Concerning Certain Issues Related to the Specific Application of Law in Hearing of Criminal Cases regarding Environmental Pollution (2006). The Interpretation by the Court is specifically issued with regard to the explanation as to what constitutes "serious loss," "particularly serious consequences," and "serious harm" in Articles 338 and 339, quantifying what they mean. The Interpretation states:

> Article 1: Any of the following situations falls under "*serious damage to public [and/or] private property*" referred to in Articles 338, 339 and 408 of the Criminal Law (1997):

1. causing damage to public [and/or] private property in the amount of more than ¥300,000 *yuan*;
2. causing the loss of the basic functions or permanent damage to basic agricultural land, protected forest land [or] forest land for special purposes of more than five *mu*, other agricultural land of more than ten mu, [or] other land of more than twenty *mu* [a Chinese measurement];
3. causing the death to forest or other forest trees of more than five cubic meters, or causing the death to more than 2,500 young trees;

> Article 2: Any of the following situations falls under "*serious consequences of personal death [or] injury*," or "*serious harm to human health*" referred to in Articles 338 and 339 of the Criminal Law (1997):

1. causing the death of more than one person, serious injury of more than three persons, [or] light injury of more than ten persons, or serious injury to more than one person and light injury to more than five persons;

2. causing the occurrence [or] spread of [a] contagious disease, or causing people being poisoned constituting a situation as classified in sub-category III of emergency public health incident as set out in the Plan of the State Emergency Response to Sudden Public Health Incidents;
3. other situations "causing serious consequences of personal death [or] injury" or "causing serious harm to human health."

> Article 3 Any of the following situations falls under "*particularly serious consequences*" referred to in Articles 338 and 339 of the Criminal Law (1997):

1. causing loss to public [or] private property of more than one million *yuan*;
2. causing the occurrence of situations involving water source pollution [or] people evacuation that are specified in the emergency environmental incidents in above subcategory II as stated in the Plan State Emergency Response to Sudden Environmental Incidents;
3. causing the loss of the basic functions or permanent damage to basic farm land, protected forest, special purpose forest land of more than 15 *mu*, and more than 30 *mu* of other land for agricultural use, [or] other land of more than 60 *mu*;
4. causing the death of forest or other trees of more than 150 cubic meters, or the death of more than 7,500 young trees;
5. causing the death of more than three persons, serious injury to more than ten persons, light injury to more than 30 persons, or serious injury to more than three persons and light injury to more than ten persons;
6. causing the occurrence [or] spread of [a] contagious disease constituting a situation above those as classified in sub-category II of emergency public health incident as set out in The Plan of the State Emergency Response to Sudden Public Health Incidents;
7. other situations with particularly serious consequences.

In the above English translation, the [or] and other words inserted are made at my discretion and they in fact constitute further uncertainty. The Interpretation thus clarifies the meaning of some of the imprecise words in the original Act. However, the Interpretation was issued in 2006, almost ten years after the original Act taking effect. It makes one wonder how the cases were decided in the intervening years. Obviously, the Chinese courts did decide cases during those years. One can speculate that the courts must have used a common-sense approach in understanding what these words entail and how ordinary people may understand how serious a particular criminal act as is commonly perceived by ordinary people and by the courts themselves in the circumstances.

Fifthly, in Articles 338 and 339, we can see there are other words of imprecision, for instance, "relevant departments," and "loss of public or private property." This is not to say that statutory provisions drafted in English in common law countries do not contain similar expressions, but normally, as is the case in English law, they are defined in the law itself. For instance, the U.K. Animal Welfare Act 2006 (c45), uses the vague adjective "appropriate" to qualify the substantive "national authority" (as in "appropriate national authority"), but the general interpretation section of the Act clearly defines what "appropriate national authority" means; that is, it refers to (a) in relation to England, [to] the Secretary of State; and (b) in relation to Wales, [to] the National Assembly for Wales (2006, para 62, 34). Another example drawn from the same Act is the use of "local authority" which is defined to refer specifically to:

> (a) in relation to England, [to] a county council, a district council, a London borough council, the Common Council of the City of London or the Council of the Isles of Scilly, among others (2006, para 35).

In general, in English statutes, when a particular word or a phrase used is general or vague but carries legal significance, their definition is expressly contained in the same statute. The same rule generally applies when an ordinary word which may carry an uncommon meaning is used in a statutory provision. For example, the interpretation provision of the U.K. Animal Welfare Act (2006) defines the ordinary word "premises" so as to include "any place and, in particular, includes—(a) any vehicle, vessel, aircraft or hovercraft; (b) any tent or movable structure" (2006, para 62, 35).[20]

In contrast, if we look at the Chinese Criminal Law (1997), general and vague words are not normally defined or described.[21] For the example cited above, the Criminal Law (1997) does not provide any definition or description as to what may constitute "loss to public or private property" in Article 338. The Supreme People's Court also recognized this and issued an explanation in the Interpretation of the Supreme People's Court Concerning Certain Issues Related to the Specific Application of Law in Hearing Criminal Cases Involving Environmental Pollution (2006):

> The "loss to public or private property" referred to in this Interpretation includes the damage and destruction to property directly caused by the environmental polluting act, the reduction of the actual value of the property, and the costs incurred for the necessary and reasonable measures adopted to prevent the expansion of the pollution and the elimination of the pollution.

Another relevant factor in relation to imprecise words used in law is that in the common law, words that are not defined or even words that are defined in a particular statute are always subject to judicial interpretation and application. Thus, for many words that are not defined in the statute proper, judicial interpretation in legal precedent is referred to and applied in subsequent cases. However, in the Chinese legal system, case law in terms of judicial interpretation does not constitute a source of law and Chinese judges do not elaborate or give reasons.

On the whole, in the Criminal Law (1997), there are many words of generality and vagueness, such as "public interest," "justified self-defense," "willful criminal act," "work units concerned," "other laws," and "other regulations." These words are not defined or elaborated. We may further note that even in the judicial interpretation by the Supreme People's Court cited above, there are further linguistic uncertainties in the use of punctuation, the use of "and/or," "other particularly serious situations," among others.

POSSIBLE REASONS FOR LEGISLATIVE UNCERTAINTY

As we have seen in the foregoing, the Chinese statutory language as represented in the Criminal Law (1997) has vague, ambiguous, general, and otherwise imprecise words and contains other linguistic features of this kind. We have also seen that such imprecision can be attributed to both the inherent linguistic features in the Chinese language in terms of grammatical and structural uncertainty and the deliberate use of the language through the choice of imprecise lexical words. In this regard, consideration of the Chinese legal system as a whole may be relevant.

Modern China law was influenced by the civil law system. Statutory laws constitute the main source of law. Unlike common law jurisdictions such as the United States or the United Kingdom, there is no strict precedential concept for case law. In theory, each case stands as its own decision and will not bind another court. Judges' decisions are usually not accompanied by lengthy written legal opinions and reasoning. Judicial decisions do not have any legally binding precedential effect on other cases. However, in practice lower people's court judges often attempt to follow the interpretations of the laws decided by the Supreme People's Courts. Case law does not constitute precedent and has no binding force, thus judicial or statutory interpretation in the common law sense of statutory provisions does not play a significant part in the legal system. The court applies the law as proclaimed by the legislature. However, an important source of law is the judicial interpretation (or judicial explanation) issued from time to time by the Supreme People's Court and the Supreme People's Procuratorate of China. Their interpretations are important guides for procurators, lawyers, and judges. These are not always interpretations arising from actual court cases. They are in the form of *jieshi* (interpretation or explanation), *yijian* (opinion), official answers, letters in reply, notices, and other similar forms, a measure that amounts to the re-creation of detailed rules and new rules (Ji, 2004).

Judicial interpretation in China dates back to 1954, shortly after the founding of the PRC. The national authorities found it necessary to issue such explanations to cope with the problems that arose in handling cases. The Standing Committee of the National People's Congress (NPC), the Chinese national parliament, passed in 1995 the Decision on Interpretation of Law which provided that those questions connected with specific application of laws and decrees should be interpreted by the Supreme People's Court. Thus the highest judicial body in China was formally conferred with the power of enacting judicial interpretation. This power was also confirmed by the legislation afterwards in the Organic Law of People's Court of the People's Republic of China in 1979. Furthermore, the Standing Committee of the NPC later adopted a resolution on the improvement of interpretation work of Chinese laws, providing:

> an interpretation of questions involving the specific application of laws and decrees in court trials shall be provided by the Supreme People's Court, and an interpretation of problems concerning the concrete application of laws and decrees in procuratorial practices shall be prescribed by the Supreme People's Procuratorate.

Furthermore, if there is any difference in principle between them, the Standing Committee of NPC will make final determination for interpretation or decision. Thus, the judicial interpretation has been considered as a formal source of law.[22]

The fundamental purpose of judicial interpretation by the Supreme People's Court and the Supreme People's Procuratorate is to clarify the issues raised in legal practice and to unify the understanding of law (Wang, 1995, p.572). The Procuratorate's interpretations of law are not binding and are of guiding nature while the Court's interpretations are binding. Specific to legal practice of criminal law, the Chinese judicial interpretation has the following functions (Wang, 1995):

1. Indicating how to correctly understand the meaning of the law;
2. Explaining the issues of the law;
3. Indicating the concrete standard of sentencing within the statutory punishments;
4. Clarifying the guilty line and line for giving a heavier punishment when the law requires "serious circumstances" or "particularly serious circumstances."
5. Clarifying the limitation of time for a particular law;
6. Explaining how to implement laws.

Wang (1995, p.575) points out that with function (4), it is typical for Chinese legislature to use "serious circumstances" in law as the threshold for convicting for an offense and to have "particularly serious circumstances" as the indicator for the heavier punishment in Chinese criminal law, and the "circumstances" need common knowledge to be understood, but it does not usually work well and therefore judicial explanation is needed for further description (Wang, 1995, p.575).

Wang (1995) further highlights that when compared with judges' opinions in case report of the courts in the United States and the Federal Republic of Germany, Chinese judicial interpretation typically covers a broader scope. The Chinese Supreme Court and Supreme Procuratorate have to do so mainly because of the general or incomplete character of the law (Wang, 1995). As in other countries, Chinese judicial explanations help to make the issues clear (Wang, 1995, p.577). Furthermore, in accordance with the tradition of continental law which Chinese law follows, a basic law should remain stable, but the changing social situations requires the law to make a timely response to them (Wang, 1995, p.577).[23]

Another consideration in the discussion of imprecise Chinese legal language is that the matter is also related to the problem of poor drafting. Peerenboom (2002, p.252) points out that, while PRC laws treat many issues in a general way, they often fail or omit to address some substantive legal issues. Presumably, such omissions are intended to afford greater flexibility in implementation or indicate a lack of consensus at the time of implementation. At other times the omission seems to be a mere oversight. Peerenboom (2002) argues that often the only possible explanation for the many omissions, inconsistencies, contradictions, and related maladies that plague much China's legislation is poor drafting, the lack of practical experience, and appreciation for law-making hierarchies on the part of the drafters.

Several judicial interpretations to the Criminal Law (1997), judicial interpretations have been issued in recent years.[24]

Most of these interpretations and opinions from the Supreme People's Court and the Procuratorate were issued to clarify vague wording in the Criminal Law (1997), or to quantify or specify what certain general, ambiguous or vague words mean, for instance, *qingjie yanzhong* (circumstances [of the offense] are serious), *qingjie jiaoqing* (circumstances [of the offense] are light or not serious), *shu'e juda* (the amount [of money involved] is huge), *shu'e jiaoda* (the amount is rather large) in relation to property damage, bribery, and others to determine appropriate punishment.

Another aspect although not directly related to the issues under consideration here is the poor and improper use of language in Chinese law in general, and in the writing of court decisions by judges in China. Chinese courts are required to publish their decisions, but many have failed to do so. One reason, as reported, for not publishing judgments by some of the courts is believed to be the numerous linguistic errors found in court decisions and the poor writing skills of judges. Some courts feel too embarrassed to publish such poorly written works. Linguistic errors found in Chinese decisions include ungrammatical or wrong usage, use of slang, inappropriate use of words, accidental omission or addition of words, typographical errors, punctuation errors, impropriate use of classical Chinese mixed with colloquialism, mistakes in writing litigants' names, among others. It was reported that some judges in Sichuan Province were accorded with disciplinary and financial sanctions in 2004 for the numerous linguistic errors in their judgments after the court in Sichuan held that a linguistic error in a court decision renders the judgment a wrong decision (see Cao, 2004).

POSSIBLE LEGAL CONSEQUENCES OF CHINESE LINGUISTIC UNCERTAINTY

A number of implications can be drawn from the foregoing discussion. Language used in law as in other areas is characterized by indeterminacy, or "open textureness" as Hart (1992 [1961]) calls it, with a core of "settled meaning" and a "penumbra of uncertainty." The English legal language is not immune from imprecise and ambiguous expressions (see Solan, 2004, Charnock, 2006). English legal jargon such as "fair and reasonable," "due process of law" is vague and elusive. So are abstract legal expressions such as "justice," "due diligence," and "reasonable endeavours". However, I see the Chinese language and legal language more indeterminate than its English counterpart. If we describe this indeterminacy in terms of Hart's "core" and "penumbra," the Chinese settled core would seem smaller and the penumbra and open textureness larger. If this is the case, then, would Chinese law be more uncertain than common law in English?

I believe that Chinese law should not be more uncertain than English law, but in reality, it is, at present and for the foreseeable future. Major reasons, I believe, are the lack of coherent and consistent legal narrative in China; the lack of precedent which may settle indeterminate cases in reference to a settled past legal history as it exists in English common law; and furthermore, the lack of an independent judiciary in China. Legal rules and judicial interpretation I refer to here differ from legislative interpretation practiced in China when the Supreme People's Court issues binding legislative interpretation to define statutory provisions. This is very different from case law determined on the basis of legal dispute and precedent.

Endicott (2000), in his study of indeterminate language and law in English, points to a paradox in law. On the one hand, he notes that, for law and the rule of law, there is a consensus about the requirements: law must be open, clear, coherent, prospective, and stable (see Raz, 1979). Law that fails to meet these requirements would not be law, and a legal system that lacks them to some degree is defective in a legal sense (Endicott, 2000, p.185). So, such linguistic "unclarity," be it vagueness, ambiguity, or generality, must be eliminated in the language used in law, otherwise law and rule of law cannot be attained and arbitrary government will result. On the other hand, linguistic uncertainty is inherent in language, and cannot be eliminated, thus is "ineliminable" from a legal system (Endicott, 2000, p.190). Furthermore, law commonly appeals to moral considerations, and such general moral evaluative considerations are necessarily vague. This is the most important source of vagueness in law (Endicott, 2003, p.114). Not every law needs to be vague, but all legal systems necessarily have vague, general, and uncertain laws. In fact, it is inconceivable for a community to be completely regulated with precise and exact laws (Endicott, 2000, p.190). Given the above dilemma, Endicott argues that a vague law does not necessarily represent a deficit in the rule of law. By the same token, replacing a vague law with a precise law does not necessarily bring a community closer to the ideal of the rule of law (Endicott, 2000, p.191). But what is important here is that the judiciary plays a critical role in making law certain and stable.

In China's case, due to historical reasons and the influence of the civil law system and other legal and political reasons, its judiciary has not been able to fulfill the necessary role in stabilizing the law. The judiciary has been perennially weak and ineffectual. Furthermore, due to the lack of established legal rules and principles as they exist in common law, uncertain laws enable authorities to make arbitrary decisions or exempt their actions from the law as it happens not infrequently throughout China's modern history. For instance, in common law, one long-established rule in contract law is the parole evidence rule, that is, written instrument is deemed as the complete and final expression of the contract parties and cannot be varied or contradicted by oral evidence. There are also numerous legal rules in legislative interpretation in common law (e.g., see Côté, 1999; Holland and Webb, 2003; Bennion, 2007). In China, courts in recent years have started to formulate legal rules, but they are not systematic and not binding. There is not yet a coherent body of legal principles or rules.

As we know, all languages are inherently uncertain, but an argument could be advanced that some languages may be more uncertain and indeterminate than others. As shown by the examples cited in this chapter, certain linguistic features in Chinese may be prone to produce more uncertainties when compared with other languages, such as English. I argue that the Chinese legal language is more uncertain than the English legal language. In this regard, a German jurist, Grossfeld (cited in Weisflog, 1987, p.206) believes that the English legal language, compared with the German legal language, is less concentrated or more "open-textured"; and English legal concepts are vaguer. There are different views as to whether one language may be more ambiguous than others. For instance, Bally (1944) was skeptical of the idea, but Jespersen (1964) did not rule out *a priori* the possibility that some languages could be less inadequate than other languages, or that ambiguities may increase with the development of a language, both cited in Kooij (1971, pp.3–4).

In addition, it seems that Chinese language users, in this case, Chinese lawmakers and legal drafters, often take advantage of linguistic uncertainty. Inappropriate and defective use of language in Chinese legislation produces more uncertainty. Another observation is that Chinese legal language tends to be ordinary, that is, very close to ordinary, nontechnical, nonspecialist Chinese. The Chinese legal language has a growing legal vocabulary. However, in terms of syntax and other grammatical features, legal Chinese is very much like ordinary formal Chinese, which is in sharp contrast to legal English with an obsession with precision, sometimes bordering on excessiveness and incomprehensibility. Legal Chinese is often just as loose as ordinary Chinese. Improvement has been noted in recent years but adequate expression in Chinese legal drafting within the linguistic constraints is critical. Further improvement in this area will undoubtedly reduce some of the uncertainties in Chinese law, even though indeterminacy in language and law can never be eliminated, in Chinese and other tongues.

NOTES

1. http://www.bloomberg.com/news/articles/2014-05-12/picking-quarrels-and-provoking-troubles-the-crime-sweeping-china.

2. This would contradict and prevail over the legal principle that the current Chinese criminal law recognizes, that is, where acts are explicitly defined as criminal acts in law, the offenders shall be convicted and punished in accordance with law; otherwise, they shall not be convicted or punished. It is a modified version of *nulla poena sine lege* (there is "no crime without law making it so and no punishment except in accordance with a statutory rule"): see Li (2010).

3. http://news.ifeng.com/opinion/special/xunxinzishi/ See also http://www.ftchinese.com/story/001060493

4. http://www.bloomberg.com/news/articles/2014-05-12/picking-quarrels-and-provoking-troubles-the-crime-sweeping-china: Chinese blind activist Chen Guangcheng, now living in exile in the United States, was charged for "gathering a crowd to disturb traffic order"; and rights advocate Xu Zhiyong, who is now serving a four-year jail term in Beijing, was charged under Article 291 with "gathering a crowd to disrupt public order"; Former rights lawyer Pu Zhiqiang was also charged

and convicted in 2015 under the offense of picking quarrels and provoking troubles among other charges.

5. http://sinosphere.blogs.nytimes.com/2015/07/27/q-and-a-chen-zhonglin-on-picking-quarrels-online/?login=email&action=click&contentCollection=AsiaPacific&module=RelatedCoverage&region=EndOfArticle&pgtype=article&mtrref=www.nytimes.com

6. https://www.law.berkeley.edu/article/picking-quarrels-casts-shadow-over-chinese-law/

7. Interpretation of the Supreme People's Court and the Supreme People's Procuratorate on Several Issues concerning the Specific Application of Law in the Handling of Defamation through Information Networks and Other Criminal Cases (2013): http://lawinfochina.com/display.aspx?id=16184&lib=law. Interpretation of the Supreme People's Court and the Supreme People's Procuratorate on Several Issues concerning the Application of Law in the Handling of Criminal Cases of Picking Quarrels and Making Trouble (2013): http://www.lawinfochina.com/display.aspx?id=14963&lib=law.See also http://sinosphere.blogs.nytimes.com/2015/07/27/q-and-a-chen-zhonglin-on-picking-quarrels-online/?login=email&action=click&contentCollection=AsiaPacific&module=RelatedCoverage&region=EndOfArticle&pgtype=article&mtrref=www.nytimes.com

8. A man in Beijing was arrested and detained in 2016 for *xunxin zishi* after he scratched 30 cars following fights with his wife: http://www.bj148.org/zzgjj/zzdt/201609/t20160914_1250720.html

9. A woman was sentenced by a court in Shaanxi Province in 2016 for *xunxin zishi* to two years' imprisonment for petitioning in Beijing related to her administrative detention as a result of a fight with another: http://www.thepaper.cn/newsDetail_forward_1526264

10. In 2014, a woman in the city of Wuhan was sentenced to four years' jail on the charge of *xunxin zishi* for assaulting and harassing medical staff related to her plastic surgery: http://www.hb.xinhuanet.com/2014-12/03/c_1113494113.htm. See also http://3g.ifeng.com/news/sharenews.f?aid=110446677&mid=&vt=5&srctag=cpz_sh_imtj_p

11. http://weibo.com/1909545300/E99357pnn

12. https://www.cpj.org/2016/06/two-chinese-journalists-detained-for-picking-quarr.php

13. Former rights lawyer Pu Zhiqiang was prosecuted and given a three year suspended sentence on the charge of "picking quarrels and provoking trouble" and "inciting ethnic hatred" for his seven Weibo posts in 2015: http://www.nytimes.com/2015/12/23/world/asia/conviction-of-pu-zhiqiang-affirms-chinas-determination-to-muzzle-rights-lawyers.html?_r=0; http://www.nytimes.com/2015/12/15/world/asia/pu-zhiqiang-china-trial-weibo-posts.html?action=click&contentCollection=Asia%20Pacific&module=RelatedCoverage&region=EndOfArticle&pgtype=article

14. See, for example, *Raffles v. Wichelhaus* 2 Hurl. & C. 906, 159 Eng. Rep. 375 (Ex. 1864); and *Frigaliment Importing Co. v. B.N.S. International Sales Corp.*, 190 F.Supp. 116 (S.D.N.Y. 1960).

15. For discussions on indeterminacy and the law see Bix (1993), Stratman (2004), Bhatia (2005).

16. Keller (1994, p.749), citing Ma Xiaohong, points out that the principles of generality and flexibility in contemporary Chinese lawmaking have a close parallel with the Chinese imperial legislative tradition. Ma Xiaohong, cited in Keller (1994), believes that the late imperial Ming and Qing legislation was characterized by generality of language, and contemporary Chinese legislative theorists often praise and invoke the views of imperial lawmakers in support of their contemporary practices.

17. Note that in Chinese court, only the law enacted in the Chinese language is valid, not English or any other translation. Thus, some of these uncertainties will not become an issue while others will.

18. See, for example, *Re Toal Application for Judicial Review* [2006] NIQB 44, para 10.

19. See Lewis (2012) for her discussion of the meaning of "huge," "extremely huge" as used in Article 395 of the Criminal Law (1997). See also Li (2010) on the meaning of "large" and "especially large," and "major circumstances" and "minor circumstances" in relation to theft under Chinese law.

20. Similarly, as Economy (2004, p.102, citing Nagle, 1996) reports, China's Water Pollution Prevention and Control Law (1984) states that "enterprises and other undertakings which cause serious water pollution must eliminate pollution within a stipulated time." What constitutes "serious" water pollution is not self-evident, nor is the meaning of "enterprises and other undertakings." The U.S. Clean Water Act (1977), by contrast, specifies in much great detail the type and amount of pollution that particular sources may emit though the procedures for establishing effluent limitations and water quality standards and through the permit process. Economy (2004, p.102) writes that it is difficult for the Chinese to know what is prohibited and what can be called to account through legal redress. In one case, when a local environmental protection bureau attempted to sue a local chemical company for failing to pay its discharge fees over a two-year period, the bureau at first could not decide whether the basis for the suit rested on the enterprise's failure to pay for small amounts of its discharge fees or its failure to pay over-standard fees. Moreover, when the local court, scheduled to hear the case, pointed out that inconsistencies between national regulations and local rules might make a suit difficult. Economy (2004, p.102) says that ambiguity in laws also permits conscious exploration by enterprises or other actors, and the Chinese even have a saying: "national policies, local countermeasures," to describe the practice of exploiting the ambiguity of national laws and regulations to figure out ways around them.

21. This is not to say that Chinese statutes do not have definitions. In fact, Chinese statutes normally give some definitions to the key terms at the beginning of statutes, for instance in the Chinese Environmental Protection Law (1989), Article 2 states: "'Environment' in this law refers to the total body of all natural elements and artificially transformed natural elements affecting human existence and development, which includes the atmosphere, water, seas, land, minerals, forests, grasslands, wildlife, natural and human historical relics, nature reserves, historical sites and scenic spots and urban and rural areas, among others." But such definitions are usually restricted to very few key terms in a statute, for example, in the Environmental Protection Law (1989), "environment" is the only definition. Furthermore, one can also

argue that many of the terms used to define the keywords need definition themselves. For instance, what would be considered "wildlife" as used in the above definition is not defined.

22. According to judicial statistical data, about 4,000 judicial interpretations have been made by the Supreme People's Court alone or jointly with the Supreme People's Procuratorate from 1949 to 2000 (Zhai, 2002).

23. Wang (1995, p.577) states that, theoretically, the Chinese legislature can make use of the method of legislative explanation to clarify or further expand the laws, which is already provided in Chinese law and is demanded by the legal circle in China, but due to the current strenuous tasks of legislative works and the legislative tradition, the Chinese legislature has not yet attended to these relatively small and routine matters.

24. For example, see the Interpretation of the Supreme People's Court and the Supreme People's Procuratorate Concerning Certain Issues Related to the Specific Application of Law in Handling Criminal Cases Involving Gambling (2005); the Interpretation of the Supreme People's Court Concerning Certain Issues Related to the Specific Application of Law in Handling Criminal Cases Involving Undermining Production Safety in Mines (2007).

Bibliography

Alexy, Robert, 1992, "Individual Rights and Collective Goods", in Carlos Nino (ed.), *Rights*, Aldershot, Dartmouth, 163–184.

Alford, William P. 1984, "Of Arsenic and Old Laws: Looking Anew at Criminal Justice in Late Imperial China", *California Law Review*, 72(6): 1180–1246.

———. 1986, "The Inscrutable Occidental? Implications of Roberto Unger's Uses and Abuses of the Chinese Past", *Texas Law Review*, 64(5): 915–972.

———. 1995, *To Steal a Book is an Elegant Offense: Intellectual Property Law in Chinese Civilization*, Stanford, Stanford University Press.

———. 1999, "A Second Great Wall? China's Post-Cultural Revolution Project of Legal Construction", *Cultural Dynamics*, 11(2): 193–213.

Alford, William P. and Liebman, Benjamin L. 2001, "Clean Air, Clear Processes? The Struggle Over Air Pollution Law in the PRC", *Hastings Law Journal*, 52: 703–748.

Allinson, Robert E. (ed.), 1989, *Understanding the Chinese Mind: The Philosophical Roots*, Oxford, Oxford University Press.

Ames, Roger T. 1988, "Rites as Rights: The Confucian Alternative", in Leroy S. Rouner (ed.), *Human Rights and the World's Religions*, Notre Dame, University of Notre Dame Press, 199–217.

———. 1991, "From Confucius to Xunzi: Ambiguity of Order in Classical Confucianism", in Roger T. Ames, Sin-Wai Chan and Mau-Sang Ng (eds.), *Interpreting Culture Through Translation*, Hong Kong, The Chinese University of Hong Kong, 1–36.

———. 2001, "New Confucianism: A Native Response to Western Philosophy", in Shiping Hua (ed.), *Chinese Political Culture (1989–2000)*, New York/London, M.E. Sharpe, 70–102.

Ames, Roger T., Chan, Sin-Wai and Ng, Mau-Sang (eds.), 1991, *Interpreting Culture Through Translation*, Hong Kong, The Chinese University of Hong Kong.

Ames, Roger T. and Rosemont, Henry, Jr. 1998, *The Analects of Confucius: A Philosophical Translation*, New York, Ballantine Books.

André, James St. 2004, "But do They have a Notion of Justice?" *The Translator*, 10(1): 1–31.

Angle, Stephen, 2002, *Human Rights and Chinese Thought: A Cross-Cultural Inquiry*, Oxford, Oxford University Press.

Anonymous, 2010, "China and the Principle of Self-Determination of Peoples", *St Antony's International Review,* 6(1): 79–102.

Aristotle. 1997, *Politics*, translated, with introduction, analysis, and notes by Peter L. Phillips Simpson, Chapel Hill, University of North Carolina Press.

Atlas, J.D. 1989, *Philosophy without Ambiguity: A Logico-Linguistic Essay*, Oxford, Oxford University Press.

Austin, John L. 1962, *How to do Things With Words*, Cambridge, Harvard University Press.

———. 1979, *Philosophical Papers*, 3rd edition, edited by J.O. Urmson and G.J. Warnock, Oxford, Clarendon Press.

Bach, Kent and Harnish, Robert M. 1979, *Linguistic Communication and Speech Acts*, Cambridge, The MIT Press.

Belkin, Ira, 2000, "China's Criminal Justice System: A Work in Progress", *Washington Journal of Modern China,* 6(2): 61–84.

———. 2011, "China's Tortuous Path Toward Ending Torture in Criminal Investigations", *Columbia Journal of Asian Law*, 24: 273–302.

Benney, Jonathan, 2013, *Defending Rights in Contemporary China*, London, Routledge.

Bennion, F. 2002, *Statutory Interpretation*, 4th edition, London, Butterworths.

Bentham, Jeremy, 1996 [1789], *An Introduction to the Principles of Morals and Legislation*, B.J.H. Burns and H. L. A. Hart (eds.), Oxford, Clarendon Press.

Bernhardt, Kathryn and Huang, Philip C.C. (eds.), 1994, *Civil Law in Qing and Republican China*, Stanford, Stanford University Press.

Bhatia, V., Engberg, J., Gotti, M. and Heller, D. (eds.), 2005, *Vagueness in Normative Texts,* Bern, Peter Lang.

Bielsa, Esperanca and Bassnett, Susan, 2009, *Translation in Global News,* New York, Routledge.

Biggerstaff, Knight, 1961, *The Earliest Modern Government Schools in China*, Ithaca, Cornell University Press.

Bix, Brian H. (ed.), 1993, *Law, Language and Legal Determinacy*, Oxford, Clarendon Press.

———. 2003, "Can Theories of Meaning and Reference Solve the Problem of Legal Determinacy?" *Ratio Juris*, 16(3): 281–295.

Black, Max, 1970 [1949], *Language and Philosophy: Studies in Method*, Ithaca and London, Cornell University Press.

Bloom, A.H. 1981, *The Linguistic Shaping of Thought: A Study in the Impact of Language on Thinking in China and West*, Hillsdale, NJ, Lawrence Erlbaum.

Bodde, Derk, 1981, *Essays on Chinse Civilization*, Princeton, Princeton University Press.

———. 1991, *Chinese Thought, Society, and Science: The Intellectual and Social Background of Science and Technology in Pre-modern China*, Honolulu, University of Hawaii Press.

Bodde, Derk and Morris, Clarence, 1973, *Law in Imperial China, Exemplified by 190 Ch'ing Dynasty Cases with Historical, Social, and Judicial Commentaries*, Philadelphia, University of Pennsylvania Press.

Bontekoe, Ron, and Stepaniants, Marietta (eds.), 1997, *Justice and Democracy: Cross-Cultural Perspectives*, Honolulu, University of Hawai'i Press.

Bowers, Frederick, 1989, *The Linguistic Aspects of Legislative Expression*, Vancouver, University of British Columbia.

Broekman, Jan M. and Backer, Larry, Cata, (eds.), 2015, *Signs in Law: A Source Book*, Berlin, Springer.

Brook, Timothy, Bourgon, Jerome, and Blue, Gregory, 2008, *Death by a Thousand Cuts*, Cambridge, Harvard University Press.

Burke, Lucy, Crowley, Tony and Girvin, Alan (eds.), 2000, *The Routledge Language and Cultural Theory Reader*, London/New York, Routledge.

Bussani, Mauro and Sebok, Anthony J. (eds.), 2015, *Comparative Tort Law: Global Perspectives*, Cheltenham, Edward Elgar.

Cai, Yuanpei, 2007 [1933], *Zhongguo lunlixue shi (History of Ethics in China)*, Nanjing, Jiangsu Literature and Art Publishing House.

Cao, Deborah, 1996, "Towards A Model of Translation Proficiency", *Target: International Journal for Translation Studies*, 8(2): 325–340.

———. 1997, "Consideration in Translating Chinese/English Contracts", *Meta*, 42(4): 661–669.

———. 1998, "The Illocutionary Act in Translating Chinese Legislation", *Babel: International Journal of Translation,* 44(3): 244–253.

———. 1999, "'Ought to' As a Chinese Legal Performative?" *International Journal for the Semiotics of Law,* 12(2): 153–169.

———. 2001, "*Fazhi* vs/and/or Rule of Law: A Semiotic Venture Into Chinese Law", *International Journal for the Semiotics of Law*, 14(3): 223–247.

———. 2002, "Finding the Elusive Equivalents in Chinese/English Legal Translation", *Babel: International Journal of Translation,* 48(4): 330–341.

———. 2004, *Chinese Law: A Language Perspective*, Aldershot, Ashgate.

———. 2007a, *Translating Law*, Foreword by Justice Michael Kirby, Clevedon, Multilingual Matters.

———. 2007b, "Inter-lingual Uncertainty in Bilingual and Multilingual Law", *Journal of Pragmatics*, 39: 69–83.

———. 2009, "Illocutionary Acts of Chinese Legislative Language", *Journal of Pragmatics*, 41: 1329–1340.

———. 2010a, *Animal Law in Australia and New Zealand*, foreword by Justice Michael Kirby, Sydney, Thomson-Reuters/Lawbook.

———. 2010b, "Legal Translation", in Alison Johnson and Malcolm Coulthard (eds.), *The Routledge Handbook of Forensic Linguistics*, London, Routledge, 74–93.

———. 2010c, "Legal Translation", in Yves Gamier and Luc van Doorslaer (eds.), *Handbook of Translation Studies*, Amsterdam, John Benjamins, 191–195.

———. 2010d, "Judicial Interpretation of Bilingual/Multilingual Laws: A European and Hong Kong Comparison", in Joanna Jemielniak and Przemysław Mikłaszewicz (eds.), *Interpretation of Law in the Global World: from Particularism to a Universal Approach*, Berlin, Springer, 71–86.

———. 2011, "Foreword: Power of and to Language in Law", in A. Wagner and L. Cheng (eds.), *Exploring Courtroom Discourse: The Language of Power and Control,* Aldershot, Ashgate, xv–xvii.

———. 2012a, *Dang gougou qingqing kuqi shi (While the Dog Gently Weeps: Humans, Law and Sentience*), Changchun, Jilin University Press.

———. 2012b, "Linguistic Uncertainty and Legal Transparency: Statutory Interpretation in China and Australia", in V. K. Bhartia, C. A. Hafner, L. Miller and A. Wagner (eds.), *Transparency, Power and Control: Perspectives on Legal Communication,* Aldershot, Ashgate, 13–30.

———. 2013a, "Legal Translation Studies", in Carmen Millan and Francesca Bartrina (eds.), *The Routledge Handbook of Translation Studies,* London, Routledge, 415–424.

———. 2013b, "Legal Translation", in Carol A. Chapelle (ed.), *The Blackwell Encyclopedia of Applied Linguistics*, London, Wiley-Blackwell.

———. 2014, "Teaching and Learning Legal Translation", *Semiotica*, 201: 103–119.

———. 2015a, *Animal Law in Australia,* Sydney, Thomson-Reuters/Lawbook.

———. 2015b, *Animals in China: Law and Society*, London, Macmillan.

———. 2015c, "Afterword: Trials and Tribulations of Legal Translation", in Anne Wagner et al. (eds.), *Ashgate Handbook on Legal Translation,* Aldershot, Ashgate, 303–315.

———. 2017, "On the Universality of Rights: Absence and Presence of Rights in the Chinese Language", *Intercultural Pragmatics*, 14(2): 277–292.

———. 2018 (forthcoming), "Desperately Seeking 'Justice' in Classcial Chinese: On the Meaning of *Yi*", *International Journal for the Semiotics of Law*.

———. 2018 (forthcoming), "Chinese Legal Thought: Mohist School", in Mortimer Sellers and Stephan Kirste (eds.), *Encyclopedia of the Philosophy of Law and Social Philosophy*, Amsterdam, Springer.

Cao, Deborah, and Mannoni, Michele, 2017, "Are There Illegal Rights in Chinese Law? On the Meaning of Feifa Quanyi", *The Chinese Journal of Comparative Law*, 5(1):190–204.

Cao, Deborah and White, Steven (eds.), 2016, *Animal Law and Welfare: International Perspectives*, Berlin/New York, Springer.

Cao, Deborah, and Zhao, Xingmin, 2006, *Lianheguo fanyi (Translation at the United Nations),* Beijing, Foreign Translation and Publishing Press.

———. 2008, "Translation at the United Nations as a Specialised Translation", *Journal of Specialised Translation,* 9(1): 39–54.

———. 2013, "Legal Translation at the United Nations", in Anabel Borja Albi and Fernando Prieto Ramos (eds.), *Legal Translation in Context*, Berlin, Peter Lang, 203–220.

Carroll, John Bissell, 1964, *Language and Thought*, Englewood Cliffs, New Jersey, Prentice-Hall Inc.

Carzo, Domenico and Jackson, Bernard S. (eds.), 1985, *Semiotics, Law and Social Science*, Rome, Gangemi editore and the Liverpool Law Review.

Ch'en, Paul Hen-Chao, 1979, *Chinese Legal Tradition under the Mongols: The Code of 1291 as Reconstructed*, Princeton, Princeton University Press.

Ch'ü, T'ung-tsu, 1965, *Law and Society in Traditional China*, Paris, Mouton & Co.
Ch'ü, T'ung-tsu, 1969, *Local Government in China under the Ch'ing*, Stanford, Stanford University Press.
Ch'ü, T'ung-tsu (Qu Tongzu), 1998, *Qu Tongzu faxue lunzhu ji (Qu Tongzu's Works on Law)*, Beijing, Zhongguo zhengfa daxue chubanshe.
Chan, Joseph, 1994a, "Making Sense of Confucian Justice", *Philosophy East and West*, 44: 559–575.
———. 1994b, "The Asian Challenge to Universal Human Rights: A Philosophical Appraisal", in James T.H. Tang (ed.), *Human Rights and International Relations in the Asia-Pacific Region*, London, Pinter, 25–38.
———. 1999, "A Confucian Perspective on Human Rights for Contemporary China", in Joanne R. Bauer and Daniel A. Bell (eds.), *The East Asian Challenge for Human Rights*, Cambridge, Cambridge University Press, 212–240.
———. 2009, "Is There a Confucian Perspective on Social Justice?" in Takashi Shogimen and Cary J. Nederman (eds.), *Western Political Thought in Dialogue with Asia*, Lanham, Lexington, 261–277.
Chang, Han-Liang, 1998, "Chinese Ideograms", in Paul Bouissac (ed.), *Encyclopedia of Semiotics*, Oxford, Oxford University Press, 114–116.
Chang, Wejen, 2016, *In Search of the Way,* Edinburgh, Edinburgh University Press.
Chao, Yuen Ren, 1959, "Ambiguity in Chinese", in *Sinological Studies Dedicated to Bernhard Karlgren*, Copenhagen, Ejar Munksgaard Copenhagen, 1–14.
———. 1968, *A Grammar of Spoken Chinese*, Berkeley, University of California Press.
Charnock, R. 2006, "Clear Ambiguity", in A. Wagner and S. Cacciaguidi-Fahy (eds.), *Legal Language and the Search for Clarity,* Berns, Peter Lang, 65–103.
Chen, Albert Hung-Yee, 1992, *An Introduction to the Legal System of the People's Republic of China*, Singapore, Butterworths Asia.
———. 1999, "Towards a Legal Enlightenment, Discussion in Contemporary China on the Rule of Law", *Pacific Basin Law Journal*, 17: 125–165.
Chen, An, 1999, *Restructuring Political Power in China, Alliances and Opposition: 1878–1998*, London, Lynne Rienner Publishers.
Chen, Jianfu, 1999, *Chinese Law: Towards an Understanding of Chinese Law, its Nature and Development*, The Hague, Kluwer Law International.
———. 2008, *Chinese Law: Context and Transformation*, Leiden, Martinus Nijhoff Publisher.
Chen, Li and Zelin, Madeleine (eds.), 2015, *Chinese Law: Knowledge Practice and Transformation, 1530s to 1950s,* Leiden, Brill.
Chen, Qiaojian, 2016, "Xiu'e, yi and zhengdang (Shame, Yi and Righteousness of Mencius)", *Journal of Sun Yat-sen University*, 56(2): 136–145.
Chen, Rong, Hu, Chunmei, and He, Lin, 2013, "*Lying* between English and Chinese: An Intercultural Comparative Study", *Intercultural Pragmatics*, 10(3): 375–401.
Chen, Zhongcheng, 2001, *English-Chinese/Chinese-English Corrective Glossary of Legal Terms*, Beijing, Law Press.
Cheng, Chung-Ying, 1989, "Chinese Metaphysics as Non-metaphysics: Confucian and Daoist Insights into the Nature of Reality", in Robert E. Allinson (ed.),

Understanding the Chinese Mind: The Philosophical Roots, Oxford, Oxford University Press, 167–208.

———. 1991, *New Dimensions of Confucian and Neo-Confucian Philosophy*, Albany, SUNY.

———. 1997, "Can We Do Justice to All Theories of Justice?" in Ron Bontekoe and Marietta Stepaniants (eds.), *Justice and Democracy: Cross-Cultural Perspectives*, Honolulu, University of Hawai'i Press, 181–198.

Child, Barbara, 1992, *Drafting Legal Documents: Principles and Practices*, St Paul, MN, West Publishing Co.

Chiu, Hungdah, 1970, "The Development of Chinese International Law Terms and the Problems of Their Translation into English", in Jerome Alan Cohen (ed.), *Contemporary Chinese Law: Research Problems and Perspectives*, Cambridge, Harvard University Press, 139–157.

Choukroune, Leïla, 2016, "The Language of Rights and the Politics of Law: Perspectives on China's Last Legal Ditch Struggle", *International Journal for the Semiotic of Law*, 29: 779–803.

Chroust, Anto-Hermann and Osborn, David L. 1942, "Aristotle's Conception of Justice", *Notre Dame Law Review*, 17(20): 129–143.

Clarke, Donald C. 1996a, "Methodologies for Research in Chinese Law", *University of British Columbia Law Review*, 30: 201–209.

———. 1996b, "Power and Politics in the Chinese Court System: The Enforcement of Civil Judgements", *Columbia Journal of Asian Law*, 10(1): 1–92.

———. 2003. "Empirical Research into the Chinese Judicial System", in E. G. Jensen, and T.C. Heller (eds.), *Beyond Common Knowledge: Empirical Approaches to the Rule of Law,* Stanford, Stanford University Press, 164–192.

———. 2010. New Approaches to the Study of Political Order in China. *Modern China*, 36(1), 87–99.

Cohen, Jerome Alan (ed.), 1970, *Contemporary Chinese Law: Research Problems and Perspectives*, Cambridge, Harvard University Press.

———. 1969, "The Chinese Communist Party and Judicial Independence: 1949–59", *Harvard Law Review*, 82(5): 967–1006.

———. 2011, "The Suppression of China's Human Rights Lawyers: Do Foreign Lawyers Care?", http://usali.org/publications/the-suppression-of-chinas-human-rights-lawyers-do-foreign-lawyers-care-2.

———. 2013a, "Introductory Reflections", in Mike McConville and Eva Pils, (eds.), *Comparative Perspectives on Criminal Justice in China*, Cheltenham, Edward Elgar, 3–12.

———. 2013b, "Politics and Criminal Justice", in Mike McConville and Eva Pils (eds.), *Comparative Perspectives on Criminal Justice in China*, Cheltenham, Edward Elgar, 439–444.

———. 2016, "A Looming Crisis for China's Legal System", *Foreign Policy*, 22 February 2016.

Cohen, Jerome Alan, Edwards, R. Randall and Chen, Fu-Mei Chang (eds.), 1980, *Essays on China's Legal Tradition*, Princeton, Princeton University Press.

Confucian Analects was translated by James Legge, 1970 [1893], *The Chinese Classics, Volume I: Confucian Analects, the Great Learning and the Doctrine of the Mean*, Hong Kong, Hong Kong University Press.

Conner, Alison W. 2000, "True Confessions: Chinese Confessions Then and Now", in Karen Turner, James V. Feinerman and R. Kent Guy (eds.), *The Limits of the Rule of Law in China*, Seattle, The University of Washington Press, 132–162.

Connery, Christopher Leigh, 1998, *The Empire of the Text: Writing and Authority in Early Imperial China*, New York/Oxford, Rowman and Littlefield Publishers.

Cooke, Maeve, 1998, "Introduction", in Maeve Cooke (ed.), *On the Pragmatics of Communication*, Cambridge, The MIT Press.

Côté, P. A. 1999, *L'Interprétation des Lois*, 3rd edition, Cowansville, Yvon Blais.

Cotterrell, Roger, 2014, "The Concept for Law for Global Legal Pluralism?" in S.P.Donlan and L.H. Urscheler (eds.), *Concepts of Law: Comparative, Jurisprudential and Social Science Perspectives*, Farnham, Ashgate, 193–208.

Covell, Ralph, 1978, *W.A.P. Martin: Pioneer of Progress in China*, Washington, DC, Christian University Press.

Creel, Herrlee G. 1953, *Chinese Thought from Confucius to Mao Tse-Tung*, Chicago, Chicago University Press.

———. 1980, "Legal Institutions and Procedures During the Chou Dynasty", in Jerome Alan Cohen, R. Randall Edwards and Fu-Mei Chang Chen (eds.), *Essays on China's Legal Tradition*, Princeton, Princeton University Press, 26–55.

Cua, Antonio S. (ed.), 2012, *Encyclopedia of Chinese Philosophy*, New York/London, Routledge.

Danet, Brenda, 1980, "Language in the Legal Process", *Law and Society*, 14(3): 447–563.

De Bary, William Theodore, 1995, "The Constitutional Tradition in China", *Journal of Chinese Law*, 9(1): 7–34.

———. 1996, *The Trouble with Confucianism*, Cambridge, Harvard University Press.

———. 1998, *Asian Values and Human Rights: A Confucian Communitarian Perspective*, Cambridge, Harvard University Press.

De Bary, William Theodore and Bloom, Irene (eds.), 1999, *Sources of Chinese Tradition*, 2nd edition, Volume 1, New York, Columbia University Press.

De Bary, William Theodore and Tu, Weiming (eds.), 1998, *Confucianism and Human Rights*, New York, Columbia University Press.

De Francis, John, 1984, *The Chinese Language: Fact and Fantasy*, Honolulu, University of Hawaii Press.

———. 1989, *Visible Speech: The Diverse Oneness of Writing Systems*, Honolulu, University of Hawaii Press.

Deng, Feng, (undated), "Corrective Justice in Confucian Legal Tradition: A Nonexistent Concept", working paper presented at Harvard-Yenching's Confucianism Workshop.

De Vattel, E. 1863, *The Law of Nations*, Philadelphia, T. & J. W. Johnsen.

Devitt, Michael and Sterelny, Kim, 1999, *Language and Reality: An Introduction to the Philosophy of Language*, Oxford, Blackwell.

Dong, Zhongshu, 2015, *Luxuriant Gems of the Spring and Autumn*, 2015, attributed to Dong Zhongshu, edited and translated by Sarah A. Queen, and John S. Major, New York, Columbia University Press.

Dunbar, Robin, Knight, Chris and Power, Camilla (eds.), 1999, *The Evolution of Culture: An Interdisciplinary View*, Edinburgh, Edinburgh University Press.

Duranti, Alessandro, 1997, *Linguistic Anthropology*, Cambridge, Cambridge University Press.

Duranti, Alessandro and Goodwin, Charles (eds.), 1992, *Rethinking Context: Language as an Interactive Phenomenon*, Cambridge, Cambridge University Press.

Duyvendak, J. J. L. 1963 [1928], *The Book of Lord Shang: A Classic of the Chinese School of Law*, Chicago, University of Chicago Press.

Dworkin, Ronald, 1977, *Taking Rights Seriously*, Cambridge, Harvard University Press.

Eco, Umberto, 1976, *A Theory of Semiotics*, Bloomington, Indiana University Press.

———. 1979, *The Role of the Reader*, Bloomington, Indiana University Press.

———. 1984, *Semiotics and the Philosophy of Language*, London, Macmillan.

———. 1992, *Interpretations and Overinterpretation*, with Umberto Eco, Richard Rorty, Jonathan Culler and Christine Brooke-Rose, edited by Stefan Collini, Cambridge, Cambridge University Press.

———. 1996, *From Marco Polo to Leibniz: Stories of Intercultural Misunderstanding*, a lecture presented to the Italian Academy for Advanced Studies in America, 10 December, 1996.

Economy, E. C. 2004, *The River Runs Black: The Environmental Challenge to China's Future*, Ithaca/London, Cornell University Press.

Edwards, R. Randle, 1986, "Civil and Social Rights: Theory and Practice in Chinese Law Today," in R. Randle Edwards, Louis Henkin and Andrew J. Nathan (eds.), *Human Rights in Contemporary China*, New York, Columbia University Press, 41–76.

Edwards, R. Randle, Henkin, Louis and Nathan, Andrew J. (eds.), 1986, *Human Rights in Contemporary China*, New York, Columbia University Press.

Empson, William, 1970, *Seven Types of Ambiguity*, 3rd edition, London, Chatto and Windus.

Endicott, Timothy A.O. 2000, *Vagueness in Law*, Oxford, Oxford University Press.

———. 2003, "Raz on Gaps: The Surprising Part", in Lukas H. Meyer, Stanley L. Paulson and Thomas W. Pogge (eds.), *Rights, Culture, and the Law: Themes from the Legal and Political Philosophy of Joseph Raz*, Oxford, Oxford University Press, 99–115.

Fang, Weigui, 2000, "Dong xi yang kou zizhu zhi li" (A Study of the Early Chinese Translations of the Western Concepts of Parliament, Democracy and Republic in the Nineteenth Century), *Zhongwai faxue* (*Peking University Law Journal*), 12(3): 257–276.

Faxue da cidian (Encyclopedia of Legal Studies), 1999, Shanghai, Shanghai cishu chubanshe.

Feinberg, Joel, 1980, *Rights, Justice, and the Bounds of Liberty: Essays in Social Philosophy*, Princeton, Princeton University Press.

Feng, Bing, 2008, "Lun Xun Zi de yizheng sixiang (On Xun Zi' Thought on Yizheng)", *Journal of Henan University*, 48(2): 41–47.

Finkelstein, David, 1970, "The Language of Communist China's Criminal Law", in Jerome Alan Cohen (ed.), *Contemporary Chinese Law: Research Problems and Perspectives*, Cambridge, Harvard University Press, 188–209.

Forrest, Robert A.D. 1973, *The Chinese Language*, 3rd edition, London, Faber & Faber Ltd.

Foucault, Michel, 1977, *Language, Counter-memory, Practice: Selected Essays and Interviews*, edited and translated by Donald F. Bouchard and Donald F. Bouchard and Sherry Simon, Oxford, Blackwell.

———. 1978, *The Archeology of Knowledge*, S. Smith, trans., London, Tavistock.

———. 1980, *Power/Knowledge: Selected Interviews and Other Writings (1972–1977)*, New York, Pantheon Books.

———. 1984, *The Foucault Reader*, edited by Paul Rabinow, New York, Pantheon Books.

Fu, Tingmei, 1993, "Legal Person in China: Essence and Limits", *American Journal of Comparative Law*, 41(2): 261–297.

Fu, Yulin, 1999, "Falü shuyu de fayi he falü gainian de jieshi" (Translation of Legal Terms and Interpretation of Legal Norms), *Peking University Law Review*, 2(1): 241–266.

Fuller, Lon L, 1969, *The Morality of Law*, New Haven, Yale University Press.

Fuma, Susumu, 2007 [1993], "Litigation Masters and The Litigation System of Ming and Qing China", *International Journal of Asian Studies*, 4 (1): 79–111.

Fung, Yu-lan 1952, *A History of Chinese Philosophy*, two volumes, Derk Bodde, trans., Princeton, Princeton University Press.

———. 1966, *A Short History of Chinese Philosophy*, New York, The Free Press.

Gadamer, Hans-Georg, 1975, *Truth and Method*, translated and edited by Garrett Barden and John Cumming, New York, The Seabury Press, originally published in 1960 as *Wahrheit und Methode*, Tübingen.

———. 1976, *Philosophical Hermeneutics*, translated and edited by David E. Linge, Berkeley, University of California Press.

Geertz, Clifford, 1983, *Local Knowledge: Further Essays in Interpretive Anthropology*, New York, Basic Books.

Goddard, Cliff (ed.), 2006, *Ethnopragmatics*, Berlin, Mouton de Gruyter.

Goddard, Cliff and Wierzbicka, Anna, 2014, *Words and Meanings: Lexical Semantics across Domains, Languages and Cultures,* Oxford, Oxford University Press.

Goodrich, Luther Carrington, 1966, *The Literary Inquisition of Ch'ien-Lung*, New York, Paragon Book.

Graham, Joseph F. (ed.), 1985, *Difference in Translation*, New York, Cornell University Press.

Guy, R. Kent, 2000, "Rule of Man and the Rule of Law in China: Punishing Provincial Governors during the Qing", in Karen Turner, James V. Feinerman and R. Kent Guy (eds.), *The Limits of the Rule of Law in China*, Seattle, The University of Washington Press, 88–111.

Habermas, Jürgen, 1987, *The Theory of Communication Action, Vol 2, System and Lifeworld: A Critique of Functionalist Reason*, Boston, MA, Beacon Press.

———. 1996, *Between Facts and Norms: Contributions to a Discourse Theory of Law and Democracy*, William Rehg, trans., Cambridge, the MIT Press.

———. 1998, *On the Pragmatics of Communication*, Maeve Cooke (ed.), Cambridge, The MIT Press.

Haft, Lloyd (ed.), 1993, *Words From the West: Western Texts in Chinese Literary Context*, Leiden, CNWS Publications.

Hall, David L. and Ames, Roger T. 1987, *Thinking Through Confucius*, Albany, State University of New York Press.

———. 1995, *Anticipating China: Thinking Through the Narratives of Chinese and Western Culture*, Albany, State University of New York Press.

———. 1998, *Thinking From the Han: Self, Truth, and Transcendence in Chinese and Western Culture*, Albany, State University of New York Press.

Hanan, Patrick, 1980, "Judge Bao's Hundred Cases Reconstructed", *Harvard Journal of Asiatic Studies*, 40(2): 301–323.

Hansen, Chad, 1983, *Language and Logic in Ancient China*, Ann Arbor, University of Michigan Press;

———. 1989, "Language in the Heart-mind", in Robert E. Allinson (ed.), *Understanding the Chinese Mind: The Philosophical Roots*, Oxford, Oxford University Press, 75–124.

———. 1992, *A Daoist Theory of Chinese Thought: A Philosophical Interpretation*, Oxford, Oxford University Press.

———. 2012, "Mohism: Later (Mo Jia, Mo Chia)", in A. S. Cua (ed.), *Encyclopedia of Chinese Philosophy,* New York, Routledge. 461–469.

Hao, Tiechuan, 1997, "Zhongguo jindai faxue liuxuesheng yu fazhi jindaihua" (China's Returned Law Students in Modern Times and its Modern Legal Development), *Faxue yanjiu (CASS Law Journal)*, 19(6): 3–33.

———. 2000, "Zhongguo jindai faxue liuxusheng yu xin zhongguo chuqi de fazhi jianshe" (China's Returned Law Students and Legal construction in the Early Years of the People's Republic of China), *Faxue yanjiu (CASS Law Journal)*, 22(2): 136–153.

Harbsmerier, Christoph, 1998, *Joseph Needham Science and Civilisation in China* - Volume 7, Part I: *Language and Logic*, Cambridge, Cambridge University Press.

Hart, H.L.A. 1979, "Between Utility and Rights", *Columbia Law Review*, 79: 828–846.

———. 1954, "Definition and Theory in Jurisprudence", *The Law Quarterly Review*, 70: 37–60.

———. 1994 [1961], *The Concept of Law*, 2nd edition, with a Postscript edited by Penelope A. Bulloch and Joseph Raz. Oxford, Clarendon Press.

———. 1968, "The Ascription of Responsibility and Rights", in Antony Flew (ed.), *Logic and Language*, Oxford, Basil Blackwell, 145–166.

Hayden, George Allen, 1974, "The Courtroom Plays of the Yuan and Early Ming Periods", *Harvard Journal of Asiatic Studies,* 34: 192–220.

———. 2004, *Falü wenhua shitan (Studies in the History of Legal Culture)*, Beijing, Shangwu yinshuguan.

———. 2014, "Falü fanyi zai Zhongguo jindai de diyici wanzheng shijian" (The First Complete Attempt of Legal Translation in Modern China", *Bijiaofa yanjiu (Comparative Law Study)*, 2014(2): 190–200.

He, Jiahong, 2016a, "Miscarriage of Justice and Malpractice in Criminal Investigations in China", *The China Review*, 16(1): 65–93.

He, Jiahong and He, Ran, 2013, "Wrongful Convictions and Tortured Confessions: Empirical Studies in Mainland China", in Mike McConville and Eva Pils (eds.), *Comparative Perspectives on Criminal Justice in China*, Cheltenham, Edward Elgar, 73–90.

He, Ni, 2014, *Chinese Criminal Trials: A Comprehensive Empirical Inquiry*, Berlin, Springer.

He, Qinhua, 2001, "Wanguo gongfa yu Qingmo guojifa" (The Elements of International Law in Chinese and International law in the Late Qing Dynasty), *Faxue yanjiu (CASS Law Journal)*, 23(5): 137–148.

———. 2016b, *Back from the Dead: Criminal Justice and Wrongful Convictions*, University of Hawai'i Press.

Head, John W. and Wang, Yanping, 2005, *Law Codes in Dynastic China: A Synopsis of Chinese Legal History in the Thirty Centuries from Zhou to Qing,* Durham, North Carolina, Carolina Academic Press.

Henderson, Dan Fenno, 1970, "Japanese Influences on Communist Chinese Legal Language", in Jerome Alan Cohen (ed.), *Contemporary Chinese Law: Research Problems and Perspectives*, Cambridge, Harvard University Press, 158–187.

Henderson, Sandra, 1997, "The Concept of Equivalence in Translation Studies: Much Ado About Something", *Target*, 9(2): 207–233.

Henkin, Louis, 1986, "Human Rights Idea in Contemporary China: A Comparative Perspective", in R.Randle Edwards, Louis Henkin and Andrew J. Nathan (eds.), *Human Rights in Contemporary China*, New York, Columbia University Press, 7–39.

———. 1998, "Epilogue: Confucianism, Human Rights, and Cultural Relativism", in William Theodore de Bary and Tu Weiming (eds.), *Confucianism and Human Rights*, New York, Columbia University Press, 308–314.

Hock, Hans Henrich, and Joseph, Biran D. 1996, *Language History, Language Change, and Language Relationship: An Introduction to Historical and Comparative Linguistics*, Berlin, Mouton de Gruyter.

Hoijer, Harry (ed.), 1954, *Language in Culture*, Chicago, University of Chicago Press.

Holland, J. A. and Weeb, J. S., 2003, *Learning Legal Rules*, 5th edition, Oxford, Oxford University Press.

Hsu, Dau-Lin, 1970, "Crime and Cosmic Order", *Harvard Journal of Asiatic Studies*, 30: 111–125, http://www.academia.edu/11544619/The_Sense_of_Justice (Goel, Shivam, The Sense of Justice (March 4, 2015). Available at SSRN: http://ssrn.com/abstract=257375chan,3 or http://dx.doi.org/10.2139/ssrn.2573753).

Huang, Liu-Hung, 1984, *A Complete Book Concerning Happiness and Benevlence*: *A Manual for Local Magistrates in Seventeenth-Century China,* edited and translated by Chu Djang, Tucson, The University of Arizona Press.

Huang, Philip C.C., 2001, *Code, Custom, and Legal Practice in China. The Qing and the Republic Compared*, Stanford, Stanford University Press.

Hulsewė, Anthony F. P. 1955, *Remnants of Han Law*, Leiden, Brill.

Hymes, Dell, 1974, *Foundations in Sociolinguistics: An Ethnographic Approach*, Philadelphia, University of Pennsylvania Press.

Idema, W. L. and Zürcher, E. (eds.), 1990, *Thought and Law in Qin and Han China: Studies Dedicated to Anthony Hulsewe on the Occasion of his Eightieth Birthday*, Leiden, Brill.

Jackendoff, Ray, 2002, "The Natural Logic of Rights and Obligations", in Ray Jackendoff, Paul Bloom and Karen Wynn (eds.), *Language, Logic and Concepts: Essays in Memory of John Macnamara,* Cambridge, MIT Press, 67–95.

———. 2006, "On Conceptual Semantics", *Intercultural Pragmatics,* 3–3: 353–358.

———. 2007a, *Language, Consciousness, Culture: Essays on Mental Structure,* Cambridge, MIT Press.

———. 2007b, "Conceptual Semantics and Natural Semantic Metalanguage Theory have Different Goals", *Intercultural Pragmatics,* 4–3: 411–418.

Jackson, Bernard S. 1995, *Making Sense in Law: Linguistic, Psychological and Semiotic Perspectives*, Liverpool, Deborah Charles Publications.

———. 1996, *Making Sense in Jurisprudence*, Liverpool, Deborah Charles Publications.

———. 1997, *Semiotics and Legal Theory*, Liverpool, Deborah Charles Publications.

Jespersen, Otto, 1964, *Language: Its Nature, Development and Origin*, London, Allen & Unwin.

Ji, W. 2004, *Space of Choice and Judicial Discretion in China: A Perspective of Comparative Legal Culture, CDAMS Discussion Paper,* Kobe, Kobe University.

Jiang, Bixin, 1985, "Shang Yang gai fa wei lü zhiyi" (Doubts on Shang Yang Changing *fa* to *lü*), DOI:10.16092/j.cnki.1001–618x.1985.05.015

Jiang, Hao, 2015, "Chinese Tort Law: Between Tradition and Transplant", in Mauro Bussani, Mauro and Anthony J. Sebok (eds.), *Comparative Tort Law: Global Perspectives*, Cheltenham, Edward Elgar, 385–411.

Johnson, Alison, and Coulthard, Malcolm (eds.), 2010, *The Routledge Handbook of Forensic Linguistics*, London, Routledge.

Johnson, Ian, 2014, "Chinese Atheists? What the Pew Survey Gets Wrong", *New York Review of Books*, 24 March, 2014, http://www.nybooks.com/daily/2014/03/24/chinese-atheists-pew-gets-wrong/

Johnson, Wallance S. Jr. 1979, *The T'ang Code: Volume I*, trans., Princeton, Princeton University Press.

———. 1997, *The T'ang Code: Volume II, Specific Articles*, trans., Princeton, Princeton University Press.

Johnston, I. 2010, *The Mozi: A Complete Translation,* Hong Kong, The Chinese University Press.

Jones, William C. 1985, "The Constitution of the People's Republic of China", *Washington Univeristy Law Quarterly*, 63(4): 707–735.

———. 1989, *Basic Principles of Civil Law in China*, trans., New York, M.E. Sharpe.

———. 1994, *The Great Qing Code*, trans., Oxford, Clarendon Press.

Jordan, Ann D. 1997, "Lost in the Translation: Two Legal Cultures, the Common Law Judiciary and the Basic Law of Hong Kong Special Administrative Region", *Cornell International Law Journal*, 30: 335–380.

Jori, M. 1994, "Legal Performative", *The Encyclopedia of Language and Linguistics*, Volume 4, Oxford, Pergamon Press.

Justinian's Institutes, 1987, translated with an Introduction by P. Birks, and G. McLeod, with the Latin text of P. Krueger, New York, Cornell University Press.

Kahn, Joseph, 2005, "Deep Flaws, and Little Justice, in China's Court System", the *New York Times*, 21 September 2005.

———. 2006, "Advocate for China's Weak Crosses the Powerful", the *New York Times*, 20 July 2006.

Kao, Karl S. Y., 1989, "Bao and Baoying: Narrative Causality and External Motivations in Chinese Fiction", *Chinese Literature: Essays, Articles, Reviews*, 11: 115–138.

Keller, Perry, 1989, "Legislation in the People's Republic of China", *University of British Columbia Law Review*, 23(3): 653–688.

———. 1994, "Sources of Order in Chinese Law", *The American Journal of Comparative Law*, 42(4): 711–759.

———. 2000, "The National People's Congress and the Making of National Law", in J.M. Otto, M.V. Polak, Jianfu Chen and Yuwen Li (eds.), *Law-Making in the People's Republic of China*, The Hague, Kluwer Law International, 75–90.

———. (ed.), 2001, *Chinese Law and Legal Theory*, Aldershot, Ashgate/Dartmouth.

Kent, Ann, 1993, *Between Freedom and Substance: China and Human Rights*, Hong Kong, Oxford University Press.

Kinkley, Jeffrey, 2000, *Chinese Justice, the Fiction: Law and Literature in Modern China*, Stanford, Stanford University Press.

Knoblock, John and Riegel, Jeffrey, 2000, *The Annals of Lü Buwei (Lüshi chunqiu): A Complete Translation and Study*, Stanford, Stanford University Press.

Kong, Xiangjun, 1999, *Hetong fa yinan anli pingxi yu fali yanjiu (Legal Analysis and Study of Doubtful and Difficult Cases in Contract Law)*, Beijing, Renmin fayuan chubanshe.

Kooij, Jan G. 1971, *Ambiguity in Natural Language: An Investigation of Certain Problems in its Linguistic Description*, Amsterdam/London, North-Holland Publishing Company.

Kuiper, Koos, 1993, "Dutch Loan-Words and Loan-Translations in Modern Chinese: An Example of Successful Sinification by Way of Japan", in Lloyd Haft (ed.), *Words from the West: Western Texts in Chinese Literary Context*, Leiden, CNWS Publications, 116–144.

Kurzon, Dennis, 1986, *It Is Hereby Performed... Explorations in Legal Speech Acts*, Amsterdam/Philadelphia, John Benjamins Publishing.

———. 1989, "Language of the Law and Legal Language", in Lauren Christer and Marianne Nordman (eds.), *Special Language: From Humans Thinking to Thinking Machines,* Clevedon, Multilingual Matters, 283–290.

———. 1997, "Legal Languages: Varieties, Genres, Registers and Discourses", *International Journal of Applied Linguistics*, 7(2): 119–139.

Lackner, Michael, Amelung, Iwo and Kurtz, Joachim (eds.), 2001, *New Terms for New Ideas: Western Knowledge and Lexical Change in Late Imperial China*, Leiden/Boston/Koln, Brill.

Lan, Rongjie, 2010, "A False Promise of Fair Trials: A Case Study of China's Malleable Criminal Procedure Law", *UCLA Pacific Basin Law Journal*, 27:153.

Lao Zi, 2003, *Laozi*, annotated by Zhu Liangzhi, Guagnzhou, Jinan Univerity Press.
Lau, D.C. 1963, *Lao Tzu: Tao Te Ching*, trans., London, Penguin Books.
———. 1979, *The Analects by Confucius*, trans., Harmondsworth, Penguin Classics.
Lee, L.T. and Lai, W.W. 1978, "The Chinese Conceptions of Law: Confucian, Legalist and Buddhist", *The Hastings Law Journal*, 29: 1307–1329.
Lee, Tahirih V. (ed.), 1997, *Law, the State, and Society in China*, New York, Garland Publishing.
Legge, James, 1970, *The Chinese Classics: With a Translation, Critical and Exegetical Notes, Prolegomena, and Copious Indexes*, five volumes: 1. *The Confucian Analects, Great Learning, Doctrine of the Mean*; 2. *The Works of Mencius*; 3. *The Shoo-king*; 4. *The She-king*; 5. *The Ch'un Ts'ew with the Tso Chuen*, reprinted from the 1893–1895 edition of Oxford University Press, Hong Kong, Hong Kong University Press.
Levenson, Joseph R. 1959, *Liang Ch'ich'ao and the Mind of Modern China*, New York, Harper & Row.
Lewis, Margaret K. 2012, "Presuming Innocence, or Corruption, in China", *Columbia Journal of Transnational Law*, 50(2): 287–369.
Lewis, Mark Edward, 1999, *Writing and Authority in Early China*, New York, State University of New York Press.
Leys, Simon, 1997, *The Analects of Confucius*, New York, W.W. Norton.
Li, Charles N. and Thompson, Sandra A. 1981, *Mandarin Chinese: A Functional Reference Grammar*, Berkeley, University of California Press.
Li, Guilian (ed.), 1999, *Zhongguo falü sixiang shi (History of Legal Thought in China)*, Beijing, Beijing University Press.
Li, Li, 2010, "*Nulla Poena Sine Lege* in China: Rigidity of Flexibility?" *Suffolk University Law Review*, 43: 655–667.
Liang, Ch'ich'ao (Liang Qichao), 1959, *Intellectual Trends in the Ch'ing Period*, Immanuel C.Y. Hsü trans., Cambridge, MA, Harvard University Press.
Liang, Linxia, 2007, *Delivering Justice in Qing China: Civil Trials in the Magistrate's Court*, Oxford, Oxford University Press.
Liang, Qichao, 2002, *Liang Qichao faxue wenji (Collection of Liang Qichao's Writings on Law)*, edited by Fan Zhongxin, Beijing, Zhongguo zhengfa daxue chubanshe.
Liang, Zhiping, 1989, "Explicating 'Law': A Comparative Perspective of Chinese and Western Legal Culture", *Journal of Chinese Law,* 3(1): 55–92.
———. 1996, *Qingdai xiguanfa: Shehui yu guojia (The Customary Law of the Qing Dynasty: Society and State)*, Beijing, Zhongguo zhengfa daxue chubanshe.
———. 1997, *Xunqiu ziran chixu zhong de hexie: Zhongguo chuantong falü wenhua (Seeking Harmony in Natural Order: Chinese Traditional Legal Culture)*, Shanghai, Shanghai renmin chubanshe.
———. (ed.), 1998, *Falü de wenhua jieshi (Cultural Interpretation of Law)*, 2nd edition, Beijing, Joint Publishing House.
———. 2004, *Fayi yu renqing* (*Meaning of Law and Sentiment of People*), Beijing, Zhongguo fazhi chubanshe.
Liao, W. K. 1959, *The Complete Works of Han Fei Tzu: A Classic of Chinese Political Science*, translated from the Chinese with Introduction and Notes by W K Liao, two volumes, London, Arthur Probsthain.

Link, Perry, 2013, *An Anatomy of Chinese: Rhythm, Metaphor, Politics*, Cambridge, Harvard University Press.

Liu, Hongying, 2003, *Falü yuyanxue (Legal Linguistics),* Beijing, Beijing daxue chubanshe.

Liu, Lydia H. 1995, *Translingual Practice: Literature, National Culture and Translated Modernity China 1900–1937*, Stanford, Stanford University Press.

———. (ed.), 1999, *Tokens of Exchange: the Problem of Translation in Global Circulations*, Durham & London, Duke University Press.

Liu, Yongping, 1998, *Origins of Chinese Law: Penal and Administrative Law in its Early Development*, Hong Kong, Oxford University Press.

Lu, Hong and Miethe, Terance, D., 2007, *China's Death Penalty: History, Law, and Contemporary Practices*, London, Routledge.

Lü, Shuxiang, 1990, "Tongguo duibi yanjiu yufa" (The Study of Grammar Through Comparative Analysis), in Yang Zijian and Li Ruihua (eds.), *Yinghan duibi yanjiu lunwen ji 1977–1989 (Essays on Comparative Studies of the Chinese and English Languages 1977–1989)*, Shanghai, Shanghai Waiyu jiaoyu chubanshe, 21–33.

Lubman, Stanley B. 1970, "Methodological Problems in Studying Chinese Communist Civil Law", in Jerome Alan Cohen (ed.), *Contemporary Chinese Law: Research Problems and Perspectives*, Cambridge, Harvard University Press, 230–260.

———. 1999, *Bird in a Cage: Legal Reform in China after Mao*, Stanford, Stanford University Press.

———. 2013, "Concluding Observations", in Mike McConville and Eva Pils (eds.), *Comparative Perspectives on Criminal Justice in China*, Cheltenham, Edward Elgar, 447–452.

Lucy, John A. 1992, *Language Diversity and Thought: A Reformulation of the Linguistic Relativity Hypothesis*, Cambridge, Cambridge University Press.

———. 1996, "The Scope of Linguistic Relativity: An Analysis and Review of Empirical Research", in John J. Gumperz and Stephen C. Levinson (eds.), *Rethinking Linguistic Relativity*, Cambridge, Cambridge University Press, 37–69.

Lynch, Elizabeth M. 2010, "China's Rule of Law Mirage: The Regression of the Legal Profession Since the Adoption of the 2007 Lawyers Law", *George Washington International Law Review*, 42: 535.

Lyons, David, 1970, "The Correlativity of Rights and Duties", *Noûs*, 4: 45–55.

Macauley, Melissa A. 1998, *Social Power and Legal Culture: Litigation Masters in Later Imperial China*, Stanford, Stanford University Press.

MacCormack, Geoffrey, 1985, "Law and Punishment in the Earliest Chinese Thought", *The Irish Jurist*, 20: 334–351.

———. 1989, "Natural Law and Cosmic Harmony in Traditional Chinese Thought", *Ratio Juris*, 2(3): 254–273.

———. 1990, *Traditional Chinese Penal Law*, Edinburgh, Edinburgh University Press.

———. 1996, *The Spirit of Traditional Chinese Law*, Athens/London, University of Georgia Press.

———. 2001, "Mythology and the Origin of Law in Early Chinese Thought", *Journal of Asian Legal History,* 1:1–23.

MacFarquhar, R. and Schoenhals, M. 2008, *Mao's Last Revolution*, Cambridge, Harvard University Press.

MacIntyre, Alasdair, 1981, *After Virtue*, Notre Dame, University of Notre Dame Press.

———. 1988, *Whose Justice? Which Rationality?* Notre Dame, University of Notre Dame Press.

MacMurray, John V.A. (ed.), 1973, *Treaties and Agreements with and Concerning China: 1894–1919*, Volume 1, New York, Fertig.

Maley, Yon, 1994, "The Language of the Law", in John Gibbons (ed.), *Language and the Law*, New York, Longman.

Malinowski, Bronislaw, 1923, "The Problem of Meaning in Primitive Languages", in C.K. Ogden and I.A. Richards (eds.), *The Meaning of Meaning: A Study of the Influence of Language upon Thought and of the Science of Symbolism*, London, Routledge and Kegan Paul, 296–336.

Martin, W.A.P. 1864, *Wanguo gongfa* (*Elements of International Law*), trans., Beijing. Chongshiguan.

Martin, W.A.P. et al., 1878, *Gongfa bianlan (A Practical Introduction to International Law)*, trans., Beijing.

Martin, W.A.P. 1900, *A Cycle of Cathay or China, South and North with Personal Reminiscences*, New York, Fleming H. Revell.

———. 1907, *The Awakening of China*, New York, Doubleday.

McConville, Mike, 2013, "Comparative Empeircl Co-ordinates and the Dynamics of Criminal Justice in China and the West", in Mike McConville and Eva Pils (eds.), *Comparative Perspectives on Criminal Justice in China*, Cheltenham, Edward Elgar, 13–69.

McConville, Mike, and Pils, Eva, (eds.), 2013, *Comparative Perspectives on Criminal Justice in China*, Cheltenham, Edward Elgar.

McKnight, Brian E. 1992, *Law and Order in Sung China*, London, Cambridge University Press.

———. 1995, "T'ang Law and Later Law: The Roots of Continuity", *Journal of the American Oriental Society*, 115(3): 410–420.

Meadows, Thomas, 1847, *Desultory Notes on the Government and People of* China, London, W. H. Allen & Co., https://archive.org/details/desultorynoteson00mead

Mellinkoff, David, 1963, *The Language of the Law*, Boston, Little, Brown and Company.

Miao, Runtian, 2003, "Lun rujia de chengxin xueshuo ji qi xiandai yiyi" (On the Confucian Notion of *Chengxin* and its Modern Significance), *Shehui kexue zhanxian (Social Science Front)*, 124(4): 11–15.

Michelson, Ethan, and Read, Benjamin L. 2011, "Public Attitudes toward Official Justice in Beijing and Rural China", in Margaret Y.K. Woo and Mary E. Gallagher (eds.), *Chinese Justice: Civil Dispute Resolution in Contemporary China,* Cambridge, Cambridge University Press, 169–203.

Millan, Carmen, and Bartrina, Francesca (eds.), *The Routledge Handbook of Translation Studies,* London, Routledge.

Minzner, Carl, 2005, "*Xinfang*: Alternative to Formal Chinese Legal Institutions", *Stanford Journal of International Law*, 42(1): 1–92.

———. 2009, "Judicial Disciplinary Systems for Incorrectly Decided Cases: The Imperial Chinese Heritage Lives On", *New Mexico Law Review*, 39: 1–25.

———. 2011, "Judicial Disciplinary Systems for Incorrectly Decided Cases: The Imperial Chinese Heritage Lives on", in Margaret Y.K. Woo, and Mary E. Gallagher (eds.), *Chinese Justice: Civil Dispute Resolution in Contemporary China,* Cambridge, Cambridge University Press, 58–90.

Montgomery, Scott L. 2000, *Science in Translation: Movements of Knowledge Through Cultures and Time*, Chicago/London, the University of Chicago Press.

Mooney, Annabel. 2014. *Human Rights and the Body,* Aldershot, Ashgate.

Morris, Marshall (ed.), 1995, *Translation and the Law*, Amsterdam, John Benjamins Publishing.

Morrison, M. 1989, "Excursions into the Nature of Legal Language", *Cleveland State Law Review*, 37: 271–336.

Moser, David, 2016, *A Billion Voices: China's Search for a Common Language*, New York, Penguin.

Mühlhahn, Klaus, 2009, *Criminal Justice in China: A History,* Cambridge, Harvard University Press.

Munro, Donald J. 1969, *The Concept of Man in Early China*, Stanford, Stanford University Press.

———. 1977, *The Concept of Man in Contemporary China*, Ann Arbor, The University of Michigan Press.

Nan, Luming and Xiao, Zhiyue, 1991, *Zhonghua renmin gongheguo dichan falü zhidu (The Land Law System of the People's Republic of China)*, Beijing, Zhongguo fazhi chubanshe.

Nathan, Andrew J. 1986, "Sources of Chinese Rights Thinking", in R. Randle Edwards, Louis Henkin and Andrew Nathan (eds.), *Human Rights in Contemporary China*, New York, Columbia University Press, 125–164.

Nelken, David (ed.), 1996, *Law as Communication*, Aldershot, Dartmouth.

———. (ed.), 1997, *Comparing Legal Cultures*, Aldershot, Dartmouth.

Nevalainen, Terttu and Traugott, Elizabeth Closs, (eds), 2012, *The Oxford Handbook of the History of English*, Oxford, Oxford University Press.

Ng, Michael, H.K. 2014, *Legal Transplantation in Early Twentieth-Century China*, London, Routledge.

Nino, Carlos (ed.), 1992, *Rights*, Aldershot, Dartmouth.

Nino, Carlos, 1989, "The Communitarian Challenge to Liberal Rights", *Law and Philosophy*, 8: 37–52.

Ocko, Jonathan K. 2000, "Using the Past to Make a Case for the Rule of Law", in Karen Turner, James V. Feinerman and R. Kent Guy (eds.), *The Limits of the Rule of Law in China*, Seattle, The University of Washington Press, 65–87.

Ogden, C.K. and Richards, I.A. 1949, *The Meaning of Meaning: A Study of the Influence of Language upon Thought and of the Science of Symbolism*, London, Routledge & Kegan Paul Ltd.

Park, Nancy, 2008, "Imperial Chinese Justice and the Law of Torture", *Late Imperial China*, 29(2): 37–67.

Peerenboom, Randall P. 1990a, "Confucian Justice: Achieving a Humane Society", *International Philosophical Quarterly*, 117(1): 17–32.

———. 1990b, "Confucian Jurisprudence: Beyond Natural Law", *Asia-Pacific Culture Quarterly*, 18(4): 12–38.

———. 1993a. "What's Wrong with Chinese Rights?: Toward a Theory of Rights with Chinese Characteristics", *Harvard Human Rights Journal*, 6: 29–57.

———. 1993b, *Law and Morality in Ancient China: the Silk Manuscripts of Huang-lao*, Albany, State University of New York Press.

———. 1995, "Rights, Interests, and the Interests in Rights in China", *Stanford Journal of International Law*, 31: 359–386.

———. 2002, *China's Long March Toward Rule of Law*, Cambridge, Cambridge University Press.

Peerenboom, Randall P., Petersen, Carole, J., and Chen, Albert H.Y. (eds.), 2006, *Human Rights in Asia*, London, Routledge/Curzon.

Peirce, Charles Sanders, 1979 [1934], *Collected Papers of Charles Sanders Peirce*, edited by Charles Hartshorne and Paul Weiss, Cambridge, The Belknap Press of Harvard University Press.

Perry Keller, 1994, "Sources of Order in Chinese Law", *The American Journal of Comparative Law*, 42: 4, 711–759.

Pils, Eva, 2013, "Disappearing China's Human Rights Lawyers", in Mike McConville and Eva Pils (eds.), *Comparative Perspectives on Criminal Justice in China*, Cheltenham, Edward Elgar, 411–438.

Pohl, Karl-Heinz, (ed.), 1999a, *Chinese Thought in a Global Context: A Dialogue Between Chinese and Western Philosophical Approaches*, Leiden, Brill.

Pohl, Karl-Heinz, 1999b, "Communitarianism and Confucianism - In Search of Common Moral Ground", in Karl-Heinz Pohl (ed.), *Chinese Thought in a Global Context: A Dialogue between Chinese and Western Philosophical Approaches*, Leiden, Brill, 262–286.

Pomerleau, Wayne, P. undated, "Western Theories of Justice", *The Internet Encyclopedia of Philosophy,* ISSN 2161–0002, http://www.iep.utm.edu/justwest/ 27 March 2017

Potter, Pitman B. (ed.), 1994, *Domestic Law Reforms in Post-Mao China*, New York/ London, M.E. Sharpe.

———. 2001, *The Chinese Legal System: Globalization and Local Legal Culture*, London/New York, Routledge.

Pulleyblank, Edwin G. 1991, *Lexicon of Reconstructed Pronunciation in Early Middle Chinese, Late Middle Chinese, and Early Mandarin*, Vancouver, University of British Columbia Press.

Qu, Wensheng, 2013, *Cong cidian chufa (Starting from Dictionaries),* Shanghai, Shanghai renmin chubanshe.

Rao, Xinxian, 1999, *Zhongguo falü shi lungao (On Chinese Legal History)*, Beijing, Falü chubanshe.

Rawls, John, 1988, "The Priority of Right and Ideas of the Good", *Philosophy and Public Affairs*, 17: 251–276.

———. 1993, "The Law of Peoples", in Stephen Shute and Susan Hurley (eds.), *On Human Rights: The Oxford Amnesty Lectures 1993*, New York, Basic Books, 41–82.

———. 1999, *A Theory of Justice*, revised edition, Cambridge, The Belknap Press of Harvard University Press.

Raz, Joseph, 1979, *The Authority of Law*, Oxford, Clarendon Press.
———. 1980, *The Concept of a Legal System: An Introduction to the Theory of Legal System*, Oxford, Clarendon Press.
———. 1984, "Legal Rights", *Oxford Journal of Legal Studies*, 4(1): 1–21.
———. 1989, "Liberating Duties", *Law and Philosophy*, 8(1): 3–22.
———. 1994, *Ethics in the Public Domain: Essays in the Morality of Law and Politics*, Oxford, Clarendon Press.
———. 1998, "On the Authority and Interpretation of Constitution: Some Preliminaries", in Larry Alexander (ed.), *Constitutionalism: Philosophical Foundations,* Cambridge, Cambridge University Press, 152–193.
———. 1999, *Practical Reason and Norms*, Oxford, Oxford University Press.
———. 2001, *Value, Respect, and Attachment*, Cambridge, Cambridge University Press.
Ren, Xin, 1997, *Tradition of the Law and Law of the Tradition, Law, State and Social Control in China*, London, Greenwood Press.
Richards, I.A. 1953, "Toward a Theory of Translating", in Arthur F. Wright (ed.), *Studies in Chinese Thought*, Chicago, University of Chicago Press, 247–262.
Rickett, W. Allyn, 1998, *Guanzi: Political, Economic, and Philosophical Essays from Early China*, a study and translation by W. Allyn Rickett, two volumes, Princeton, Princeton University Press.
Riles, Annelise, 1991, "Spheres of Exchange and Spheres of Law: Identity and Power in Chinese Marriage Agreements", *International Journal of the Sociology of Law*, 19: 501–523.
Roetz, Heiner, 1999, "The Dignity within Oneself: Chinese Tradition and Human Rights", in Karl-Heinz Pohl (ed.), *Chinese Thought in a Global Context: A Dialogue between Chinese and Western Philosophical Approaches*, Leiden, Brill, 236–261.
Rorty, Richard, 1997, "Jusice as a Larger Loyalty", in Ron Bontekoe and Marietta Stepaniants (eds.), Justice and Democracy: Cross-Cultural Perspectives, Honolulu, University of Hawai'i Press, 9–22.
Rosemont, Henry Jr. (ed.), 1991, *Chinese Texts and Philosophical Contexts: Essays Dedicated to Angus C. Graham*, La Salle, Open Court.
———. 1988, "Why Take Rights Seriously? A Confucian Critique", in Leroy S. Rouner (ed.), *Human Rights and the World's Religions*, Notre Dame, University of Notre Dame Press, 167–182.
———. 1998, "Human Rights: A Bill of Worries", in William Theodore de Bary and Tu Weiming (eds.), *Confucianism and Human Rights*, New York, Columbia University Press, 54–66.
Ross, Claudia, and Ross, Lester, 2000, "Language and Law: Sources of Systemic Vagueness and Ambiguous Authority in Chinese Statutory Language", in Karen Turner, James V. Feinerman and R. Kent Guy (eds.), *The Limits of the Rule of Law in China*, Seattle, The University of Washington Press, 221–270.
Rubenstein, Daniel, 1997, "Legal and Institutional Uncertainties in the Domestic Contract Law of the People's Republic of China", *McGill Law Journal*, 42: 495–536.
Ruskola, Teemu, 1992, "Moral Choice in the *Analects*: A Way Without a Crossroads?", *Journal of Chinese Philosophy*, 19: 285–296.

———. 2002, "Legal Orientalism", *Michigan Law Review*, 101(1): 179–234.
———. 2003, "Law Without Law, Or Is "Chinese Law" An Oxymoron?" *William & Mary Bill of Rights Journal*, 11(2): 655–669.
———. 2013, *Legal Orientalism: China, The United States and Modern Law*, Cambridge, Harvard University |Press.
Sandel, Michael, 1982, *Liberalism and the Limits of Justice*, Cambridge, Cambridge University Press.
Sandel, Todd L. 2003, "Linguistic Capital in Taiwan: The KMT's Mandarin Language Policy and its Perceived Impact on Language Practices of Bilingual Mandarin and Tai-gi Speakers", *Language in Society*, 32: 523–551.
Sapir, Edward, 1921, *Language*, New York, Harcourt, Brace & World.
———. 1993, *The Psychology of Culture: A Course of Lectures*, reconstructed and edited by Judith T. Irvine, Berlin, Mouton de Gruyter.
Sarcevic, Susan, 1997, *New Approach to Legal Translation*, The Hague, Kluwer Law International.
Schak, David C. and Hudson, Wayne (eds.), 2003, *Civil Society in Asia*, Aldershot, Ashgate.
Schane, S. 2002, "Ambiguity and Misunderstanding in the Law", *Thomas Jefferson Law Review* 25: 1, 167–194.
Schauer, Federick (ed.), 1993, *Law and Language*, Aldershot, Dartmouth.
Scheffler, Israel, 1979, *Beyond the Letter: A Philosophical Inquiry into Ambiguity, Vagueness and Metaphor in Language*, London, Routledge & Kegan Paul.
Schoenhals, Michael, 1992, *Doing Things with Words in Chinese Politics: Five Studies*, Berkeley, China Research Monograph.
Schwartz, Benjamin I. 1964, *In Search of Wealth and Power: Yen Fu and the West*, Cambridge, MA, Harvard University Press.
———. 1985, *The World of Thought in Ancient China*, Cambridge/London, The Belknap Press of Harvard University Press.
Scogin, Hugh T. Jr. 1990, "Between Heaven and Man: Contract and the State in Han Dynasty China", *Southern California Law Review*, 63(5): 1325–1404.
———. 1994, "Civil Law in Traditional China: History and Theory", in Kathryn Bernhardt and Philip C.C. Huang (eds.), *Civil Law in Qing and Republican China*, Stanford, Stanford University Press, 13–41.
Searle, John R. 1969, *Speech Acts: An Essay in the Philosophy of Language*, Cambridge, Cambridge University Press.
———. 1976, "A Taxonomy of Illocutionary Acts", *Language in Society*, 5: 1–25.
———. 1979, *Expression and Meaning: Essays in the Theory of Speech Acts*, Cambridge, Cambridge University Press.
———. 1984, *Minds, Brains and Science*, Harmondsworth, Penguin.
———. 1998, *Mind, Language and Society: Philosophy in the Real World*, New York, Basic Books.
Searle, John R., Kiefer, Ferenc and Bierwisch, Mandred (eds.), 1980, *Speech Act Theory and Pragmatics*, Dordrecht/London/Boston, D. Reidel Publishing Company.
Seidman, A. and Seidman, R. B. 1996, "Drafting Legislation for Development, Lessons from a Chinese Project", *American Journal of Comparative Law*, 44(1): 1–44.

Sejersted, Francis, 1988, "Democracy and the Rule of Law", in Jon Elster and Rune Slagstad (eds.), *Constitutionalism and Democracy*, Cambridge, Cambridge University Press, 131–152.

Setton, Mark, 2000, "Ambiguity in the *Analects*: Philosophical and Practical Dimensions", *Journal of Chinese Philosophy*, 27(4): 545–569.

Seymour, James, and Patrick Yuk-tung Wong, 2015, "China and the International Human Rights Covenants", *Critical Asian Studies*, 47(4): 514–536.

Shambaugh, David, 2007, "China's Propaganda System: Institutions, Processes and Efficacy", *The China Journal,* 57: 25–58.

Shankman, Steven and Durrant, Stephen W. (eds.), 2002, *Early China/Ancient Greece: Thinking Through Comparisons*, New York, State University of New York Press.

Shao, Jingmin, 1999, "Qiyi: yufa yanjiu de tupokou" (Ambiguity: Breakthroughs in the Study of Grammar), in Ma Qingzhu (ed.), *Yufa yanjiu rumen (Introduction to the Study of Grammar)*, Beijing, Shangwu yinshuguan, 362–381.

Shapiro, I. (ed.), 1994, *The Rule of Law*, New York, New York University Press.

Shapiro, Sidney, 1990, *The Law and the Lore of China's Criminal Justice*, Beijing, New World Press.

Shen, Gui, 2001, *Xianfa tongzhi shidai de kaishi - Xianfa diyi an cunyi (The Beginning of the Rule by the Constitution: Doubts about the First Constitutional Case)*, htttp://www.chinalaw.com.

Shen, Zhengtao, 1999, "Hai zi du liang yin, jiufen shang fating" (With the Two Pronunciations of Hai, the Dispute Goes to Court), *Fazhi Ribao (Legal Daily)*, 14 March, 1999.

Shi, Youwei, 2000, *Hanyu wailaici (Foreign Words in Chinese)*, Beijing, Shangwu yinshuguan.

Shore, Bradd, 1998, "Semiotics of Culture", in Paul Bouissac (ed.), *Encyclopedia of Semiotics*, Oxford, Oxford University Press, 165–168.

Solan, Lawrence, 2004, "Pernicious Ambiguity in Contracts and Statutes", *Chicago-Kent Law Review*, 79(1): 859–888.

Staunton, Sir George, 1966 [1810], *Ta Tsing Leu Lee; Being the Fundamental Laws, and a Selection from the Supplementary Statutes, of the Penal Code of China; Originally printed and published in Pekin, in various successive editions, under the sanction, and by the authorty, of the several emperors of the Ta Tsing, or present dynasty. Translated from the Chinese; and accompanied with an appendix, consisting of authentic documents, and a few occasional notes, illustrative of the subject of the work; by Sir George Thomas Staunton, bart. F.R.S,* Taipei, Ch'eng-Wen Publishing Co.

Steiner, George, 1998, *After Babel: Aspects of Language and Translation*, 3rd edition, London, Oxford University Press.

Stephens, Thomas, B. 1992, *Order and Discipline in China: The Shanghai Mixed Court 1911–27*, Seattle/London, University of Washington Press.

Stone, Christopher D. 1981, "From a Language Perspective", *The Yale Law Journal*, 90: 1149–1192.

Stratman, J. F. 2004, "How Legal Analysts Negotiate Indeterminacy of Meaning in Common Law rules: Towards a Synthesis of Linguistic and Cognitive Approaches to Investigations", *Language and Communication,* 24: 23–57.

Su, Li. 1998, "Ershi shiji zhongguo de xiandaihua he fazhi" (Modernization and Rule of Law of China in the Twentieth Century), *Faxue yanjiu (CASS Law Journal)*, 20(1): 3–15.

Sullivan, Ruth, 2002, *Sullivan and Driedger on the Construction of Statutes*, Toronto, Butterworths.

Sun, Shiyan, 2007, "Gongmin ji zhengzhi quanli guoji gongyue de liangfen zhongwenben: wenti,bijiao yu chulu", *Huanqiu falu pinglu*, 6, http://www.hrol.org/Documents/ChinaDocs/Obligations/2012–11/272.html

Sung, Tz'u (Song Ci), 1981, *The Washing Away of Wrongs: Forensic Medicine in Thirteenth-Century China*, McKnight, Brian E. trans, Ann Arbor, Center for Chinese Studies, The University of Michigan.

Svarverud, Rune, 2001, "The Nations of 'Power' and 'Rights' in Chinese Political Discourse", in Michael Lackner, Iwo Amelung and Joachim Kurtz (eds.), *New Terms for New Ideas: Western Knowledge and Lexical Change in Late Imperial China*, Leiden/Boston/Koln, Brill, 125–146.

Tan, Sor-hoon, 2014, "The Concept of *Yi* in the Mencius and Problems of Distributive Justice", *Australasian Journal of Philosophy*, 92(3): 489–505.

Tiersma, Peter Meijes, 1999, *Legal Language*, Chicago, Chicago University Press.

Toolan, Michael (ed.), 2002, *Critical Discourse Analysis: Critical Concept in Linguistics*, New York, Routledge.

Tsao, Feng-fu, 1999, "The Language Planning Situation in Taiwan", *Journal of Multilingual and Multicultural Development,* 20(4/5): 328–375.

Turner, Karen, 1990, "Sage Kings and Laws in the Chinese and Greek Traditions", in P.S. Ropp (ed.), *Heritage of China, Contemporary Perspectives on Chinese Civilization*, Berkeley, California University Press, 86–111.

———. 1992, "Rule of Law Ideals in Early China?" *Journal of Chinese Law*, 6(2): 1–44.

———. 1993, "War, Punishment, and the Law of Nature in Early Chinese Concepts of the State", *Harvard Journal of Asiatic Studies,* 53(2): 285–324.

Turner, Karen, Feinerman, James V. and Guy, R. Kent (eds.), 2000, *The Limits of the Rule of Law in China*, Seattle, The University of Washington Press.

Turner, Karen, Gao, Hongjun and He, Weifang (eds.), 1994, *Meiguo xuezhe lun Zhongguo falü chuantong (American Scholars on Chinese Legal Tradition)*, Beijing, China University of Political Science and Law Press.

Twiss, Sumner B. 1998, "A Constructive Framework for Discussing Confucianism and Human Rights", in William Theodore de Bary and Tu Weiming (eds.), *Confucianism and Human Rights*, New York, Columbia University Press, 27–53.

Tymoczko, Maria and Gentzle, Edwin (eds.), 2002, *Translation and Power,* Amherst/Boston, University of Massachusetts Press.

Unger, Roberto M. 1977, *Law in Modern Society: Toward a Criticism of Social Theory*, New York, Free Press.

Vanderveken, Daniel, Kubo, Susumu (eds.), 2001, *Essays in Speech Act Theory*, Amsterdam, John Benjamins Publishing.

Van Norden, Bryan, 2017,"Mencius", in Edward N. Zalta (ed.), *The Stanford Encyclopedia of Philosophy* (Spring 2017 Edition), https://plato.stanford.edu/archives/spr2017/entries/mencius/, Stanford University.

Venuti, L. (ed.), 1992, *Rethinking Translation: Discourse, Subjectivity, Ideology*, London, Routledge.

Venuti, L. 1995, *The Translator's Invisibility: A History of Translation*, London, Routledge.

Vincent, R.J. 1986, *Human Rights and International Relations*, Cambridge, Cambridge University Press.

Von Jhering, Rudolph, 1915, *The Struggle for Law*, translated from the 5th German edition by John J. Lalor, with an introduction by Albert Kocourek, Chicago, Callaghan.

Wagner, Anne and Broekman, Jan M. (eds.), 2012, *Prospects of Legal Semiotics*, Berlin, Springer.

Wagner, Anne, Werner, Wouter and Cao, Deborah (eds.), 2007, *Interpretation, Law and the Construction of Meaning*, Berlin/New York, Springer.

Waismann, Friedrich, 1968, "Verifiability", in Antony Flew (ed.), *Logic and Language*, Oxford, Basil Blackwell, 117–144.

Waley, Arthur, 1938, *The Analects of Confucius*, London, George Allen & Unwin.

———. 1939, *Three Ways of Thought in Ancient China*, London, George Allen & Unwin.

Wan, Margaret B. 2015, "Court Case Ballads Popular Ideals of Justice in Late Qing and Republican China", in Li Chen and Madeleine Zelin (eds.), *Chinese Law: Knowledge Practice and Transformation, 1530s to 1950s,* Leiden, Brill, 287–320.

Wang, Chenguang and Zhang, Xianchu (eds.), 1997, *Introduction to Chinese Law*, Hong Kong/Singapore, Sweet & Maxwell Asia.

Wang, Guanghui, 2000a, "Xianfa wei genben fa zhi yanjin" (Constitution as a Basic Law and its Evolution), *Faxue yanjiu (CASS Law Journal)*, 22(2): 127–135.

———. 2000b, "New Contract Law in China", *Journal of Contract Law*, 15: 242–267.

Wang, Gungwu, 1991, "Power, Rights, and Duties in Chinese History", in Wang Gungwu (ed.), *The Chineseness of China: Selected Essays*, Hong Kong, Oxford University Press, 165–186.

Wang, Huaiyu, 2009, "The Way of Heart: Mencius' Understanding of Justice", *Philosophy East and West*, 59(3): 317–363.

Wang, J.C. 1966, *Chinese Intellectuals and the West: 1872–1949*, Chapel Hill, The University of North Carolina Press.

Wang, Jian (ed.), 2001, *Xifa dongjian: Waiguoren yu zhongguo fa de jindai biange (Western Law Going East: Foreigners and the Reform of Modern Chinese Law)*, Beijing, Zhongguo zhengfa daxue chubanshe.

Wang, Lei, 2000, *Xianfa de sifahua (Constitutional Law Applied in Courts)*, Beijing, Zhongguo zhengfa daxue chubanshe.

Wang, Liming (ed.), 2000, *Minfa (Civil Law)*, Beijing, Zhongguo renmin daxue chubanshe.

Wang, S. 1995, "The Judicial Explanation in Chinese Criminal Law", *The American Journal of Comparative Law*, 43(4): 569–579.

Wang, S. 2004, "Environmental Crime and Environmental Criminal Law in the People's Republic of China", *European Journal of Crime, Criminal Law and Criminal Justice*, 12(2): 150–165.

Wang, Tay-Sheng, 2000, *Legal Reform in Taiwan under Japanese Colonial Rules: 1895–1945, the Reception of Western Law*, Seattle, Washington University Press.
Wang, Yugen, 2011, "The Limits of Poetry as Means of Social Criticism: The 1079 Literary Inquisition Against Su Shi Revisited", *Journal of Song-Yuan Studies*, 41:29–65.
Watson, Alan, 1974, *Legal Transplant, An Approach to Comparative Law*, Edinburgh, Scottish Academic Press.
Watson, Burton, 1971 [1962], *Early Chinese Literature*, New York/London, Columbia University Press.
———. 1967, *Mo Tzu: Basic Writings*, trans., New York/London, Columbia University Press.
———. 2003, *Han Feizi: Basic Writings*, trans., New York/London, Columbia University Press.
Watt, John R. 1972, *The District Magistrate in Late Imperial China*, New York, Colombia University Press.
Weatherley, Robert, 1999, *The Discourse of Human Rights in China: Historical and Ideological Perspectives*, London, Macmillan Press.
Weisflog, W.E. 1987, "Problems of Legal Translation", paper presented at the XIIth International Congress of Corporate Law, Zürich, 179–218.
Weston, Martin, 1991, *An English Reader's Guide to the French Legal System*, Oxford, Berg.
Wheaton, Henry, 1878 [1836], edited by A.C. Boyd, *Elements of International Law*, London, Stevens and Sons.
Whorf, Benjamin Lee, 1956, *Language, Thought and Reality: Selected Writings of Benjamin Lee Whorf*, edited by John B. Carroll, Cambridge, MA, The MIT Press.
Wierzbicka, Anna, 1996, *Semantics: Primes and Universals*, Oxford, Oxford University Press.
———. 2002, "Right and Wrong: from Philosophy to Everyday Discourse", *Discourse Studies*, 4(2): 225–252.
———. 2003a, *Cross-Cultural Pragmatics: The Semantics of Human Interaction*, 2nd edition, Berlin, Mouton de Gruyter.
———. 2003b, "Reasonable Man and Reasonable Doubt: the English Language, Anglo Culture and Anglo-American Law", *Forensic Linguistics*, 10(1): 1–22.
———. *English: Meaning and Culture*, Oxford, Oxford University Press.
———. 2007a, "Theory and Empirical Findings: A Response to Jackendoff", *Intercultural Pragmatics*, 4(3): 399–409.
———. 2007b, "NSM Semantics versus Conceptual Semantics: Goals and Standards (A Response to Jackendoff)", *Intercultural Pragmatics*, 4(4): 521–529.
———. 2010a, "Cross-Cultural Communication and Miscommunication: The Role of Cultural Keywords", *Intercultural Pragmatics*, 7(1): 1–23.
———. 2010b, *Experience, Evidence, and Sense: Hidden Cultural Legacy of English*, Oxford, Oxford University Press.
———. 2014a, "Can There be Common Knowledge without a Common Language? German *Pflicht* versus English Duty", *Common Knowledge*, 21(1): 141–171.
———. 2014b, *Imprisoned in English: The Hazards of English as a Default Language*, Oxford, Oxford University Press.

Wilder, G.D. and Ingram J.H. 1974 [1922], *Analysis of Chinese Characters*, New York, Dover Publications.

Williams, Raymond, 1976, *Keywords: A Vocabulary of Culture and Society*, London, Fontana.

Williamson, T. 2001, "Vagueness, Indeterminacy and Social Meaning", *Critical Studies,* 16: 61–76.

Wilt, Idema, 2009, *Judge Bao and the Rule of Law: Eight Ballad-Stories from the Period 1250–1450,* Singapore, World Scientific Publishing Co.

Wittgenstein, Ludwig, 1997, *Philosophical Investigations*, 2nd edition, G.E.M. Anscombe trans., Oxford, Blackwell Publishers.

Woo, Margaret Y.K. and Gallagher, Mary E. (eds.), 2011, *Chinese Justice: Civil Dispute Resolution in Contemporary China,* Cambridge, Cambridge University Press.

Wright, Arthur F. (ed.), 1967 [1953], *Studies in Chinese Thought*, Chicago, University of Chicago Press.

Wright, David, 2000, *Translating Science: The Transmission of Western Chemistry into Late Imperial China, 1840–1900*, Leiden, Brill.

———. 2001, "Yan Fu and the Tasks of the Translator", in Michael Lackner, Iwo Amelung and Joachim Kurtz (eds.), *New Terms for New Ideas: Western Knowledge and Lexical Change in Late Imperial China*, Leiden/Boston/Koln, Brill, 235–256.

Wu, Daying, Ren, Yunzheng, and Li, Lin, 1992, *Bijiao lifa zhidu (Comparitive Leal Studies of Legal Systems),* Beijing, Qunzhong chubanshe.

Wu, Guoping, 2014, "Yi zhaodao Zhongwen zhong 'tianfu renquan' zuizao chuchu" (Found the Earliest Use of 'tianfu renquan' in Chinese), http://www.oldkids.cn/blog/view.php?bid=697544

Wu, Laurence C. 1986, *Fundamentals of Chinese Philosophy*, Lanham/New York, University Press of America.

Wu, Shuchen, 2011, "Qin Gai fa wei lü yuanyin kao" (On the Reasons for Changing fa to lü in Qin Dynasty), *Faxuejia*, 2011(2): 28–40.

Wu, Wei, and Vader Beken, Tom, 2012, "The Evolution of Criminal Interrogation Rules in China", *Internaional Journal of Law, Crime and Justice*, 40(4): 271–295.

Wu, Yingcai and Li, Yude, 1997, *Xiandai hanyu de qiyi (Ambiguity in Modern Chinese)*, Ningxia, Ningxia renmin chubanshe.

Xia, Yong, 2011, *The Philosophy of Civil Rights in the Context of China* (translated from Chinese), Leiden, Martinus Nijhoff Publishers.

Xiao, Jianyi, 2000, "Kong, Meng, Xun yili sixiang bijiao yanjiu (A Comparative Study of Yi and Li in Confucius, Mencius and Xun Zi), *Journal of Xi'an Foreign Language University*, 8(4): 98–103.

Xiao, Yang, 1997, "Trying to Do Justice to the Concept of Justice in Confucian Ethics", *Journal of Chinese Philosophy*, 24: 521–551.

Xiong, Yuezhi, 2001, "Liberty, Democracy, President: The Translation and Usage of Some Political Terms in Late Qing China", in Michael Lackner, Iwo Amelung and Joachim Kurtz (eds.), *New Terms for New Ideas: Western Knowledge and Lexical Change in Late Imperial China*, Leiden/Boston/Koln, Brill, 69–89.

Xu, Xianming, 1996, "Lun fazhi goucheng yaojian" (The Concept, Principles and Elements of Rule of Law), *Faxue yanjiu* (*CASS Law Journal*), 18(3): 37–44.

Xu, Songyan, 2001, "Lun Mozi sixiang zhong de yi" (On Yi in Mohism), *Journal of Liaoning Normal University*, 24(2): 93–95.

Xu, Xin, 2015, "Shenyuan: wuguzhe jihua jiqi tuijin celue (Redressing Injustice: Innocence Project and Strategies for its Promotion", *Ha'erbin gongye daxue xuebao*, 2015(2): 20–24.

Xu, Zhongming, 2000, *Faxue yu wenxue zhijian* (*Between Law and Literature*), Beijing, Zhongguo zhengfa daxue chubanshe.

Xunzi, translated into modern Chinese by Zhang Jue and translated into English by John Knoblock, 1999, Hunan/Beijing, Hunan People's Publishing House and Foreign Languages Press.

Yan, Fu, 1981 [1931], *Fayi* (Montesquieu's *De l'esprit des lois*), Beijing, Shangwu yinshuguan.

Yang, S. And Huang, Y.Y. 2004, "The Impact of the Absence of Grammatical Tense in L1 on the Acquisition of the Tense-Aspect System in L2", *International Review of Applied Linguistics,* 42: 49–70.

Yang, Xue, 2015, "The Confucianization of Law and the Lenient Punishments in China", *International Journal of Criminal Justice Sciences*, 10(1): 32–47.

Ye, Zhengdao, 2004, "Chinese Categorization of Interpersonal Relationships and the Cultural Logic of Chinese Social Interaction: An Indigenous Perspective", *Intercultural Pragmatics*, 1(2): 211–230.

———. 2006, "Why the "Inscrutable" Chinese Face? Emotionality and Facial Expression in Chinese", in Cliff Goddard (ed.), *Ethnopragmatics*, Berlin, Mouton de Gruyter, 127–169.

———. 2013, "Understanding the Conceptual Basis of the 'Old Friend' Formula in Chinese Social Interaction and Foreign Diplomacy: A Cultural |Script Approach", *Australian Journal of Linguistics*, 33(3): 365–385.

———. 2014, "Opposites in Language and Thought: A Chinese Perspective", Selected Papers from the 4th UK Cognitive Linguistics Conference, http://www.uk-cla.org.uk/files/proceedings/Zhengdao.pdf

Yeh, His-nan, Chan, Hui-chen, and Cheng, Yuh-show, 2004, "Language Use in Taiwan: Language Proficiency and Domain Analysis", *Journal of Taiwan Normal University*, 49(1): 75–108.

Yu, Hua, 2011, *China in Ten Words*, translated from the Chinese, London, Duckworth Overlook.

Yu, Jiang 2001, "Jindai Zhongguo faxue yuci de xingcheng yu fazhan" (Formation and Development of Modern Chinese Legal Language and Terms), *Zhongxi falü chuantong (Chinese and Western Legal Tradition)*, volume 1, Beijing, Zhongguo zhengfa daxue chubanshe, 24–66.

———. 2000, "Qingmo minfaxue de shuru yu chuanbo" (The Introduction and Propagation of Civil Law during the Late Qing Dynasty in China), *Faxue yanjiu (The CASS Law Journal*), 22(6): 141–149.

Yu, Ronggen, 1999, *Daotong yu fatong (Rule According to Dao and Rule According to Law)*, Beijing, Falü chubanshe.

Zang, Kehe, 1998, *Hanzi danwei guannian shikao shu (Historical Study of the Unit Concept of Chinese Characters)*, Shanghai, Xuelin chubanshe.

Zarrow, Peter, 1998, "Citizenship and Human Rights in Early Twentieth-Century Chinese Thought: Liu Shipei and Liang Qichao", in William Theodore de Bary and Tu Weiming (eds.), *Confucianism and Human Rights*, New York, Columbia University Press, 209–233.

Zeng, Xianyi, 2005, *Zhongguo fazhi shi (The Legal History of China)*, Beijing, Beijing daxue chubanshe and Beijing gaodeng jiaoyu chubanshe.

Zeng, Xianyi and Ma, Xiaohong, 2006, "A Dialectic Study of the Structure and Basic Concepts of Traditional Chinese Law and an Analysis of the Relationship between *li* (ceremony) and *fa* (law)", *Frontiers of Law in China*, 1: 34–52.

Zhai, J. 2002, "Judicial Information of the People's Republic of China: A Survey," http://www.llrx.com/features/chinajudicial.htm.

Zhang, Jue, 1995, *Han Feizi quanyi (The Complete Modern Chinese Translation of Han Feizi)*, two volumes, Guiyang, Guizhou renmin chubanshe.

Zhang, Jue and Knoblock, John, 1999, *Xunzi,* two volumes, translated into modern Chinese by Zhang Jue, and translated into English by John Knoblock, Hunan and Beijing, Hunan People's Publishing House and Foreign Languages Press.

Zhang, Zhongqiu, 1999, *Zhongxi falü wenhua biaojiao yanjiu (A Comparative Study of Chinese and Western Legal Cultures)*, Nanjing, Nanjing daxue chubanshe.

———. 1999, *Zhongxi falü wenhua bijiao yanjiu (Comparative Studies of Chinese and Western Legal Cultures)*, Nanjing, Nanjing daxue chubanshe

Zhongxi falü chuantong (Chinese and Western Legal Tradition), 2001, Volume 1, Beijing, Zhongguo zhengfa daxue chubanshe.

Zhou, Caizhu and Qi, Ruiduan, 1995, *Mo Zi Quanyi (The Complete Modern Chinese Translation of Mo Zi)*, annotated and translated by Zhou Caizhu and Qi Ruiduan, Guiyang, Guizhou renmin chubanshe.

Index

About the Author

Deborah Cao is a professor at Griffith University, Australia. She is a linguist and legal scholar. She has published in areas including legal theory, legal semiotics, legal translation, the philosophical and linguistic analysis of Chinese law, and legal culture and animal law. She is editor of *International Journal for the Semiotics of Law*. Her major books in English include *Chinese Law: A Language Perspective* (Ashgate, 2004), *Translating Law* (Multilingual Matters, 2007), *Animal Law in Australia and New Zealand* (Thomson Reuters, 2010), *Animal Law in Australia* (Thomson Reuters, 2015), and *Animals in China: Law and Society* (Palgrave Macmillan, 2015). She is also active in social media in China and writes about Chinese culture, society, and animals, and was named one of the 200 most influential bloggers in China in 2012.

www.ingramcontent.com/pod-product-compliance
Ingram Content Group UK Ltd.
Pitfield, Milton Keynes, MK11 3LW, UK
UKHW040154091026
15587UKWH00018B/171

9 781498 503952